Contents

Acknowledgments

RESEARCH FOR THIS BOOK was funded by the Wenner-Gren Foundation for Anthropological Research, a Dean's Research Grant from New York University, and the Pionier Program in Mass Media and the Imagination of Religious Communities at the University of Amsterdam.

While in Nigeria I was affiliated with the Kano State History and Culture Bureau and Arewa House Centre for Historical Documentation in Kaduna. I am very grateful for their help and commitment to facilitating research on all aspects of northern Nigerian history and culture. Abdullahi Mahadi and Hamid Bobboyi, former directors of Arewa House, Abdullahi Maradun, archivist at Arewa House, and Auwalu Hamza, director of research at the Kano State History and Culture Bureau, were especially generous with their time and effort. My gratitude for their logistical and intellectual help runs deep.

The book could not have been written without the help and support of many of the young, creative talents of the Hausa literary and video world. The novelists and filmmakers Ɗan Azumi Baba, Adamu Mohammed, and Yusufu Lawan were all generous with their time. I especially thank Ado Ahmad, chairman of Gidan Dabino Publishers, and Yusufu Adamu, novelist and university professor, without whom this research would not have been possible. Ado Ahmad, along with the late directors Aminu Hassan Yakasai and Tijani Ibraheem, the author and actor Adamu Mohammed, and the camera operator Bashir Muɗi, introduced me to the world of Hausa film. I extend special thanks to the publisher, editor, and novelist Ibrahim Sheme and to Abdalla Uba Adamu, whose work on Hausa cinema has overlapped with and informed my own. Alhaji Aminu Ɗan Bappa; the *'yan toxics*, Nura, Usman, Abdulhamid, Kabiru, Abdulkadir, and Kabiru; Philip Shea and Yusufu Adamu of Bayero University Kano; and Abdulkarim Ɗan Asabe and Fatimah Palmer of the Federal College of Education, Kano, were largely responsible for making my stay in Nigeria so memorable, for which I thank them all.

I was preceded in Kano by a burst of young Western researchers—Alaine Hutson, Jonathan Reynolds, Conerly Casey, Katja Werthmann, Rudi Gaudio, Peter A. Rogers, and Mathias Krings—and followed by Shobana Shankar, Sean Stilwell, Moses Ochonu, Steven Peirce, and Susan O'Brien. We rarely were in Kano at the same time, but I have learned much from them. Since my first predissertation trip, Jonathan Haynes has shared my sense of the importance of Nigerian video film.

During my research a number of people helped me with interviews (and gaining access to interviews). They include Abdullahi Maradun, archivist at Arewa House, Dalha Waziri of Bayero University, Abdulkarim 'Dan Asabe of the Federal College of Education, and especially Usman Aliyu Abdulmalik. Their efforts and ideas improved the quality of my research and prevented me from making social blunders. Moses Ochonu helped me with archival research, and Usman Aliyu Abdulmalik helped me with translation and interviews.

At Barnard College and Columbia University I have had the support and help of many great colleagues, including Nadia Abu El-Haj, Marco Jacquemet, Paul Kockelman, Mahmood Mamdani, Gregory Mann, Brinkley Messick, Rosalind Morris, Beth Povinelli, Nan Rothschild, Lesley Sharp, Sandhya Shukla, Paul Silverstein, Maxine Weisgrau, and Paige West. Many of the ideas in this book were aired in courses I taught on urban African culture, media, and technology and on spaces of globalization taught with Reinhold Martin. I would like to thank all the students from these classes for their insights and their willingness to experiment and Reinhold for his stimulating ideas.

Over many years, I have had the enormous good fortune to learn from Birgit Meyer of the Vrije Universiteit Amsterdam, both in her written work and in person. I was particularly lucky to spend a year in Amsterdam as a fellow of the Pionier Project in Mass Media and the Imagination of

Religious Communities under Birgit's directorship. Ze D'Abreu, Sudeep Das Gupta, Marleen De Witte, Francio Guadaloupe, Lotte Hoek, Martijn Oosterbaan, Peter Pels, Rafael Sanchez, Patricia Spyer, Matthias van de Port, and Jojada Verrips all made that stay one of the most stimulating and enjoyable of my life. I have worked so closely with Birgit Meyer and learned so much from her that many of her ideas are woven into this text.

Despite all this learning, the foundations and architecture for this project were laid during my graduate years at New York University. I was lucky to arrive at NYU at a time when people were trying to develop new ideas and ways of thinking about media and society, about the traffic in culture and material objects. This text is very different from the dissertation I submitted there, but the excitement and desire to learn, and the ideas that run through it, all bear the mark of that formation. I would like to thank my advisors, Lila Abu-Lughod, T. O. Beidelman, Fred Myers, Bambi Schieffelin, and especially Faye Ginsburg, for all their help and advice and for making this project what it is. While at NYU I benefited from the support and insight of a great graduate cohort: Alison Griffiths, Maureen Mahon, Tony Rossi, Lotti Silber, Sarah Teitler, and Erica Wortham. Teja Ganti, on whose generosity and capacious knowledge of Indian film I have continually depended, deserves special thanks. I would also like to thank Kate Baldwin, Jennifer Cole, Brian Edwards, and William Mazzarella for friendship and support over the years.

Chapters 4 and 7 originated as the articles "Theaters of the Profane: Cinema and Colonial Urbanization," *Visual Anthropology Review* 14.2 (1998–99): 46–62; and "Degraded Images, Distorted Sounds: Nigerian Video and the Infrastructure of Piracy," *Public Culture* 16.4 (2004): 289–314. Stefan Andriopoulos, Toby Dodge, Andy Podell, and Meg McLagan read portions—or in the case of Andy, all—of the book at different times. I am very grateful for their critical insights and for putting their own work aside when I asked them. I would also like to thank Caroline McLoughlin and Sumaiya Itahalique for helping me with copyedits and Lorene Bouboushian for tracking down image rights. I appreciate the careful work of my editors and copyeditors at Duke University Press.

Throughout this project Meg McLagan has provided me with emotional and intellectual support, encouraging me to develop my ideas and providing me with criticism and love so this could happen. Sinéad and Annie Larkin have lived with every iteration of both the book and me. Together with Meg they have made the life in and around the book worth living.

Finally, I want to thank my parents, to whom I dedicate this book in recognition of everything they have given me.

emergence

- Media technologies intro'd to Nigeria by colonial regimes in an attempt to shape political subjects and create modern, urban Africans

- Intro of media + electrical plants, RRs → part of the wider infrastructural project of urbanism.

- Media in Kano is the outcome of technology's encounter w/ social formations of northern Nigeria + w/ norms shaped by colonialism, postcolonial nat'lism + Islam.

- Media technologies produce the modes of leisure + cultural forms of urban Africa → Hindi films to Muslim Nigeria, leisure practices of Hausa cinemagoers in Kano, + the dynamic emergence of Nigerian video films.

- Diverse, unexpected media forms thriving in urban Africa

- Mix of anthro + media to see media's place in urban life.

- "Infrastructure" as a rubric for understanding macro- + micro-level operations that generate + sustain media cultures, specifically w/ Kano.

- "Infrastructure" = "totality of both technical + cultural systems that create institutionalized structures whereby goods of all sorts circulate, connecting + binding people into collectivities."

Introduction

After the introduction of Islamic law in Kano state, northern Nigeria, Wapa Cinema was shut down along with all other cinemas in Kano city. As part of their attempt to institute a new form of Islamic urbanism, authorities separated Christian areas more firmly from Muslim ones, divided buses and taxis by gender, and closed down un-Islamic institutions from brothels to beer parlors to movie theaters. Cinemas were problematic urban places because of what they did, creating a space for mixed-sex activities, and for what they bred, prostitution and other un-Islamic activities that fed on the crowds drawn by the theater.

What was it about cinema that occasioned such disquiet among politicians in charge of defining a new religious order? It was not an issue of form—of conservative Islamic iconophobia rejecting the images of cinema. Representational images continued to be freely available through magazines, stickers, calendars, videocassettes, and a wide variety of other media. Nor was the issue one of content, as the Indian and American films shown at the cinema could easily be seen on television or bought on video. Rather, what made authorities anxious were the sorts of practices that had grown up around the social space of cinema among Hausa people in northern Nigeria. Cinema draws people because of the narratives and spectacles of the films it shows, but the *experience* of going there is greater than the films themselves. It is this excess, the immaterial experience of cinema emerging from the assemblage of built space, film, and social practice, that became the target of regulation. One cannot understand this decree without realizing that what Hausa authorities saw as un-Islamic was not the cinema theater itself but the aura that hung over it, not the just built space or the bright images shown there but the assemblage of these into a social event which generated an electrical charge of excitement.

A few months later, theaters in Kano were reopened after a series of procinema campaigns. Exhibitors promised to ban women, removing the clearest legal obstacle. They complained about the negative effect on their livelihoods, arguing they were being punished economically with no clear religious reason. Next, together with Hausa filmmakers, they challenged authorities to provide the legal reasoning behind the ban, given that cinema is legal in most Islamic societies. The state closure of cinema was a populist response of Hausa politicians, who felt that theaters were an easy and highly visible target that would highlight the moral nature of the new legal regime. But precisely because legal regimes are legal, the closure had to be justified in the logic of Islamic law, and this proved hard to do. Cinema is a marginal but accepted part of Hausa society. The controversy over the cinema's place under shari'a law was the latest in a series of such controversies that had taken place since the medium's emergence in Nigeria in the 1930s. After shari'a, cinema emerged reorganized for a new era, ready to be the arena for new sets of experiences, the continuing site of cultural debate, and a fecund place for arguments over the shape and limits of Hausa religious and cultural norms.

This book analyzes the cultural work of media technologies and their role in producing what we call urban Africa—specifically the Muslim Hausa city of Kano, northern Nigeria. Media technologies are more than transmitters of content, they represent cultural ambitions, political machineries, modes of leisure, relations between technology and the body, and, in certain ways, the economy and spirit of an age. Yet at the same time, media such as television, cassettes, and cinema provide the infrastructure to facilitate and direct transnational flows of cultural goods and the modes of affect, desire, fantasy, and devotion these goods provoke. They create technical and institutional arrangements, each directing what sort of media (Islamic preaching, sporting events, Indian films, Hollywood) will travel and what the arrangements of their exhibition and reception will be. In this way, media create unique aural and perceptual environments, everyday urban arenas through which people move, work, and become bored, violent, amorous, or contemplative. This book unpacks the cultural logics of media technologies in Nigeria and their unintended consequences, which create the particular experience of urban life in colonial and postcolonial Nigeria.

Technologies are unstable things. We think we know what a radio is, or what a cinema is used for, but these phenomena, which we take for granted, have often surprising histories. What media are needs to be interrogated and not presumed. The meanings attached to technologies, their technical functions, and the social uses to which they are put are not an inevitable consequence but something worked out over time in the context of considerable cultural debate. And even then, these meanings and uses are often unstable, vulnerable to changing political orders and subject to the contingencies of objects' physical life. The recent shari'a ban on cinema and its rescission is a clear example of this. Debates about what media are, and what they might do, are particularly intense at moments when these technologies are introduced and when the semiotic economies that accompany them are not stable but in the process of being established (Gitelman and Pingree 2003). I focus on these moments when technologies were first introduced in order to foreground the material and epistemic instability of media.

It did not have to be that in Kano cinema theaters were closed down for being immoral, just as it was not inevitable that cinemas in Europe and the United States became socially acceptable after initial periods of intense moral concern. Technologies' affect on social life is the outcome of a series of processes. Of great importance are the intentions and ideologies that go into conceiving and funding any specific technology. Media systems are sponsored and built to effect social action, to create specific sorts of social subjects. When British colonialists built radio networks or mobile cinemas, for instance, they did so with the intention of educating and developing Nigerians into "modern" colonial citizens. One aim of this book is to examine the systemic efforts of governments to stabilize the symbolic logic of infrastructure and thereby examine the relation between infrastructural technologies and modes of rule. Yet the material qualities of these technologies, while working to implement those designs, also create possibilities outside the imagination of their designers. As these media get taken up and used in everyday life, they spin off in wholly unexpected directions, generating intended and unintended outcomes. If to understand how it is technologies come to have meaning we first need to understand the ideologies governing their sponsorship, we next must keep a keen analytic awareness of the technologies' autonomous power, which create technical and social potentials outside their sponsors' control. Which aspects of technologies' technical and social potential are brought into being depends on the intentions going into their construction, their technical capacity, and the social and religious contexts they inhabit. Each of these conditions helps determine how technology exists and makes meaning. None can finally control what is at stake.

The narrative movement of the book starts with the creation of a radio network and the use of mobile cinema units during the colonial period. It focuses on the tight link between the introduction of media and the modernizing ambitions of the colonial state (see also Abu-Lughod 2004; Mankekar 1999; and Rajagopal 2001). The middle chapters examine how media technologies, specifically cinema, are shaped and transformed by the social and religious practices of Hausa society. At the end, I examine the contemporary period, which has seen the rise of piracy and the striking success of Nigerian video films. The first chapters analyze the colonial state's ambitions to produce modern Hausa subjects by disembedding them from their rooted cultural world and "exposing" them (through the mediation of technology) to the circulation of ideas from around the world. The middle shows the disordering of these ambitions and a reordering of technology in Hausa social life. The end examines the emergence of a new era of Nigerian media outside of state control, representing new sets of relations between neoliberalism, the informal economy, and Nigerian politics and society. In the narrative movement from state control of media to its general absence from many of today's key media forms lies one of the key features I wish to examine of media systems and media technologies: their dynamic and processual nature over time.

Examining how technologies work is a powerful way of finding out what it is to live as an African urban subject. Technologies have material, sensual qualities: the wooden radio cabinet, a satellite dish perched monumentally on a roof, a small plastic transistor, the clean modern lines of a cinema theater, the tangle of cables stealing electricity from neighborhood pylons. These qualities are key to the significance of how media operate. Cassettes playing in buses or taxis, loudspeakers relaying religious recitations over the rooftops and through the streets, televisions playing continuously in cafes and restaurants create new ambient sounds and spectacles that make up the city's mediated environment (Hirschkind 2006; Spitulnik 2002). Media are key ingredients in popular life, in the everyday pleasures and affective engagements that make up the urban experience everywhere. They are also important in stimulating new aesthetic forms that borrow from older ones, adapting and reworking them, creating new forms from old. In facilitating the emergence of new leisure habits and helping to innovate cultural practices, communication technologies share, with all urban infrastructures, the role of providing physical networks through which the goods, ideas, religions, and people that make up urban life are trafficked. To understand how this occurs it is fruitful to examine how media operate as part of a wider networked infrastructure that facilitates and mediates the goods that travel along its paths.

MEDIA, INFRASTRUCTURE, AND URBANISM

Kano, Northern Nigeria, is a sprawling city on the edge of the Sahel desert. In this dominant economic, political, and religious center, Sufi orders, Lebanese businessmen, Ibo traders, and Hausa politicians interact but are embedded in discrete networks that extend in different directions over the world. The city itself takes shape as a node of these different circuits. It becomes the site of many differing forms of exchange, some in mutual competition, all moving at different rates, so that an intensification in Islamic practice is coextensive with the rise in materialism and a perceived drop in spirituality; Islamic law is introduced at the same time as forms of popular culture in which Hausa actors mimic Hindi cinema.

Infrastructures are the material forms that allow for exchange over space, creating the channels that connect urban places in wider regional, national, and transnational networks (Graham and Marvin 2001). Systems of economic exchange need means of transport, whether camels, trucks, railroads, or planes, and these in turn need the roads and rail lines, the warehouses and shops, the personnel speaking Arabic or English, that allow this exchange to occur. These grids dictate the sets of cultural, religious, and economic networks with which the city is involved, and indeed the physical shape of the city emerges from the layering of these infrastructures over time (Graham and Marvin 1996, 2001; Harvey 2000; Lefebvre 1991). At the most basic level, infrastructures are technical systems of transport, telecommunications, urban planning, energy, and water that create the skeleton of urban life. Analyzing media as technical infrastructures gives greater analytic purchase on how these technologies operate as technical systems. Infrastructures are the institutionalized networks that facilitate the flow of goods in a wider cultural as well as physical sense. AbdouMaliq Simone (2004) has written about this in regards to the knowledge circulating in African networks of ethnic migrants that connects these migrants to each other and to a homeland. Infrastructures can also be "soft," such as the knowledge of Arabic, or a particular sort of religious learning, the performance of a cultural style that allows one to participate in a "diaspora aesthetic" (Diawara 2002). *Infrastructure*, in my usage, refers to this totality of both technical and cultural systems that create institutionalized structures whereby goods of all sorts circulate, connecting and binding people into collectivities.

Much of what we experience as urban reality is mediated by how infrastructural networks connect urban areas into wider cultural, religious, and economic networks. The historical development of cities is structured by successive technological revolutions: transport by camels, then ships, railways, telegraphs, roads, and fiber optic cables. Even "virtual cities," the instantaneous real-time linkage of diverse urban centers into electronic networks, only exist due to the laying of cables across oceans, the digging up of cities to feed in pipes, or the construction of relay stations and the launching of satellites. These infrastructures have mediating capacities. Newly developed networks do not eradicate earlier ones but are superimposed on top of them, creating a historical layering over time (Lefebvre 1991). This is why Henri Lefebvre argues that when we look at the city we are confronted not by one social space but by many, all clashing and feeding off of each other at the same time. Stephen Graham and Simon Marvin (1996) term this mediation "enhancement," referring to how new technologies do not simply destroy older forms of communication but call into being new mobilities and sometimes intensify older ones. At any one point urban space is made up of the historical layering of networks connected by infrastructures. These are the conduits that dictate which flows of religious and cultural ideas move and therefore which social relations get mobilized in their wake. Their historical layering helps explain why dormant cultural, religious, and economic forms can suddenly gain purchase again, be reawakened and reenergized in a new situation. When we think of the urban experience, partly what we are referring to is the particular assemblage of networks that forms the unique configuration of a city and the preconditions that allow for the emergence of cultural and religious ideas. Infrastructures are not simply neutral conduits, then; they mediate and shape the nature of economic and cultural flows and the fabric of urban life. One powerful articulation of this mediation is the monumental presence of the infrastructures themselves.

TECHNOLOGY

In the David Lean film *The Bridge on the River Kwai*, Alec Guinness plays Colonel Nicholson, the officer in charge of British prisoners of war forced to build a railway bridge to aid a Japanese war offensive. At first, British prisoners passively try to sabotage construction by working slowly and inefficiently, but over time this attitude is transformed by the colonel into a fevered commitment to building the bridge in as fast and technically excellent a way as possible. He ceases to conceive of the bridge in narrowly technical terms—as transporting Japanese troops and supplies from one side of a river to the other—and begins to see it as deeply symbolic. Here, infrastructure is used as representation to "prove" to local natives and to the Japanese a fundamental racial superiority expressed through British technical expertise. For Nicholson, the bridge embodies qualities of organization and order that characterize military life and British civilization. In a tender scene, he wanders over the newly completed bridge at sunset, admiring it, stroking its hard supports, patting its railing. The Japanese commander joins him, thinking Nicholson is taking an evening stroll. Gazing at the sunset he turns to Nicholson and observes, "Beautiful, isn't it?" "Yes," replies Nicholson as he looks not at the sun but at the bridge itself, "It really is a first-rate job."

This film powerfully captures the representational logic of infrastructure embodied in the colonial arena, with its roots in the civilizing mission of colonial development and its potential for modernizing colonial subjects. It reveals the workings of what I term in chapter 1 the "colonial sublime," the use of technology to represent an overwhelming sense of grandeur and awe in the service of colonial power. Technology represented a world order in which the immaterial workings of God and his spirits were subordinated to the power of science to rationally order and control the natural world. British mastery of it was part of the conceptual promise of colonialism and its self-justification—the freeing of natives from superstitious belief by offering them the universalizing world of science. The construction of complex technological projects is seen in this light as part of the spectacle of colonial rule. In Lean's film, Nicholson's desire to use the bridge as representation becomes excessive, so much so it overwhelms his sense of its technical function—the transportation of Japanese troops to facilitate a war effort. This is carried so far that the British organize a commando team to destroy the bridge and at the climax of the film Nicholson, horrified that his work is to be destroyed, fights against the commandos, reacting to their attack as if it were an assault on all the ideologies of British workmanship, technical expertise, and civilizational superiority congealed in the material form of the bridge. Made in the 1950s, Lean aims the film at the fault line where the British commitment to science is revealed to be a fetish, a hysterical icon of colonial rationality and technology run amuck. Nicholson dies ambiguously, falling on the dynamite plunger, making him responsible for the bridge's destruction but leaving open the question of whether he ever realized that his commitment to the bridge led him astray.[1]

The ideological development of contemporary infrastructures has its roots in the Enlightenment project of rationally engineering the world, ordering it according to the free circulation of goods and ideas (Mattelart 1996, 2000). This is one of two ways infrastructure came to function in the colonial arena. Infrastructure created the connecting tissue linking disparate territories into a state and facilitating the rise of a centralized political administration. But as David Lean's film dramatizes, infrastructure was just as important as a representation, evidence of the civilizing promise of colonial technical superiority (Adas 1989; Mitchell 2002; Mrázek 2002; Prakash 1999). In the early years of radio and cinema in Northern Nigeria this was explicit in that media both depicted infrastructures (in films and in radio talks about engineering projects) and *were* infrastructures that conjoined scientific rationality with spectacle.

The tie between the representational logic of infrastructure and the state was not loosened with the end of colonialism but intensified, only now infrastructure came to represent the promise of independent rule rather than colonial supremacy. Government after government in sub-Saharan Africa came to independence with the ambition of building a modern African nation. As Okwui Enwezor (2001) has shown, during this period new public buildings in Nigeria followed the international style, as nationalist leaders were less interested in emphasizing Africa's cultural difference than in asserting its presence in a common cosmopolitan internationalism. In this context radio stations and television networks, like road networks and steel plants, were infrastructural evidence of the political success of independence, the icons of new postcolonial nations. The nationalist leaders' assertion that Africa too was modern was both a direct response to the colonial sublime, the use of technology to represent an ideology of superiority, and also an internalization of its logic.

Anthropological and African studies analyses of technology, or, more precisely, analyses of stories of African reactions to technology, have tended to stress how Africans understand and "indigenize" foreign technologies in their own conceptual schema. This classic anthropological move is a powerful corrective to stereotypes of African "first contact" with technology—the circulation of stories about the inability of natives to understand modern technologies whether they be photographic images, printed texts, clothing, or domestic items like soap.[2] Timothy Burke (1996) argues that Ndebele and Shona people in Southern Rhodesia in the 1950s who smeared stork margarine over their bodies instead of eating it were simply incorporating new commodities into existing regimes of cleanliness (protecting the skin through the use of oils and fats). Rumors that African medics were using their ambulance and medical technologies to steal blood and sell it represented not a misunderstanding of what those technologies were used for but a way of marking cultural difference (L. White 2000). This move at unmasking the simplicity of European reports of African encounters with technology is important, but it often downplays the autonomy of objects and the very real uncertainties and epistemic instabilities of objects themselves. I was struck in my research how often people referred to their previous "ignorance" about objects. When I asked many older people about ideas that the cinema projected images of spirits, or that radio broadcasts were magic—people were sanguine and often amused by these responses. "We were ignorant then," the prominent Sufi cleric Shaikh Nasiru Kabara said simply when I asked why many opposed listening to the radio and watching cinematic images.[3] I heard the same explanation of religious resistance to many technologies, from riding bikes to watching television. For Kabara, the idea that previous clerics were mistaken is not something that makes him defensive or that he needs to justify. This was only for a momentary period ("We were ignorant *then*") and can be spoken about from a contemporary position of knowledge, where the anxiety-provoking capacities of new technologies have been domesticated. For Kabara this position of knowledge and familiarity with technology is not just the result of Hausa people's becoming more Westernized and more familiar with Western technology but also, significantly, because of their better education *Islamically*. The ignorance he was referring to was not about how to use technology but how to understand the legal status of technology in Islamic law. Objects generate anxiety. Their technical capacity offers possibilities that are unknown and potentially threatening. One major theme in Cary's (1939) novel *Mr. Johnson* is the tension between the desired benefits and feared results of building a road connecting a small town to the great urban centers of Northern Nigeria. For the colonial officer, Rudbeck, "to build a road, any road, anywhere is the noblest work a man can do" (Cary

1939: 46). His senior, Blore, by contrast, considers "motor roads to be the ruin of Africa, bringing swindlers, thieves and whores, disease, vice and corruption, and the vulgarities of trade, among the decent unspoilt tribesmen" (46). Cary represents local authorities, the emir, and the *waziri* as fearing that the road will bring "thieves and swindlers" and transformations that will undermine their authority. The central tension in the book is one of potential, open-endedness, and inability to know exactly what the future will bring. It is about the contingencies technologies bring about and the attempt to stabilize them. When colonial administrators try to fix the symbolic logic of radio in an Enlightenment tradition of exposure to the free flow of ideas, when Nasiru Kabara mobilizes an Islamic legal system to explain technology, what is at stake are the competing traditions mobilized to institutionalize and control this instability. This is not to argue that Africans did not domesticate and indigenize technologies—as in many cases they did—but it is worth hesitating before looking at this process. By paying attention to the incomprehension that greeted many innovations, and by examining the social efforts that went into regulating and producing technologies as objects that have meaning, we gain a greater sense of these moments of instability and avoid an invocation of social agency without a sense of the limits on that agency. To read through African incomprehension too quickly is to fail to realize the autonomy of the objects themselves, the fact that attempts to domesticate them take time and social effort, and while they do their potential looms large and unpredictable.

THE STRUCTURE OF THE BOOK

This book's title, *Signal and Noise*, operates on several levels. At its base it focuses attention on the capacity of media technologies to carry messages (signals) and on the technical interference and breakdown that clouds and even prevents that signal's transmission (noise). I also use *noise* to refer to the interference produced by religious and cultural values, the historic configurations in which technologies and cultural forms are made manifest. Finally, on a more metaphoric level, the title refers to the connection between media and modes of rule (signals) while keeping in mind the unstable consequences media bring about (noise). In chapter 1, I examine the effects of the colonial sublime, the way that technology was made to be an explicit part of colonial political spectacle. I focus on the building of grand infrastructure projects as a way of understanding how the British invested in making technology sublime, overwhelming peoples' senses with the spectacular achievements of science. The erection of immense factories, the construction of bridges, roads, and rail, indeed the terrifying ability to remake landscapes and the natural world, were the ways in which the sublime was produced as a necessary spectacle of colonial rule. The consequence of this for many Hausa is that these infrastructures not only began to redefine the fabric of urban life, but they did so as machines invested with their owners' identity. Because of this, many Hausa reacted ambivalently to these technologies, arguing that they were specifically Christian and therefore un-Islamic. When media technologies such as radio or cinema were introduced, they entered into a highly contested social field in which electronic technologies were associated explicitly with Christianity and with colonial rule.

In the next two chapters I examine the consequence of this origin by tracing the building of the radio network in Nigeria (chapter 2) and the introduction of mobile cinema units traveling to urban and rural areas showing documentaries on agriculture, health, and colonial citizenship (chapter 3). These chapters continue to examine the relation between technology and colonial rule, but at the same time they tease out how these media began to generate new forms of leisure in urban Nigeria, creating cultural possibilities that threatened and sometimes overwhelmed this logic. I do this by tracing the concrete material features of these technologies and how they were used in the urban North. Radio, for instance, was part of the technologizing of public urban space. In its early years it was not a domestic technology but a public one, with receiving sets nailed to the walls of prominent places blaring out signals over urban streets. It was part of a new era of technologized urban form when local spaces were increasingly opened up to the forms of leisure and information coming from elsewhere. Chapter 2 traces this material history of radio by looking at the place of the object in Hausa society and its changes over time.

Like radio, mobile cinema was explicitly political, and indeed enormous effort went into separating mobile film from its commercial cousin, entertainment cinema. I examine the political address of mobile cinema to explore in detail the links between cinema and a form of political rule—colonialism. For most Nigerians, their first experiences of cinema came through the traveling film units of the Nigerian government. I explore how these screenings operated in practice, what their aesthetic forms were, and how this film form continued into the postcolonial era. In many ways, my work engages with some of the key thematic elements of what has come to be called early cinema (Elsaesser and Barker 1990; Gunning 1986, 1994; M. Hansen 1991): the "first contact" of audiences with cinematic technology, foregrounding the spectacle of the technology over the content of films and highlighting the linkage between cinema and wider transformations of modernity. I draw on this work to question a bedrock assumption of mainstream cinema history: that the emergence of cinema should be examined in relation to that ur-form of industrial modernity, the commodity. In this chapter I use the context of colonial rule in Nigeria to provide a different genealogy for the emergence of cinema, one that examines the mode of cinematic exchange as governed not by commodity but by political relations. The political use of cinema, moreover, did not simply disappear with the end of colonialism; it was fully adopted by postcolonial Nigerian leaders, who realized its usefulness in propagating a very modern form of political power—mediated publicity (McLagan 2003).

Chapters 4 and 5 shift away from how media technologies were introduced with the aim of serving colonial rule to how these technologies began to be shaped and reimagined by Nigerians—and the limits in that process. Chapter 4 argues that Hausa in the 1940s and 1950s saw the introduction of cinema theaters in urban Kano as an imposition of colonial urbanization on Muslim space. Cinema halls, like beer parlors, theaters, and public gardens introduced new modes of modern mixed-sex association into Hausa life. In a strict Muslim area this upset existing spatial hierarchies, creating new modes of stronger sociability that had to be regulated. Chapter 4 examines this regulation. It explores the built form of cinema theaters—how they were constructed, in which parts of the urban area they were located—as a means of analyzing the nature of colonial urbanization. Looking at conflicts over where cinemas were placed, who could attend, and rumors about the spiritual and physical consequences of cinema-going, I argue that conflicts over the opening of cinemas became a key way for urban Hausa to contest the transformation in urban order imposed under colonial rule.

Chapter 5 looks at the consequences of this for contemporary experiences of cinema-going. It moves from examining urban space as built form to a greater attention to the immaterial forms of urbanization that also make up city life. These are the affective dimensions crucial to city space—the pleasures and fears, the states of arousal and boredom that congeal around certain areas and certain institutions. I argue that cinema is one such institution. If chapter 4 looks at how cinema came to be, chapter 5 analyzes what it means for contemporary urban Nigerians by looking at cinema-going as an affective practice in Kano. There, cinema-going is perceived as an immoral activity charged with illicitness, eroticism, danger, and excitement. I tack between the material specificity of cinema—the relations of lighting, vision, and movement inside and around it—and the modes of sociability and leisure it promotes. My interest is in how material structures produce immaterial forms of urbanism—the senses of excitement, danger, or stimulation that suffuse different spaces in the city and create the experience of what urbanism is.

Chapter 6 examines the rise of perhaps the most dynamic visual media form in postcolonial Africa: the Nigerian video film. Focusing on English-language Southern films and Hausa-language Northern ones, I argue that these cultural forms, across a variety of genres, draw on ideas of emotional, financial, and spiritual corruption that index the vulnerability and insecurity of contemporary Nigerian life. Southern films, I argue, rely on an aesthetics of outrage, a mode of cinematic address that rests on the outrageous abrogation of deep cultural norms to generate shock and anger in the viewer. Resting on norms of melodrama, these films provide fantastic narratives about Nigerian life in order not just to reflect that life but, by evoking bodily reactions, to constitute a living experience of this as well. Narratives about businessmen who belong to cults in order to become successful, about fraudsters who mask themselves to betray unsuspecting victims, about grandmothers who ensorcell their children and grandchildren, all represent a world in which people who appear one way turn out to be something else. In this world the visible grounds of daily experience cannot be taken at face value and vertiginous success and disaster are all too common.

In northern Nigeria, Hausa films have dealt with these issues of instability and vulnerability through the very different idiom of Indian film. Perhaps one of the most striking and unexpected results of the introduction of commercial cinema into northern Nigeria has been the massive success of Hindu Indian films with a Muslim African audience. Hausa filmmakers have pioneered a film genre wholly different from its Southern cousins, and they have done so famously, and controversially, by borrowing heavily from the narratives, songs, and style of Indian films. Their success has, in turn, spawned a fierce backlash among intellectuals angered at the infiltration of Indian film into Hausa culture. The very fact that the rise of this film form emerged at the same time as a movement toward Islamic revitalization leading to the imposition of Islamic law itself indicates the complexity and diverse cultural assemblages that make up urban Nigeria.

Nigerian video films are a national media form that emerged free from the control of the state. Chapter 7 examines the roots of the video film phenomenon in the rise of piracy in Nigeria. I see piracy not simply in legal terms but as a mode of infrastructure that facilitates the movement of cultural goods. In the case of Nigeria, I argue that piracy has generative as well as destructive qualities, and that the infrastructure created by piracy brought about the emergence of a video film industry in the North. I also explore a wider issue, arguing that piracy is not simply a neutral conduit but imposes particular conditions on the recording, transmission, and retrieval of data. Constant copying erodes data storage, degrading image and sound, overwhelming the signal of media content with the noise produced by the means of reproduction. Pirate videos are marked by blurred images and distorted sound, creating a material screen that filters audiences' engagement with media technologies and the senses of time, speed, and space that result. In this way piracy creates an aesthetic, a set of formal qualities that generate a particular sensorial experience of media marked by poor transmission, interference, and noise.

If the beginning of this book examines the rise of media technologies as part of the infrastructural project of the Nigerian colonial state, the end looks at what happens when media get dislodged from those state projects. The rise of Hausa video films is one part of the efflorescence of media that make up contemporary urban experience in Nigeria. When taxi drivers play cassettes of Islamic preachers, or youths get together to visit video parlors, these are the ephemeral ways that urban space becomes mediated, and not just because of the sounds played or images shown.

In *Signal and Noise* I develop an anthropological approach toward media and a broad analysis of how technologies come to mean in society. To do this I have had to combine theoretical and methodological approaches from a number of different disciplines. This is because I am not just interested in texts but in the conditions of possibility that allow texts to have meaning. To trace this, I have gone back to tease out what was at stake when technologies like radio and cinema were first introduced to colonial Nigeria. What was at stake in that encounter between new infrastructural technologies and Hausa colonial subjects? How did this develop and mutate over time? To answer such questions I have had to combine archival analysis with ethnography. I have tried to maintain a proper concern for the analysis of cultural texts but also for the materiality of the technologies which transmit those texts and a sense of the wider social configuration that gives those texts purchase and social force. Throughout I have been guided by a desire to start from the ground up in examining how media exist in the particular context of northern Nigeria. I seek not to take for granted histories of media that privilege their origins in Europe and the United States but critically to engage with them. I hope to discover where their insights have force and where their analytical assumptions turn out to be socially specific rather than universal to a technology. Nigeria is a vibrant, diverse, and provocative nation, continually experimenting and producing new forms of urban life, new sounds, sights, and experiences that constitute the physical ambient for its citizens. *Signal and Noise* traces out the role media and the social practices surrounding them have played in shaping that life.

1

Infrastructure, the Colonial Sublime, and Indirect Rule

In 1932 Kano city unveiled its new Water and Electric Light Works. Based in Pan Shekara, an area just outside the city, it not only was intended to bring the infrastructural benefits of colonialism to Nigeria but was the first project of its size and ambition financed entirely by the Native Administration,[1] at a cost of more than a third of a million pounds (Crocker 1937). Befitting such an important moment, European dignitaries traveled from Britain and from around Nigeria; the emir of Kano, chief of the Native Authority, presided over a number of Hausa-Fulani notables and the senior British officer of the North, the lieutenant governor, headed a distinguished European contingent. The opening was a spectacular event. As Mallam Dauda described it in a newspaper account, "The Southern gate of the Emir's house was magnificently decorated. Date palms had been put there and look as if they had grown there on the spot; brightly colored cloths were hung up, red, white, green, blue, and yellow and different places were railed off for people to stand in. Electric lights were put all the way around from the office of the Galadima to the Tax Office, the whole place was a mass of lights and coloured cloths of all sorts" (*Northern Provinces News* [NPN], 14 November 1931, 6). Along with this, stands were built for European and Hausa-Fulani dignitaries; a fountain was erected in front of where the ceremony was to take place, and near where the emir of Kano was sitting a large metal frame had been built with lights on it forming Arabic letters.

In his report, Mallam Dauda stressed the scale of the event and the size of the crowd: "There were so many that some were unable to see anything. . . . The dust rose up so that one could scarcely breathe and the number of people could not be counted" (ibid). The British were more precise, fixing attendance at over fifty-three thousand (NPN, 1 December 1935, 14), though Dauda's imprecision gives a more tactile sense of the overwhelming nature of the spectacle. This was a simply enormous number of people congregated to watch the event of a work of colonial infrastructure being opened. C. W. Alexander, the lieutenant governor of Northern Nigeria, made a speech to the assembly, pointing out that many had said that this project was a waste of time,[2] but that now everyone could see for themselves just what had been accomplished. With that, the emir of Kano threw the switch and thousands of colored lights hung over the wall and along the streets exploded into florescence. Fireworks erupted from the rooftops, "and the whole place was a blaze of light and very beautiful to see" (ibid.). There was a gasp from the crowd and shouts of "*Lantiriki, ya kama*—the lamps are alight." Water came gushing out of the fountain, and at the center of it all a frame of tiny lights spelled out, in Arabic script, *Sarki ya gaisheku* (The king [emir] greets you all).

For Muslim Hausa, Hausa written in Arabic script (*ajami*)—the standard mode of literacy until the British introduced Hausa written in roman script (*boko*)—was, and is, a domain of religion and tradition, a reserve from which the modern advances of colonialism were kept well away.[3] The sign, "The king greets you all," thus represents the coming together of two discrete realms. On the one side, Arabic Hausa represents an intimate domain of tradition. The statement itself references the emir's power and the continuing legitimacy of precolonial modes of government. But the material the letters are made from, electric lights, represents the spectacular heart of modernity. When the emir addresses his subjects in this fashion he is melding his traditional legitimacy with a new form of government emanating from colonial rule. Engineered into these thousands of colored lights, into the streetlamps and fountains, was a new sort of authority located in technology as the visible evidence of progress. For the British, the Water and Electric Light Works was evidence of their success in promoting modernizing improvements which they were increasingly using to legitimize their suzerainty. The Works was also a public display to the people that the emir of Kano and his administration recognized the importance of progressive infrastructural projects such as this.[4] In the latter stages of colonial rule, when colonization had to be justified to its mounting critics in the colonies and the homeland, British colonial government legitimated itself by an argument of exchange: the giving of "voluntary" political subjection in return for technological progress. What every streetlight and tap in Kano now made clear is that this form of exchange had been reproduced in Hausa society itself. The lights and fountains were not just effects of colonial rule; they were a mode of it. Mallam Dauda's account of the opening of the Water and Electric Light Works sums up the success of the initiative: "Now the waterworks and electric light have done much good to Kano. Everywhere there are stand-pipes and washing places have been built, some for men, some for women and some for children. If anyone wants these things in his house they are brought there for him and he pays for them every month. If you were to see Kano now at night you would say that it is like the stars on a summer night" (ibid.).

What must it have been like to live in Kano at that time and see the coming of electric light? To grow up with the busyness of daytime curtailed by the oncoming of night, and then one day know that night would never be the same again? What would the feeling be to know that such things as electric light existed, but until that time they always existed elsewhere in a world where Europeans lived? The coming of electricity effected a split in Nigeria between electrified and modern towns and those that remained without electric power. Those conurbations now became cities yet to be electrified, pregnant with the future, yet remaining in the past. A year after the Kano opening, one Halilu Bida wrote a short piece for the newspaper depicting the town of Ilorin. In it, he described the town's great size and admired the broadness of its new roads. "But," he enthused, "the most marvelous and splendid feature of Ilorin is its electric light. . . . There are more than a hundred lamps on standards set up in the market which is held at night. The light from these lamps is very powerful and one can see everything in all directions, while people moving about in the glare of the electric light look quite unreal, and their white garments shine brilliantly"

(*NPN*, 9 April 1932, 17). Frozen in aspic inside this short description is the sense of the experience of electricity, the excitement of seeing something for the first time. Electrification can only carry this excitement for a short time before the sense of wonder becomes exhausted and, like a bulb, goes dark. As electricity becomes familiar, possessing it will no longer make Ilorin exceptional. The adjective *electric* before the noun *light* will become unnecessary and cumbrous—stating the obvious—rather than an exciting piece of description. Yet at this point, for Halilu Bida, technology and the life it creates are charged with force. Electricity has the power to recast a mundane world and present it again to one of its inhabitants in a new way so that real people look "unreal" and everyday garments seem to shine "brilliantly" and one can see "everything in all directions" even though it is night. That moment must have been an exciting one indeed.

Grand openings of infrastructural projects like the Kano Water and Electric Light Works are both a visual spectacle and a political ritual. They possess their own codified genres: the parade of military bands, processions by British troops and by the traditional emirate cavalry, speeches by eminent dignitaries, firework displays, and the spectacular presentation of modern technologies such as the wireless and the cinematograph. Rituals like these are moments where the public display of colonial authority is made manifest (A. Apter 2002, 2005; Cohn 1983; Ranger 1983). But openings were also about the spectacle of technology itself. They celebrated the completion of long, complex projects and focused attention on the existence of the object at hand—a power plant, a bridge, or a railroad. In colonial Nigeria, an object such as a bridge was intended to operate on several levels simultaneously: it had a technical function of facilitating transport from one side of a river to another; it trained a class of workers versed in the technical skills necessary to complete the job; it embodied successful bureaucratic organization; it confirmed that Northern aristocrats understood the benefits of modern infrastructures; and it displayed British scientific superiority and, by contrast, the gulf in education and civilization separating ruler from ruled, implicitly legitimizing the rule itself. Just as the ritual surrounding the opening of the Kano Water and Electric Light Works was designed to represent the plant as a technical object, so that plant was itself involved in a representational project intended to signify the future and promise of an electric Nigeria, bright and modern.

Understanding the provision of infrastructures as a work of state representation as well as a technical process pushes us to examine the conceptual mechanism that lay behind infrastructures and translated these objects into cultural forms. In this, the erection of bridges and the building of railways in colonies such as Nigeria had much in common with infrastructures back home in Britain. What was different in Nigeria was the context of colonial rule and the way these technologies were tied to that rule. It is this link to rule that gave rise to the planning, funding, and completion of infrastructural projects and created an aura surrounding them, guiding how Nigerians and British related to them. Yet because technologies have their own material shape and design, they can never fully be reduced to the intentions with which they were constructed. They do not simply enact relations of ideology. Because they give rise to what the historian Rudolf Mrázek describes as the "sensing of colonial modernity," the phenomenal, lived experience of a world undergoing colonial modernization, the material qualities of these technologies are excessive, creating possibilities and setting in motion forces that cannot quite be contained. Mrázek (2002) gives an example of this in his account of road building in the Netherlands East Indies. Hard, dark, and smooth, these well-built highways embodied the speed and rationality of colonial rule, and stood in contrast to the mud and dust of the chaotic Indonesian world they replaced. "The newness, the hardness and cleanness" are the material qualities that embodied the roads' modernity, Mrázek argues. "Cleanness of the roads, in this logic, was the purity of the times, democracy even" (8). Mrázek's aim here is to tie the sensate experience of the objects to the larger logic of rule they express. But once in place, that logic has to jostle with competing modes of reasoning. Just as the railroad was introduced for the elite but taken up far more quickly by the poorer classes, roads were introduced in Indonesia to facilitate a fast, modern world but quickly gave rise to *vrachtautos*—native trucks. Traveling too fast to be safe, overladen with goods and people, in poor repair with frequent breakdowns, these trucks disrupted the streamlined, modern world of which they were meant to be part. Europeans saw these buses and trucks as "wild," renegades from the proper behavior that road traffic was intended to inculcate. The existence of the road, intended as a model of ordering, thus gave rise to new machineries that seemed, to European eyes, bowdlerized copies of the vehicles they should have been. Yet sleek Dutch trucks and decrepit Indonesian ones were both products brought about by the road and both equally modern. This dynamic, whereby the agency of the object (Latour 1993) has an independence from the intentions governing its introduction, opens up the sensate, material world of the technology itself.

For a book on media and urban life, dwelling in detail on the administration of colonial rule might seem an unnecessary burden. Yet one cannot really understand what the Hausa reaction to cinema, or to radio, was without understanding the structure of politics in Northern Nigeria. Such understanding moves analysis away from the inherent universalism often associated with modern technologies and toward the idea that technologies come to be within specific historic conjunctures. But by insisting on the mediating capacity of infrastructural technologies—how they operate as objects—I also wish to insist that these objects cannot be reduced to their contexts or to the order with which they were invested—in this case the colonial order in the first half of the twentieth century in Nigeria. Media are messier than that. The British use of infrastructure was not about simply staging the representation of rule; it was about addressing and producing a particular sort of modern colonial subject. Technologically adept, forward thinking, mutable, this subject was formed by the criss-crossing of new communication networks. Railways, roads, and radio broadcasts were erected to bring into being a technologically mediated subject proud of his past but exposed to new ideas, open to the education, knowledge, and ideas traveling along this new architecture of communication. By the 1950s, there emerged the modern salaried office worker, an ideal of colonial development, well educated, speaking English, working in a modern technological office, and spending his leisure time at the cinema or in private clubs. In a sense, it is this imagined subject that is immanent in the building of new infrastructures, the fantasy to which those structures are addressed. It was a subject position with which many Nigerians were uncomfortable, while others saw it as an object of desire. When, in the 1950s, a young Hausa man went to the cinema, stood in front of the post office to listen to the radio, or took the train to a nearby city, an encounter took place between subject and technology. This chapter will tease out what was at stake in such encounters to explore why infrastructural technologies took on the shapes and meanings they did in Hausa society. To do this one needs to understand the politics of indirect rule in Nigeria.

PRESERVATION AND TRANSFORMATION: THE DIALECTICAL LOGIC OF INDIRECT RULE

Northern Nigeria was conquered by the British in 1903 and established, initially, as a country wholly separate from Southern Nigeria. In 1914, these states were amalgamated to become one nation, Nigeria, ruled from the capital in the South, Lagos. The country was divided into three semiautonomous areas, the North (mainly Hausa-Fulani), West (mainly Yoruba), and East (mainly Igbo). Each region, as they came to be called, had its own lieutenant governor, its own regional assembly, and its own capital. Famously, the North of Nigeria was administered through a policy of indirect rule, a system by which the British attempted to rule through existing structures of political authority and to preserve existing cultural and religious lifeways. At the time, this was seen as a contrast to previous forms of rule which had resulted in a much more thoroughgoing transformation of indigenous life. Indirect rule was intended to avoid the "mistakes" of overly rapid transformation and was guided by the ambivalent British reaction to the growing class of Western-educated, nationalist colonial subjects in differing parts of the Empire.

In the North, the British administratively ended up creating a sort of double state. They preserved the precolonial structure that divided the land into a series of emirates, each under the control of an emir and all subject to the authority of the sultan in Sokoto. Onto this structure they mapped a British administration, renaming the areas "provinces," imposing British "residents" alongside emirs and district officers next to traditional *hakimai* (district heads [DH]) in rural areas. The Nigerian authority was renamed the Native Administration, and in theory each authority had its own well-defined powers and functions.

Scholarly arguments about indirect rule have been divided. Some assert that under the British, the emirs lost their sovereignty but in return gained powers they never had, raising the authority of the emir at the expense of his council, and imposing emirate rule over animist populations that had long rebelled against the emirs' claims of authority (Crowder 1964; Fika 1978; Yakubu 1996). Many have seen a "class" alliance between British colonialists and the Northern aristocracy in that British rule was so intimately tied to emirate authority that any critique of emirs by their subjects was seen as tantamount to an attack on colonial rule itself. Southern nationalist politicians argued fiercely that, as the Yoruba leader Obafemi Awolowo put it, under colonial rule, emirs were "clothed with powers and prestige far in excess of what they ever wielded or enjoyed before the advent of British conquest" (cited in Tibenderana 1988: 68). And in this he was supported by many Northerners. In a conversation with the retired Lord F. D. Lugard, Abubakar Imam, one of the most famous Hausa intellectuals of his time, told Lugard that in the name of "preservation," the British had not only made emirs more powerful than ever before, but that by reflexively supporting emirate authority they were creating a system where nepotism and incompetence flourished and where merit and achievement were largely irrelevant.[5] Imam represented an emerging modern-oriented, Western-educated Hausa elite, eager to modernize Northern Nigeria, and whose emerging power base was seen as a threat by the aristocracy—a situation described in detail by the historian Mahmood Yakubu (1996). For the British, one aim of colonial rule was to produce just such a modern Hausa elite.

Arguing against the idea of a class alliance and unbridled royal power, others have stressed the pressure the British maintained on emirate authority. While Northern leaders were undoubtedly given great freedom, any emirs who refused to support British control, or who were perceived as too conservative and opposed to change, were removed from office and replaced. Indirect rule was rarely as "indirect" as it claimed (Shea 1982–85; Tibenderana 1988; Umar 1997). While British colonialists complained of having to defer to the authority and status of emirs, these aristocrats were, in turn, clearly involved in a constant struggle to maintain their authority and well aware that to go against British wishes would mean replacement and likely exile. To them, the power of the Native Authority must have seemed constantly under threat.

Embedded in this debate is a contradiction at the heart of indirect rule, revolving around the simultaneous promise to preserve existing Hausa society and to transform it. The British annexation of Northern Nigeria came late in imperial history, when conquest could not be justified by might or civilizational superiority alone but had to be legitimated through the logic of bringing "progress." The British justified violent annexation by promising to "liberate" Hausa peasants from the evils of slavery and the autarchic repression of royal elites. They then legitimized colonial rule by vowing to raise Africans to the educational, political, and social plane of the "modern" world—to make backward peoples modern. The contradiction at the heart of indirect rule is how one can both preserve and transform political and religious lifeways. This issue was at the heart of Lugard's epic on colonial administration, *The Dual Mandate in British Tropical Africa* (1922), what the political scientist Robert Shenton (1986: 121) has referred to as "the bible of expansion and preservation, modernization and tradition."

These issues have figured prominently in recent debates on postcoloniality and the conflict over whether colonial rule was operated through a presumption of irreconcilable difference between rulers and ruled, or through one of identity and synthesis. Mahmood Mamdani (1996) powerfully argues that indirect rule effectively isolated African societies—"containerizing" them—by granting them special legal and political status. Preserving the unique heritage and customary structure of a group entailed creating a dual system where white settlers were ruled through civil law and colonial administration, while African societies were split into a series of discrete ethnic groups each ruled by their own legal system (customary law), and their own political institution (the Native Administration). Partha Chatterjee (1993: 18) has referred to this isolating effort as the "the rule of colonial difference," where the attempt to construct a modern, liberal state in colonial societies was disrupted by the necessity of maintaining a fundamental racial separation between ruler and ruled. Against these arguments more recent scholarship has argued that colonialism operated through the logic of governmentality, the process whereby rule is exercised through not brute subjection but the creation of a space for the apparent exercise of free will and the incorporation and assent of individuals who voluntarily act in this space (Foucault 1991; Prakash 1999; D. Scott 1999). Instead of insisting on the preservation of difference between colonizer and colonized, this line of argument looks at the mechanisms whereby colonized subjects were drawn into the political and social orbit of a single society. Colonialism did not "preserve" or maintain native societies in a state of alterity; it "disable[ed] old forms of life by systematically breaking down their conditions" and "constructing in their place new conditions so as to enable . . . new forms of life to come into being" (D. Scott 1999: 26).

The pendulum swing between whether colonial rule reified colonial subjects as inherently different through an emphasis on preservation or whether it transformed those subjects by incorporating them into the political and cultural forms of modern liberalism is an enduring problem. Part of the reason for this is clearly the instability of colonial rule itself. When Mamdani (1996: 50) argues that "European rule in Africa came to be defined by a single-minded and overriding emphasis on the customary," he is drawing on extensive evidence that British colonialists used indirect rule to relentlessly emphasize the difference of African societies and their inability to be assimilated into modern society. But in establishing this as a principle, Mamdani passes over the fact that British rule was often split, at various points in its history, between those who wished to preserve the uniqueness of native institutions and those who wished to transform them radically. This split could be manifest in the different emphasis of a differing administration over time, but it was just as present in contending points of view within the same administration and often could be manifest in warring principles within the same person. It comes down to the inherent contradiction in the principle of indirect rule: to preserve while at the same time to transform. The preservation of difference was always at war with the recognition that transformation was necessary and inevitable, just as the desire to make Africans modern was haunted by the fear of what sort of subjects those modern Africans might become. Examining the British in Nigeria, this contradiction was especially acute.

In 1911 the governor of Northern Nigeria, Sir Hesketh Bell, published an essay in the *Journal of the African Society* titled, "Recent Progress in Northern Nigeria." The essay takes the form of a report, summarizing conditions in the area and emphasizing colonial development. He describes Zungeru, the proposed new capital of Nigeria, as formerly being "a desolate waste" which "only ten years ago [was] the scene of all the horrors of the slave trade." Nowadays," he continues, "we have electric light, motor cars and ice-machines" (384). This binary is given iconic force in his selection of images comparing "ancient" modes of communication—the horse—with icons of modernity such as the dark lines of a tarmac road cutting diagonally through the bush and the hard, straight lines of the railroad disappearing over a bridge (see figures 1 and 2). This split between an "ancient" way of life and a future-oriented one materialized in ice machines, electric light, and motorcars is a cliché of colonial rule, yet even as he makes this argument, Bell shrinks away from its logical consequence. After showing that colonial rule is based, as David Scott argues, on the fundamental uprooting of the conditions of precolonial life, Bell concludes that this rule must be instituted in "such a manner as to interfere as little as possible with the traditions and customs of the people" (391). Bell understands his role is to bring change, but at the same time he is fearful of its product: "We want no violent changes, no transmogrification of the dignified and courteous Moslem into a trousered burlesque with a veneer of European civilization. We do not want to replace a patriarchal and venerable system of government by a discontented and irresponsible democracy of semi-educated politicians" (ibid.).

One of the fundamental aspects of colonial rule was its future orientation. It operated in the present, but with a powerful sense of the range of possible futures open to it. Its actions were geared toward shaping how that future might be. The fear, constantly iterated, was that progress could spoil as much as it could improve society. This is especially the case in Northern Nigeria, which the British quickly grasped as a site for experimentation. In other parts of the Empire, such as India and Southern Nigeria, there had been extensive contact between Europeans and local populations

A Fulani Horseman in an Ancient Shirt of Mail.

New Motor-Road to the Tin Fields of Bauchi.

FULANI CHIEFS SALUTING THE GOVERNOR.

A BRIDGE ON THE BARO-KANO RAILWAY LINE.

To face p. 389.

1 and 2. Images of communications in northern Nigeria "before" and "after" British rule. Used to illustrate the essay, "Recent Progress in Northern Nigeria," by Governor Hesketh Bell (1911).

economically, politically, and culturally. This had produced ambivalent results: tremendous development but also a class of educated, nationalist, or protonationalist colonial subjects. For Northern colonialists, this figure was represented by the Southern Nigerian, who embodied a possible future for Northern Nigeria. Dressed in suits, not native gowns, literate, contemptuous of manual work, future oriented, nonpliant, ever ready (so it seemed to the British) to contest decisions with an unceasing series of petitions, Southerners were resented by the British and stereotyped as the antithesis of what the colonizers wanted Northerners to become. The ghost of the Southerner haunted every decision over the proper nature of colonial transformation, its speed, and its direction. For many Northern colonialists, from the beginning of British rule until its end a half-century later, Southerners represented a failure of British rule and one the British were determined to learn from. Northern Nigeria was different and offered the potential for an alternative colonial future.[6] "It was a clean slate," as Sir Richmond Palmer (1934: 38), governor of the North, argued. Because it was untouched it could be a site for experiment. As Bell (1911: 391) concluded, "We hope, if possible, to prevent in Northern Nigeria some of the evils that have been brought about in other parts of Africa, by an overhasty adoption of European methods and customs."

While the fundamental structural tension between preservation and transformation was never fully resolved by colonialists, in the first few decades of British rule the commitment to preservation and the holding up of "indirect rule" as a mantra famously came to mark Nigerian administration. These ideals evolved into a highly elaborate set of political, social, and bodily relations between British colonialists and Hausa-Fulani aristocrats. Politically, the British heightened the powers of Native Administrations; they forbade missionization in Muslim areas, and they restricted and tightly controlled institutions of Western education. They developed a ritual system in which the authority of the emir was to be observed and performed at all levels. British officers were commanded to shun violent gestures and loud speech in front of royal figures and they were instructed to force their wives to veil so as not to offend religious sensibilities (Yakubu 1996). Protocol meant that an emir's representative accompanied the district officer (DO) whenever he went on tour so that the DO could not speak to anyone officially without the emir's representative present. When communicating formally to a *hakima* (district head), who was a member of the Native Administration and thus under the emir's authority, the DO could not speak directly to him, but only through the emir's representative.

Margery Perham (1937: 326), a theorist of colonial administration writing in the 1930s, summed up the result: "A policy of preserving the very special identity of the Northern Provinces was consciously followed. . . . The northern people were encouraged in their natural desire to resist external influences whether upon their religion, dress, architecture, or way of life generally."

Policy in the North was in marked distinction from that in the South, and this difference was fostered as a means for Northern colonialists to define a separate set of powers controlled wholly in the North. Southern colonialists saw indirect rule as an abnegation of colonial responsibility, a means of propagating the backwardness of what amounted to a feudal elite. Northern colonialists raised it to an article of faith, seeing the Islamic subjects of the North as socially superior to the Southern Nigerians, who, in becoming European, had lost the independence of their race. Moreover, the more they asserted the "special conditions" of the North, and its unique character, the more they could argue that laws made in Lagos, while suited to Southern Nigeria, were wholly inappropriate farther north. Conflict between the British administering the different provinces ran deep. One former resident of the Kano emirate recalled, "It was stupidly, ignorantly, and wrongly the custom in the Northern Provinces to sneer and laugh at the Legislative Council [which ruled from the South]. . . . This attitude was encouraged by those who should have known better and was still going on in 1942."[7] The tension was such that an American visitor pointed out that "if the Africans were to leave Nigeria, fighting would break out among the British" (Foot 1964: 107).

The consequence of this is that for many Northern colonialists, indirect rule was raised to the level of a moral good. Promotions were judged on whether "one was imbued with the true spirit of indirect rule" (Kirk-Greene 1970: xi). According to one officer, district officers or residents who found themselves in conflict with emirs were labeled as "non-indirect," with the likely consequence that their career would be stalled and they would be banished to outlying "pagan" areas (Crocker 1937). As late as 1945, in his handing over notes, one departing district officer instructed his successor that he should always have a representative of the emir with him when questioning any Hausa person. And, he continued, "Do everything possible to avoid giving the impression that you are short-circuiting the DH and do nothing to impair the latter's authority in any way."[8] Scholars have rightly questioned how much autonomy Northern rulers actually had, given that resistance to British innovations could lead to investigation and dismissal. Nevertheless, indirect rule was still the available mechanism whereby emirs could make claims on the state and get rid of unsuitable district officers or even residents—a fact starkly clear to colonial officials working with them. Generations of colonialists labored under the assumptions of indirect rule, agonizing at length how far its logic extended, believing fervently that they were preserving political rule even as they were also involved in taking it away. In the 1930s, the resident of Kano, J. H. Carrow, tried to ban the playing of the British national anthem at a bridge opening ceremony because it might offend the emir by undermining the idea of Northern "independence." Reflecting back on those moments in the 1960s, Carrow saw them as ridiculous, an example of the extreme lengths to which ideas of indirect rule were taken (measures that included forcing white women to veil at state occasions so as not to offend Muslim sensibilities).[9] In the competition between colonialists in Southern and Northern Nigeria, the South lampooned this attitude as promoting a "Sacred North" that could not be touched or altered and which preserved the most backward political structures while preventing any real movement toward progress. It is in this light that infrastructural endeavors such as the Kano Water and Electric Light Works should be seen: the Work's importance for the British lay not just in its functioning but, because it was financed by a Native Administration, it "proved" that indirect rule could promote progressive modernization.

The ideology of indirect rule, no matter how contradictory, had immense consequences that are still felt in contemporary Nigeria. On an immediate, everyday level, the absence of missionization and the relatively light cultural burden of colonialism have been felt in matters of dress, deportment, and language, as Northerners did not feel the same pressure as Southerners to become Christian and Western. On a political level it meant that the British colluded and fostered the tendency among the Hausa to remain separate from their counterparts in the South. Where Northerners (British and Nigerian) looked down on Southerners as "black Europeans," Southerners derided the North as backward and poorly educated, stereotypes still largely in place today. Indirect rule also meant that the vast majority of the technical and clerical class trained by the British under colonial rule was Southern; this instituted a divide, again still largely in place, in which the South is seen as the more developed and technologically advanced. Perhaps most important, it inaugurated the practice of emphasizing Northern exceptionalism whenever the central government was controlled by the South as a means of avoiding the imposition of Southern authority. This was fostered during the colonial period by both British and Nigerians and through the period of independence with the policy of "one North." J. H. Carrow, former resident of Kano and Sokoto, argued that the regionalism problem that emerged with the *sardauna*[10] had its roots in the more radical policy of indirect rule promoted by Lieutenant Governor Palmer in the 1920s, which urged the creation of a "Separate Independent Holy North" free of all control by the South.[11] When a Southern Christian, Olusegun Obasanjo, was elected president of Nigeria in 2000 (after decades of rule by Northerners), it is no coincidence that a short while after, several Northern states declared shari'a law. In this they followed a long tradition in Nigeria of insisting on Northern exceptionalism and using religion to establish domains of action over which the federal government was expected to have little authority.

By creating a new educational system, by promoting a transition toward a new Western-educated bureaucracy, and by restricting the bulk of that transformation to one part of society, the British were digging themselves into a hole. Criticism of these policies, even among Northerners, was sustained. W. R. Crocker (1937: 110), a northern district officer, wrote a series of scathing critiques of colonial administration, lashing out at what he saw as an ultraconservative bias that turned indirect rule from a pragmatic starting point to an ossified "theological formula to be discussed only by the hierarchs," resulting in a "pro-Fulani[12] and pro-Moslem creed of a fervor and a singleness unseen since Ɗan Fodio's days." In a later book, he blamed pro–indirect rule governors, who "discouraged, sometimes they banned, the teaching of English and of modern trades and techniques and who insulated the people from all outside contacts and knowledge in the Holy Name of Indirect Rule" (Crocker 1949: 59). Crocker realized that this "is why in the North today most of the clerks in Government and commerce and most of the technicians and employees in the Posts and Telegraph, the Public Works Department, and the Railways are not Northerners but Southerners" (ibid).

This was acknowledged forcefully when Sir Donald Cameron took over as governor of Nigeria in 1931. Cameron came to Nigeria from Tanganyika, where he initiated a pro–indirect rule policy (Mamdani 1996). But Cameron had previously worked in Southern Nigeria and had no time for the exaggerated policies of the North. In a famous speech to the Legislative Assembly in 1933 he pointed out starkly the problems in administration, attacking the idea that "Moslem Administrations should be sheltered as far as possible from contact with the world." This resulted, he argued in "an unreformed 'feudal monarchy'" that "could not be expected to stand up against the natural forces of a Western civilization that was gradually but quite perceptibly creeping further north" (cited in Gailey 1974: 117). The task of government, as Cameron saw it, was to provide machinery for constructive change and to quick-start the North on a march to modernization. His critique had a perceptible effect on the young administrators who came to power in the 1930s and began to realize the educational and technological gulf separating Southern from Northern Nigeria (see Yakubu 1996).

The British desire for a pristine, untouched Northern Nigeria inevitably conflicted with their desire to generate change. This conflict between preservation and "progress" was a structural tension at the heart of indirect rule and how this policy was enacted from governor to governor, resident to resident, and over the course of colonial rule. At times colonialism operated through the logic of separation, demarcating citizen from subject and awarding different rights based on these categories. Yet this was not a fundamental but a situational part of rule, and accounts that reify one aspect of the duality fail to recognize the dialectic. Progress and preservation, identity and difference, were in mutual contest, now one dominant, now the other. This was played out not just in stages over time (so that Northern Nigerian colonialists emphasized preservation in the 1920s and transformation in the 1950s) but within the same administrations and, in the case of people like Cameron, within the same person. The desire for separation and preservation was always in tension with another equally strong desire for "progress" rooted in the nineteenth-century evolutionary idea of mutability. This was the socialism undergirding the Fabian notion of imperial rule, which asserted the role of government in promoting what would come to be called development and which in Britain (and Nigeria) came to fruition in the postwar 1945 Labour government. Sir Arthur Creech-Jones, secretary of state for the colonies in the 1940s, announced that "British policy is to bring African territories to self-government" through representative democratic institutions that involved self-rule. He argued that indirect rule was "now obsolete because by its very nature it was static in conception and this is not suitable for a dynamic policy of development or progress" (Idahosa and Shenton n.d.).

The concept of progress acknowledged the reality that Africans would move into the situations and positions of power now occupied by Europeans, thus, in the context of a Labour government, building in the idea of an end to colonial rule itself. This progressivism derived from the Enlightenment view that human society was in constant movement, open to change, and that individuals, like societies, were potentially perfectible through rational self-achievement. Colonialism, as a form of power, operated not through isolation and separation alone but through this transformative idea of improvement and assimilation. Progress can thus be seen as a mode of social ordering, of governmentality in Foucault's sense that power works not by repression but by incorporation and internalizing modes of rule. Colonialism based on institutional segregation, the fact that Africans could never and perhaps should never be like Westerners, was in tension with colonialism that insisted Africans had to become like Westerners. Doctrines like indirect rule, rather than conceptually and politically constant, are best seen as messy, internally contradictory, and in sustained tension internally and externally.

In Nigeria this dialectic between preservation and transformation was expressed through the tropes of isolation and connection. The media theorist Armand Mattelart (1996, 2000) makes the argument that all ideas of progress from the Enlightenment are necessarily based on representations of a world in movement, where the free flow of ideas (enlightenment) merges with the free flow of goods (liberalism) to aid the development of societies. Certainly British colonialists came to believe that the possibility of social and economic transformation was based on ending the North's "isolation." Crocker's complaint (above) that champions of a "Holy North" insulated Northerners from change by refusing to teach them modern techniques or even the English language mimics Resident Carrow's protest against the effort to keep the Northern Territories "isolated and protected from so-called undesirable influences outside of their boundaries."[13] Empire linked Nigerians into a network that connected the most outlying rural area to a wider set of systems. Modernization meant to be connected to a network, and infrastructures were the necessary material bases of those connections. Where Crocker views the English language as the infrastructural mechanism for bringing change, others saw this effort engineered into the pylons, tarmac, and concrete of infrastructural development. This is why technologies were rarely invisible in Nigeria but were invested with intense representational loads, their quotidian technical functions overlain by the swirling contest over change and preservation, Christianity and Islam, indirect and direct rule. It is why technologies were not neutral objects but invested with dense—if unstable—symbolic meaning (see figures 3, 4, and 5).

ARRIVAL OF HIS EXCELLENCY'S TRAIN.

THE GUARD OF HONOUR.

3, 4, and 5. Celebrations and decorations surrounding the opening of the railway bridge at Jebba in 1916 by Governor of Nigeria, Lord Lugard. From E. D. Morel, *Nigeria: Its Peoples and Its Problems* [1911] London: Frank Cass and Co. Ltd., 1968.

THE COLONIAL SUBLIME

To understand the role colonial rule played in the representation of technology and of technology as representation it is useful to think of a concept of the colonial sublime. The sublime, for Edmund Burke and Immanuel Kant, is the individual or collective response to a confrontation with phenomena or events outside of the imagination's possibility to comprehend. Most usually, this was associated with the natural world and the greatness of mountains, volcanoes, or hurricanes. For Kant (1952: 91), the sublime is about a representation of limitlessness, an appreciation of something so great it overwhelms our power to comprehend it; in consequence it performs, in the translation of James Creed Meredith, "an outrage on the imagination." In his *Critique of Judgement*, Kant divides the concept of the sublime into the mathematically sublime and the dynamically sublime. The mathematically sublime involves a sense of magnitude, the awe that comes with experiencing something "absolutely great." This experience of greatness, though, rests on the relational, subjective character of appreciation and judgment. Unlike Burke, who located the sublime in the grand and terrifying natural objects themselves, Kant argued that the sublime can never exist in the object but only in the apperception of objects by a judging subject. Objects become sublime because we judge them in relation to other objects. Inherent to this is not size in and of itself but a relation between things. As Kant (1987: 105) argues, "that is sublime in comparison with which all else are small"; so the sublime resides not in the object itself but in our ideas about it and in "the disposition of the soul." This relational character is key because, in the case of colonialism, it emphasizes that there the sublime could only work by having a comparative pole, tradition—something to which it is greater. If one vests an idea of the sublime in the greatness of technology, this necessitates technologically ranking and ordering society and culture. It means dividing what is great from what is worthless.

The issue of power implicit in this idea is foregrounded even more in Kant's conception of the dynamically sublime. Here the sublime is experienced not so much through a sense of its absolute greatness but through the overwhelming physical powerlessness individuals feel in the face of something overpowering and terrible. It is the sense of power and fear that provokes Kant's recognition of the ambivalent nature of the sublime, which inspires a simultaneous appreciation of beauty, awe, and terror, what Jean-François Lyotard (1994: 127) refers to as "an admixture of fear and exaltation." The dynamically sublime operates through an assertion of might and power that can be terrifying and which is impossible to oppose. We can picture resistance to it, Kant tells us, but at the same time we realize that resistance is useless.

One intent in using infrastructural technologies in colonial rule was to provoke feelings of the sublime not through the grandeur of nature but through the work of humankind.[14] The erection of factories; the construction of bridges, railways, and lighting systems; indeed the terrifying ability to remake landscapes and force the natural world to conform to these technological projects by leveling mountains, flooding villages, and remaking cities; these were the ways in which the sublime was produced as a necessary spectacle of colonial rule. The colonial sublime is precisely intended to indicate the sense of power—the feeling of submission and prostration that Kant sees as integral to how the sublime operates as a mode of representation. And there is some evidence to suggest that many Muslim Hausa, at least in certain periods, reacted to new technologies and indeed to colonial rule as a whole with the mixture of horror and incomprehension that marks the sublime. But the colonial sublime carries within it two distinct modes of colonial rule. One is based on difference and the sharp separation between colonizer and colonized when technology is used to incite awe. The other proffers technology as a mode of development. It proffers access, through education and training, that domesticates the sublime and thus destroys it. This mode collapses otherness through the lure of technology as a way of becoming modern.

An early and powerful expression of this came to Northern Nigeria with the construction of the Baro-Kano railway between 1907 and 1911. The railroad was designed to link the territory of Northern Nigeria to the Niger River, where it would meet steamers coming up from the port at Lagos. The building of the railway was an immensely important endeavor in Nigerian history as it fundamentally linked the two territories of Southern and Northern Nigeria and reoriented the Northern economy away from its traditional northern routes across the Sahara and south toward Lagos and export to a European market. It inaugurated the migration of Southern Christian Nigerians to Northern Muslim cities and involved administrative reorganization, so that some emirates along the railway line were reshaped to streamline construction. Percy Girouard was selected as governor of Northern Nigeria solely because of his expertise in railway construction. Indeed, there is a fair argument that the railway brought about the nation of Nigeria itself (Girouard 1908; Kirk-Greene 1984). The "railway imperative" (Kirk-Greene 1984) referred to the open rivalry between the two competing railway systems of Southern and Northern Nigeria. Like most large technologies, railways generate sociotechnical conditions—economic, political, and juridical—that allow them to exist. In this case, the need to finance the railway forced the amalgamation of two separate territories, Southern and Northern Nigeria, into one nation, Nigeria (Morel 1968; Shenton 1986). The "imperative" for amalgamation was driven by the need to unify the burden of debt incurred in building the project (Jaekel 1997, esp. chap. 4; Oshin 1988; Shenton 1986: 63–70; Umar 1997).[15] But this work was conducted at an enormous cost to those living along the route: as land was taken over for the line, 8 million cubic yards of soil was removed for earthworks, and thousands of farmers in each district were directed by their emirs to work as forced labor on the line. The dislocation was immense.[16]

Muhammad Sani Umar (2005), in his study of Muslim intellectual response to British imperialism, provides a fascinating account of the Islamic scholar and emir of Zaria, Aliyu Ɗan Sidi, arguing that his response to the building of the railway encoded a deep and complex reaction to the experience of colonial domination. As all emirs along the territory of the railway were expected to compel farmers to leave their fields and work on the railroad, Ɗan Sidi visited the site of construction in Nupeland in 1909 when construction was it its height to see what was involved. In just that one district more than three thousand men were pressed into working on the project. As an emir, Ɗan Sidi was well aware of the intense pressure the British were placing on all royal authorities to produce the necessary labor—often under the threat of removal from office. On his return, Ɗan Sidi wrote a poem, "Waƙar diga (The Song of the Digger), that Umar translates and analyzes at length for its commentary on colonial rule:[17] "After the conventional opening with an appropriate doxology (lines 1–3), Aliyu Ɗan Sidi states that news of the advent of the railway has caused fear and terror among people, and he went to see for himself the construction sites, even as he too was fearful about the railway" (132–33).

> 18) O Brother, what a wonder I saw:
> Steel cutting steel in the work of the digger!
> 19) Here trains without limit,
> More limitless was the cutting of steel for railways.
> . . .
> 23) All the heads of districts and villages
> Were terrified by the railway.
> . . .
> 24) Women and children and the mischief-makers,
> Used to say that the country is dispersed because of the digger.
> 25) The advance of the attacking enemy does not move the forest
> Much less for the rural areas to be dispersed for the digger.

Ɗan Sidi couches his response to the might of the railway in the form of the sublime. Only a few years after military conquest, he writes that even armies do not "move the forest" or the "rural areas" as the building work had done. Instead, now there are "trains without limit," and for those at the receiving end of British policy, seeing their landscapes and lives turned upside-down by this work, the only response is fear. Umar points out that in another poem, "Waƙar Zuwa Birin Kano," (Poem on Going to Kano) Aliyu Ɗan Sidi depicts steel as a symbol of raw strength and "uses the predator's application of strength to subdue its prey as an indicator of the power" of steel, and by extension, of the colonizer. In "Waƙar diga," Ɗan Sidi narrates his journey down to the construction site, the terror many had of the railway, and lists at great length the different people—the elderly, children, youth, women, district heads, village heads, ward heads, laborers, and common people—who were caught up in this project. What comes across is the immense scale of the construction. Steel is produced limitlessly for rails and bridges; forests are felled and the landscape is remade; whole villages are broken up and dispersed to make way for the railroad. Other villages are torn apart to produce labor for it.

Colonialism, in Ɗan Sidi's account, is presented as a sublime force, limitless in nature with huge powers at its disposal to control the natural and social world. In the realm of technology, it is at the moment these new forces are introduced that the sublime is most keenly felt, as they are not yet encapsulated in preexisting conceptual categories. Lyotard argues that the sublime creates an event "for which the mind will not have been prepared, which will have unsettled it" (cited in Ray 2004). The colonial sublime was an effort, by colonialists, to use technology as part of political rule and as evidence of the supremacy of European technological civilization. As the historian David Nye (1994: 60) argues, "the technological sublime does not endorse human limitations; rather, it manifests a split between those who understand and control machines and those who do not." But the weakness of technology is that as it becomes familiar its scale is reduced and the feeling of sublime dissipates. At the moment of technological innovation we are fixed by the "terror of their novelty," as the media theorist Friedrich Kittler (1999: xl) has it, but that terror is transient: the sublime can only be maintained for a short duration before petering out. The colonial sublime, while deeply powerful, was also surprisingly fragile, undermined by the very technological processes its power rested on. Perhaps unsurprisingly, given the regime of representation technologies operated under during colonial rule, they inspired intense ideological and cultural divisions. This was fully understood by Muslim jurists, who made technology, in many disparate forms, a key symbolic form dividing the faithful from the *kafir*.

In Northern Nigeria, this resistance was evident in a widespread and sustained attack by religious scholars on colonialism that focused precisely on its material culture. Early Islamic scholars inveighed against Muslims who consorted with Europeans through their technologies. The historian Mervyn Hiskett translated the work of one Islamic scholar, Umaru Wanda, whose poem "A Warning against Paganism and Innovation (*Bid'a*)"[18] provides a long list of forbidden activities associated with colonialism: wearing shorts, or shirts with collars, using a walking stick or (mass produced) soap, wearing a watch or using electric lamps or battery torches. "Even if you pray a thousand times," Wanda declares, the result will still be perdition for those who refuse to maintain separation.[19] Wanda represents a strident voice in a contested field of political and symbolic responses to the onset of colonialism, but the uncertainty many Muslims had, even educated ones, over whether new technologies brought by Europeans were Islamically permissible was real and sustained. Whether one could attend Western schools, work for Western companies, dress in suits and ties, speak English, or go to the cinema or theater were all subject to intense debate in the early years of colonial rule and for quite a few decades after. This wariness makes clear, as does the reaction of Aliyu Ɗan Sidi to railway construction, just how dense the association of technology with Christianity and unbelief was in the colonial period. Umar's analysis of Ɗan Sidi's poetry points out that his invocation of the greatness and limitlessness of colonial power was, in fact, a rhetorical means of setting up the point that no matter how technologically powerful the British were, supreme power finally rested with Allah in a domain where British power had little purchase. For Umar, the poem is ultimately subversive and a subtle way (for a powerful emir closely watched by his British overlords) to argue against colonial rule. Given this divisive context, the Europeans' claim that technology was part of a neutral, universal world of science was undermined by their equally insistent presentation of technology as specifically European (and, to Muslims, Christian).

WONDERS, MARVELS, AND EUROPEAN TECHNOLOGIES

The colonial sublime was represented in Nigeria through the tropes of wonder (in Hausa, *mamaki*) and fear (*tsoro*) and circulated through rumors, published reports, and newspaper accounts. Among Europeans, tales of the fantastical reactions of Africans to European technologies became a stereotype. Stories that African audiences ran away from a film close-up of a mosquito (see chap. 3) or refused to have their photograph taken for fear their soul would be stolen comprise a genre that many scholars argue tells us more about the fantasies of Europeans than the actual reactions of Africans. That may be, but I am less interested in these stories as evidence of African reactions, though it is worth pointing out that wonder, awe, and fear are affective responses common to the introduction of technology and mark the reactions of Europeans and Americans as much as they do Africans. My interest is in the fact that colonialists worked hard to record those reactions, printing them in newspapers, broadcasting them on the radio, and spreading them through tales and stories. It reveals how invested the British were in having Africans react to technology as a sublime force and shows the social effort they placed into making sure these reactions were recorded and circulated.

In 1932, the *Waziri* of Zaria, a senior royal figure, wrote for the colonial newssheet the *Northern Provinces News* an article titled "A Great Wonder" about his astonishment at the coming of an airplane to Zaria: "Had anyone told me that something was coming which would fly up into the air like a bird but which was not a living thing, I should have said, 'It is not true'" (9 April 1932, 15). A year later, in Bauchi Province, the chief of Dass wrote about his first trip in an airplane: "I was filled with wonder and fear and thought I should not be able to enter" (*NPN* 7 January 1934, 4). Perhaps the most famous report in this genre was of the trip of Muhammadu Dikko, the Emir of Katsina, to London, where his first flight was recorded by the Pathé news service: the white robes and turbans of the emir, his retainers and his children standing out against the dark uniforms of the Royal Air Force and the streamlined biplanes behind them.[20] In recounting this experience in a later trip (where he got to watch sound film for the first time) he recalled, "When I alighted the white men asked me what I thought about aeroplanes and I said, "Truly they are very wonderful. If they are brought to Hausaland I shall be the first to buy one" (*NPN*, 29 July 1933, 18). And he repeated the same sentiments about cinema concluding, "And what, you readers, could be more wonderful than that? Nothing" (ibid.).

Stories like these are more important for their performative than their referential function. While one can accept that these new technologies did astonish, there is no hiding the explicitly colonial function fulfilled by the stories, and indeed the newspaper they were printed in. When Muhammadu Bauchi, the chief Islamic judge of Bauchi Emirate, wrote of the coming of airplanes to Bauchi, he concluded (as he was no doubt expected to), "This is truly an astonishing thing, and every person of intelligence should realize that nothing is too much for the Europeans" (*NPN*, 23 July 1932, 23). The British toured their planes around to different provinces, flying royal elites into the air and then recording their reactions. These stories were printed in the *Northern Provinces News*, a newspaper aimed at "Residents and Native Chiefs" and almost wholly dedicated to representing the infrastructural achievements of British rule and the modernizing tendencies of Northern royal elites. The first issue announced it was to be written by Northerners, translated from Hausa into English and Fulfulde (and vice versa) by Northerners, and that even the paper itself was to be printed in Kaduna on a new press using Northern expertise. In both content and form, *NPN* was aimed at, and enacted, precisely the sort of colonial subject the British wished to build—progressive, interested in modern developments, literate, and cosmopolitan, yet still deeply Hausa (see figures 6, 7, and 8). Along with the flights of airplanes, the newspaper regularly described the coming of electricity, the building of roads, the immense power of the railway engines, and the speed at which emirs and chiefs could move about the country. It was here that the infrastructural transformations of urban life were recorded and spectacularized and their sublimity given force by depicting technologies through the amazed reactions of Nigerians who witnessed them.

The historian Luise White (2000) has written at length of the rise of fantastic rumors and stories told by East Africans in the 1950s as a form of narrative inquiry into the moral nature of technology and colonial rule. The stories she deals with tell of Africans working with the fire department who were accused of kidnapping people and draining their bodies of blood, or of Europeans believed to kidnap people in Tanganyika, smuggle their bodies onto Sabena airline flights, and cut them up and can them on flights to the Congo. White sidesteps the question of whether these fantastic stories are true, focusing instead on the fact that, true or not, these stories present a vulnerable world in which technologies of extraction and transport (needles, trucks, airplanes) were made objects of narrative focus and their role in everyday life questioned. They "reveal popular ideas about the interaction between culture and technology, between bodies and machines" at a time when the vast majority of Africans were ignorant of the closed world of technological expertise (L. White 2000: 132). It was a climate of anxiety in which rumor flourished. In a similar vein, the anthropologist Adeline Masquelier (2002) has examined rumors about spirits that haunt the tarmac roads of Niger, possessing people and causing fatal accidents. She argues that part of the ambivalence about roads comes from the historical memory of road building and the forced labor used in construction. These stories link "the road and its deadly spirits to the region's history of civil engineering, emergent capitalism and religious transformation" and the ambivalent history of infrastructures in colonial societies (834; see also Masquelier 1992, 2000). The narratives of wonder about the coming of the airplane and electricity revolve just as much around the relationship between technology and colonial rule but offer a different sort of insight. They are more about the fantastic ways Europeans fetishized technology than they are about African modes of belief. The colonial sublime is about Europeans' tactile and symbolic effort to make technology mean. This was a sustained effort and can be parsed out through the rituals surrounding the openings of infrastructural projects and the constant need to foreground infrastructural achievements. But the project was inherently unstable. What is sublime one day is domesticated and banalized the next. Mohammed Sani Umar (1997), writing about Dikko's accounts of several trips to England, notes how impressed the emir was on his first visit and how in later accounts he grew increasingly silent about the "wonders" of European technologies. Dikko himself was nothing if not quickly able to delight in technology without attendant emotions of awe and fear and just as quick to domesticate technology by purchasing it and turning it into a means to exalt his own person. Awe produced by technology, while mighty, is at the same time vulnerable and short-lived.

CONCLUSION: INFRASTRUCTURE AND TECHNOPOLITICS

One of the great promises of colonialism in its latter days, when political domination had to be legitimated by the promise of "progress," was transformation through infrastructural innovation. Here the erection of material infrastructures offered what seemed an unmitigated good: the supplanting of mud architecture with concrete; the provision of electricity and running water; the construction of railways, bridges, and roads. These were the brute facts on the ground that bore witness to the work achieved by colonial administration and also indicated the whole world of reason and science that colonialism could offer. In this logic of progress, the difference between colonizers and colonized was profound but, importantly, not absolute. Despite engrained ideologies of racial superiority, the tenacious enlightenment ideal of liberalism was based on a fundamental idea of mutability, the belief that all societies could evolve, develop, and mature. While many can point to how hollow the idea was, its operation as a mode of power rested in the gift of development it proffered. Technology, and its use in colonial arenas, materialized that idea of progress in that Africans, through careful training, could be trained to master this world of technical competence. In this way, technology had a double function: its technical one of transmitting radio waves, or moving people faster from one place to another, and its ideological mode of address, hailing people as new sorts of political subjects. This is how technology functioned in its governmental mode, promising a coming together (at some point, always in the future) of colonizer and colonized, where power operated not by difference but by the cultivation of sameness. This promise of sameness

6. Advertisement from the magazine *West African Annual* depicting the new subjects of colonial Africa: educated, white-collar workers, future oriented, progressive and technologically engaged. Image courtesy of Bodleian Library, University of Oxford.

7. Advertisement from the magazine *West African Annual*. Note the technology of the wired office and the communicative excess of the United Africa Company logo. Image courtesy of Bodleian Library, University of Oxford.

8. Advertisement from the magazine *West African Annual*. Image courtesy of Bodleian Library, University of Oxford.

existed at the same time and in constant tension with its opposite, the use of technology as sublime, based on separation and difference and materialized through spectacular openings and the sheer profusion of statistics that gave a dizzying sense of these projects' magnitude.

The intimacy between infrastructural projects and the ideological needs of the Nigerian state reveals how colonial rule was enacted through structures of technology and science and the technical workings of these new machineries. Here the technological organization of society through roads and rail, telegraph networks and phone lines, was intended as a political means of subjection, what Patrick Joyce (2003) and Timothy Mitchell (2002) have referred to as "techno-politics" (see also J. Scott 1998; and Prakash 1999). For Joyce, techno-politics rests on the idea that liberalism is a mode of politics that functions through invisibility—meaning the lack of overt intervention by governmental bodies in everyday affairs. In their place, liberalism seeks proxies in technological regimes—building sewers, organizing libraries, mapping, counting censuses—which are political precisely because they are seen as technical and so outside of political processes. In the colonial arena, while technology was certainly caught up with ideas of political rule, the great difference with the idea of techno-politics is that technology was visibly and constantly foregrounded by both colonizer and colonized as evidence of the separation between European and African. Every bridge built, every electric streetlamp erected, was intimately involved in overt representational as well as technical work. Such projects became a form of monumentalism that defined postcolonial African governments as much as colonial ones.

The way out of the simple instrumentalism of seeing infrastructures solely through the lens of colonial rule is to pay attention to the technical features of the technologies themselves. The materiality of media, their physical properties and the possibilities these properties create, stands in a complex relation of complicity and independence from the intentions that go into its construction. These intentions do not easily go away, and long after haunt technologies by shaping the conceptual horizons of what people expect them to be. They need to be understood precisely so one can comprehend how people react to them. But they cannot totally determine. In the rise of the radio stations—built by a colonial regime according to many of the ruling ideas laid out in this chapter—we see the mutability of technologies, their unruliness and capacity to create possibilities in excess of their expected use, as well as how these tensions between order and possibility, object and intention played out and evolved over time.

2

Unstable Objects

THE MAKING OF RADIO IN NIGERIA

IN 1944, ENGINEERS IN KANO began to erect loudspeakers on the walls outside the emirate council office, the public library, the post office, and other prominent public places. The words and music coming from these speakers were radio broadcasts, mainly from England, which were captured by a central receiver and amplifier, relayed by wire to individual households and public loudspeakers, and then discharged into urban space for any in earshot to hear. Radio, which we tend to think of now as a domestic phenomenon, began its life in Nigeria as a public technology. In its early years, the vast majority of Hausa could only listen to the radio by gathering around public loudspeakers at certain times of the day. Even the listening experiences inside households were quasi-public in that large numbers of extended family gathered together to hear the broadcasts. According to the main programmer for the Northern Region, "twenty or thirty listeners per set" *inside* the domestic household, "was quite normal."[1] But this number was dwarfed by the large crowds gathered around the loudspeakers outside. At first people were attracted by radio's novelty and sat around listening to broadcasts in English, which most could not understand. Later, programs of Hausa music were added and proved to be highly popular along with broadcasts of greetings sent home from Hausa soldiers overseas.[2]

Radio diffusion—the wired relay of radio signals—continued the process of mediating urban space in Nigeria. The voices and music of radio overcoded urban streets and houses (Manovich 2001), injecting new sorts of sounds that were not there before, creating new types of aural experience, reorganizing the spaces of urban leisure so that people came to meet and congregate in places organized by the presence of the loudspeaker. The loudspeaker also became an object connecting those present to places elsewhere, inserting them in overlapping, sometimes competing, circuits of political identity where the urban competed with the regional, the regional with the national, and the nation with Empire itself: music was programmed in Kano, news broadcasts came from the center of the Northern Region at Kaduna, national news came from Lagos, while the BBC overseas service addressed Kano as part of a larger imperial circuit. Loudspeakers thus formed part of the tactile, everyday world of colonial urban life and created channels of radio waves, cables, receiving sets, and sound waves that connected that world to a larger network. Like all infrastructures, radio was about making things mobile and placing them in circulation. But as with other infrastructures, that space of circulation was not neutral but encoded a relation between the state and its subjects. In the North of Nigeria, the emergence of radio coincided with (and was brought about by) an internal shift in British colonialism that gave rise to a new modernizing class of colonial officer impatient with the slowness of indirect rule and averse to its tendency to separate and detach Northern Nigerians from wider regional and imperial rule. Radio was one of a host of infrastructural changes designed to end this isolation and make the North mobile. When groups of Hausa began to congregate outside the emirate council offices to listen to radio, these tensions between isolation and circulation, ignorance and knowledge, past and future were at play in the sounds and sight of the radio itself.

Wired broadcasting was first used in Britain in the 1920s and was introduced in Nigeria in the 1930s. The first radio signals in the North were captured when engineers used the masts of the Benue River bridge to pick up BBC broadcasts. Proposals were made to establish radio diffusion in the main urban centers of the country and were resisted, proposed again, and finally began to be realized when the first Radio Distribution Service (RDS)[3] opened in Lagos in 1935, picking up the BBC signal from Britain and relaying it via a land line to individual subscribers. From the perspective of our present, when the ontology of radio seems so firmly tied to the idea of broadcast, wired rediffusion seems a peculiar thing, and indeed it was relatively short-lived: by the 1950s, radio in Nigeria switched to wireless. Yet what now seems an experimental period throws into relief the contingency of radio and the technological order of reality it creates. The service that we know now, where radio is broadcast from large antennae erected on the highest hills in the region, where the waves run in narrow channels just below and above other channels crowding the spectrum with different programs, and where these are received by listeners with sets that can be tuned from station to station, is not the inevitable shape of radio but something that only came to pass in Nigeria after a series of tense and sustained discussions. And indeed the recent adoption of fixed channel radio sets handed out by Christian missionaries in Africa suggests that the mutation of radio has not finished.[4] The technical shape of radio emerged from the conflict within colonial rule between the pace and shape of cultural preservation and colonial transformation played out in the amplifiers and wires of the RDS. Radio was an infrastructure placed into service to meet the propaganda and cultural needs of a colonial regime. It was an information order, to be layered on top of older orders, intended to enounce, through the sublime nature of its technology and the authoritative nature of its content, the power and promise of modern life. How then did radio actually operate in places like Kano, Northern Nigeria?

URBAN RADIO

Radio was part of the technologizing of public urban space in Kano. While ornate radio sets could define the aesthetics of a modern colonial house (Mrázek 2002; Spitulnik 1998–99), in its early years in Nigeria, radio was a public not a domestic thing. It broadcast its flow of sound onto the city streets and to the people listening, passing by, or working around it (see figure 9). Radio overlaid new data-flows onto the built space of a city that was already undergoing an aural transformation brought by motorcars, railroads, and a range of new industrial sound. The peculiarity of radio as a medium was the separation of sound from source, of voice from body. This

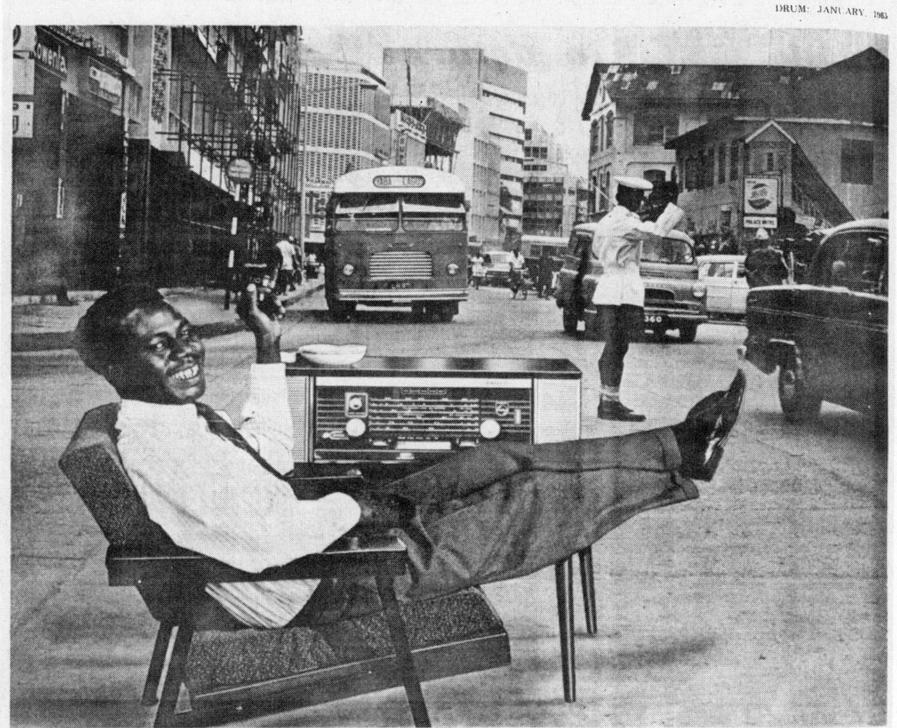
DRUM: JANUARY, 1963
This big-sound Philips can be heard anywhere! Listen to a powerful Philips radio. Anywhere. Don't concentrate, just relax. You'll hear every word, every note, because Philips big-sound loudspeakers are quality-built for powerful performance and full, clear tone. Whether you're dancing, talking, driving, or just listening, you can always *hear* a Philips.
Get big sound, big value in a PHILIPS
PHILIPS
Symbol of Quality—Sign of Perfection
PHILIPS (NIGERIA) LTD., HEAD OFFICE: P.M.BAG 1136, APAPA. BRANCH OFFICES: P.O.B. 76, PORT HARCOURT. P.O.B. 335, KADUNA

9. Advertisement from the magazine *Drum* (Nigeria) evoking the new sounds of urban life. Image courtesy of Bodleian Library, University of Oxford.

medium was aimed at listeners addressed not by ethnicity or religion (at least, not all the time) but who were, in principle, equivalent members of a public. In a curious way, radio also embodied leisure time. In a place where agrarian rhythms dominated rural life and religion was the prime demarcation of time, the colonially imposed division between work and nonwork as organizing principles of the day was new and yet to be internalized. By dividing radio broadcast into a foreign-language service during work hours and a vernacular service that came on when the workday (as defined by Europeans) was finished, radio materialized leisure time in sound waves, its broadcast creating a new experiential rhythm to the day.

In its first few decades radio feed was carried by cable, not broadcast over the airwaves, so radio sets were little more than loudspeaker boxes that could not be tuned to other stations. Programming was largely restricted to the BBC. Individual subscribers were limited mostly to expatriates and the highly educated; the vast majority of Hausa listened to the radio at public listening stations. The very wealthy could, of course, purchase their own wireless sets and tune into any station they could capture, but at this point there was no service broadcast from Nigeria. And no matter how expensive the sets were, the distortion and interference on wireless could not compete with the better sounding signal from the RDS. In the late 1930s, local programming was added to the BBC's *General Overseas Programme*: news broadcasts and announcements in Hausa, "vernacular" records (in different Nigerian languages), and even Indian music.[5] The addition of local programming was a response to the mixed reception RDS was getting from colonial officials at the provincial level. For many "indirect rulers" in administration, radio was seen at best as a waste of resources and effort and at worst as a threat to the independence and cultural integrity of the North. Vernacular broadcasts helped assuage that fear by foregrounding local culture, and local news broadcasts gave colonialists a useful channel for propaganda.

Radio was part of the economy of circulation in the imperial era, moving ideas and propaganda around a series of circuits aimed at constituting differing levels of political identity. As I noted earlier, Nigeria was at this time a nation-state subject divided into three regions (the West, East, and North), each with its own government and governor general. These regions themselves were divided into a series of provinces, with a dual leadership of a British resident and, in the North, a local emir. In its early years, radio diffusion operated at the imperial level (the BBC) and at the local, provincial level (vernacular news broadcasts and music). Perhaps what is most striking and easy to ignore about radio in its first few decades of operation is its unintelligibility. The small amount of local programming was overwhelmed by the relay of BBC programs made in England, BBC Arabic broadcasts, and Indian and English records, all broadcast to a target population overwhelmingly ignorant of those languages. Maitama Sule, an early broadcaster and later a major Northern politician, said that the popularity of radio rested heavily on its use of Hausa music, and that the rest was just confusing. In the early 1940s, Maitama recalled that those without a set would throng to listening stations or at the houses of those who possessed one to listen to Hausa singers like Hamisu Maiganga and, later, the great Mamman Shata, but it is unclear what impression those long periods of incoherence made.[6] This programming creates a splitting effect in a population by introducing noise, the unintelligible signal, as a regular part of media flow. Whether the programming was the BBC, English-language Nigerian broadcasts, or Hindi music, Hausa listeners were being habituated to a medium where they were addressed as the unintended objects of messages not created for them. Major linguistic variation in Nigeria meant that in the early days even "vernacular broadcasts" were incomprehensible to large numbers of listeners who could not understand the main languages of Yoruba, Hausa, or Igbo. Noise is still communicative, however, as unintelligibility does carry in it a promise. Its very distortion enacts the colonial ideal of progress by suggesting that while the signal is incoherent now, the future of individuals and of society as a whole is comprehension. The RDS signal in this sense is not pure noise; rather it is yet to be understood language, addressing contemporary native subjects as future colonial citizens.

By sending unintelligible signals to a Northern Hausa population, the RDS, by implication, highlighted the presence of classes of Nigerian society that could understand these messages: the small number of Western-educated Hausa and the large and growing number of Southern Nigerian migrants in the North. Through its use of language, radio materialized cleavages in society where lack of understanding was not a neutral position but placed one in a hierarchy of ignorance vis-à-vis others. Listening to radio and comprehending it was one of the myriad practices that confirmed the modern orientation of Southern Christians and the continuing "backwardness" of the majority of Muslim Hausa. This split was reiterated in a different way by the small but influential class of young, Western-educated Northern Muslims who in Kano came together to form radio listening clubs. Most of these were middle school teachers, the highest-educated Northerners at the time, and graduates of Katsina College, the elite private school modeled on Eton.[7] They represented an emerging elite, the *'yan boko* (Western-educated elites) who, though they spoke English, were invested in having Hausa news broadcast on modern technologies such as the radio and were cosmopolitan enough to take interest in the wider war news and the comedies and quizzes coming from England. *ITMA*, the Tommy Handley radio comedy, set in the Office of Twerps in the Ministry of Aggravation and Mysteries, was the most popular program—to the bemusement of colonial officers skeptical of whether these youths could "really" understand what was going on.[8] These listeners represented an emergent new collective, one with future on its side, but at that point squeezed between colonial and traditional hierarchies. These youths' delight in Tommy Handley and programs like it is no doubt a mark of distinction, a demonstration of their ability to work among the new circuits of information discharged onto Kano by the new medium. It may be that these listeners could not understand the broadcast in the way British listeners could, but unintelligibility and noise is a constituent part of all urban living and especially so in colonial situations undergoing intense change.[9]

The erection of a radio network entered into an increasingly differentiated and contested social field in colonial Kano, where the emerging class of 'yan boko clashed with the existing aristocratic elite (supported by the British) and the *ulama*, the religious leaders (some of whom were royal aristocrats) who were part of the establishment, but who had more autonomy and less direct connection to colonial administration. For the British, this class was the natural product of their endeavors, the modern-minded but still religious Hausa-Fulani subject who could combine the best elements of the Western tradition without destroying Hausa culture. These were the people who were to staff the radio networks, move into the bureaucracy, and run the schools. But, as Mahmood Yakubu examines at length, as this class moved into more powerful positions, royal elites became suspicious of this "counterelite," leaving the British with a thorny problem. They could support the modern class that the entire logic of colonial rule had been dedicated to producing, but to do so would threaten the aristocracy's authority with which the British were so firmly allied. 'Yan boko complained bitterly about Native Administrations which they saw as inept, conservative, and riddled with nepotism, corruption, and incompetence. They believed that the British had made these administrations far more powerful than in precolonial times, and so while these elites were Western educated and modern minded, they often were also fiercely critical of British rule.

The new technological order of radio was introduced into this contested field, and the physical and conceptual shape the medium came to take was intimately tied to these competing groups and their conflicted relation with British rule.

Radio's implication with colonialism meant that, perhaps inevitably, while 'yan boko were in strong favor, the technical features of the medium were interpreted by many Hausa through the lens of religious suspicion. While radio never occasioned the fierce backlash that cinema did, it inevitably came up against the religious questioning all new technologies faced. For the more conservative, radio was *ipso facto* Christian, broadcasting *kafir* (un-Islamic) sounds into the Islamic heart of Kano's old city. Adamu Salihu, who worked for the Zaria RDS during its early years, recalled that some mallams argued for the permissibility of radio, saying they were like talking drums and merely a neutral medium for the transmission of information. More conservative mallams questioned the ontology of radio itself and its legal status under Islamic law. Central to this was the conception of reproduction. If a voice is encoded in one place, transmitted by radio waves to a different city, relayed from pole to pole by cables, and then finally wired into an individual box, is the sound that issues from that box a *reproduction* or an *extension* of a voice? This was key, Salihu argued, because certain mallams argued that if the broadcast was an extension of a person, then a male voice coming into the domestic arena contravened the Islamic separation of the sexes—they did not want their wives listening to the voices of unrelated men.[10] This issue went to the ontology of radio sound, its physical and scientific properties, and the question of whether a data stream can ever be severed from its origin. For other religious figures, radio raised the entirely different issue of magic and whether the separation of sound from person could be achieved without magical help. Sheikh Nasiru Kabara, a senior Islamic cleric in Kano and himself a onetime member of the RDS advisory board, argued that many conservative clerics saw the medium as occult, that if you could not see the person talking then it must be magic and that all magic was explicitly un-Islamic.[11] The separation of data stream from person also raised political issues. Emir Abdullahi of Kano, for instance, banned recitations of the Qur'an that were relayed from Britain despite the fact they were recited by eminent clerics. Before electronic mediation, official Qur'anic reciters were appointed by the emir himself, and he had full knowledge of the moral standing of the person reciting as well as his family background. Radio replaced the embodied, socially rooted sound of the reciter with that of an anonymous, impersonal medium, one that was crucially outside the emir's control, affecting his status in matters of religion—precisely where his authority was supposed to be strongest.[12]

Religious dissension indicates how technical capacities of media—in this case the separation of sound from body, its transmission and broadcast—have to be negotiated in a society. Radio had a colonial provenance that provoked the religious reaction to it, and conservative reaction to it provoked, in turn, its own responses as the status of radio was debated both in the religious hierarchy and between the ulama and other elite classes in Hausa society. Radio produced categories of listeners as modern or conservative based on their acceptance or rejection of the technology and the leisure habits that went with it.

By binding Northern Nigerians into wider national and imperial circuits, radio imposed a new information order over existing ones. This order was not based on the interpersonal exchange of information; it was abstract, nonlocal, and outside the control of both Nigerians and, to a degree, British administrators. To a colonial bureaucracy that had insisted on the exceptionalism of the North as a way of keeping it isolated, one can see how radio's ability to link people into new "clusters of relationships" (Lefebvre 1991: 86) could be seen as potentially destabilizing.

MAKING RADIO

Instrumentally, the decision to introduce radio created a powerful channel for propaganda, but it was also part of the larger project of opening up Nigeria to ideas and concerns from outside its borders, making it more cosmopolitan and more tightly integrated into the wider world. Before beginning this process in the 1930s, the government of the Northern Region in Kaduna sent out inquiries to residents at the provincial level asking whether they thought the project was advisable, whether there would be enough subscribers to make it viable, if there was enough electricity to run it, and whether it would be valuable to administration. Unfortunately for the modernizers in the government, reaction to the idea of radio was mixed. In 1939 the resident of Kano poured cold water on the idea. Well-to-do Africans already had wireless sets, he argued, and leaders in both Kano's old city (the Muslim heart) and the Sabon Gari (the new town built for Southern Christian migrants) rejected the idea of having public loudspeakers. In his opinion, the technology was too expensive, there was little indigenous interest, and the matter should be dropped. Kano, it should be remembered, was the economic powerhouse of the North, with the wealthiest and most diverse population. If radio could not thrive there then its chances elsewhere in the North were small. In 1941, when the Northern government approached him again, pointing out the advantages in using radio to broadcast news and disseminate propaganda as well as to educate people, he was equally dismissive. He reiterated his objections and claimed, for the first time, that the emir was opposed, too. The best way of relaying news, he wrote, was the established way. Kaduna should instruct him, he would inform the emir, who would tell his district heads, who would tell those below them. Evidently broadcast, with its cheeky avoidance of established lines of hierarchy, was unnecessary.[13]

As occurred with surprising frequency during colonial rule, the arrival of a new resident in Kano brought a quick and decisive reversal in policy. J. H. Carrow, who came to Kano in 1943, was a long-serving official who had previously been resident in Sokoto, the seat of the sultanate but a more religiously oriented, less economically aggressive city than Kano. In his earlier career, Carrow had been a devout supporter of the idea of a "sacred North" that should be preserved from Southern Nigeria and "anything strange from the outside world,"[14] but he had come to realize the limitations of that policy and now desired "progress" and modernization of Hausa society. In this Carrow was exemplary of the shifting balance of power in wartime Nigeria between colonialists who opposed change and those who saw it as necessary to the North's future. These "modernizing" colonialists were aided by the fact that the generation of Hausa rulers that had been trained under the British was beginning to move into positions of power and was less opposed to the introduction of Western education and technological change.

On taking full control of Kano, Carrow made support of the RDS a key symbolic part of his vision for the city's future, decisively rejecting his predecessor's conclusion and arguments:

> I regard the matter [of opening a Kano RDS station] as most important. . . . I have to record that I do NOT consider the opposition to public loudspeakers at key points to be found in previous comments in this file as in any way final.
>
> Kano is a most important cosmopolitan trade center. We certainly cannot oppose every modern development. It is our duty to teach the leaders the important value of such matters.[15]

The decision to fund RDS stations in Nigeria was driven by the propaganda needs of the Second World War, but for colonialists like Carrow, radio materialized a theory of rule and administration, a new relationship between the state and its subjects. Radio was a potent means of communicating with large numbers of people. Propaganda was decisive in securing funds and releasing political energy, but there was a great cultural belief in the transformative power of radio and the modernizing influence of new technologies. This belief borders on fetish and is a powerful aspect of the technophilia that often accompanies the introduction of new technologies into African societies, from the radio to the computer: that modern technologies make people modern. Not content with opening an RDS station in Kano, Carrow went over the objections of the resident of Sokoto to advocate for the opening of an RDS station there. "There is always the tendency for Sokoto, Gwandu and Argungu to be parochial and wholly disinterested in matters outside their own area," he wrote to the provincial secretariat in Kaduna. "The Sultan has a difficult enough task as it is to keep up without preventing him from obtaining such modern aids to progress as radio diffusion."[16]

Behind Carrow's complaint about the "parochialism" of Hausa-Fulani society was a powerful belief in the organization of modern society as part of a circulatory system. For Carrow and other colonialists, modernity was most clearly expressed through the tropes of exposure and connection. Radio connected Nigerians to wider symbolic circuits; its role was to produce a "progressive interest in affairs happening outside the community" and to make people "more knowledgeable and curious of events further afield."[17] This belief draws on the deep history of the role the concept of circulation plays in ideas of the Enlightenment and in liberalism. As the communications scholar Armand Mattelart (1996, 2000) has argued, circulation was central to the idea of a world freed from the fixed hierarchical relations of feudal society; the concept represented a world in movement and open to change. The Enlightenment was based on the idea of the mutability of human society, its perfectibility governed by the free flow of ideas unfettered by church and state and, as Kant crucially argued, circulated through the mechanism of the reading public. Liberalism itself is based on the idea of wealth being freed from its tie to land and realized instead through the circulation of commodities (Marx 1990). Circulation encodes ideas central to the mythic constitution of modern societies—"circulating civilization," as Mattelart (1996) refers to it—but for movement to exist, it requires the constitution of technical systems of canals, roads, railways, and telegraphs, which create the material channels through which movement can occur. Mattelart analyzes these at length, his interest focused on the fact that circulation is about standardization, rationalization, regulation, bureaucracy, and the state. The technical operation of these systems generates the laws and personnel necessary to maintain them, the national languages to make them work, the ordering of time, and the regulation of space. Modernization theory drew heavily on these ideas, and one can see the link between Carrow and 1950s political scientists in their common belief that media would provide the infrastructural system to produce a mobile subject capable of psychic mutability. "Exposure" in the light of these concepts is not just access to ideas from elsewhere; it is a positive good in and of itself. Circulation has a mediating force all its own (see figure 10).

The British hoped that radio would end the parochialism of conservative Islam and expose people to new ideas, new ways of thinking coming from different nodes in the circuit. They hoped it would abolish insularity and replace the slow connections made via the camel caravans and itinerant preachers of past information orders with the electronically organized, European-focused networks of colonial modernity. In this they shared with academic scholars a belief in the transformative cultural and psychic nature of radio. But where modernization theorists (e.g., Lerner 1958a, 1958b) viewed the change as overcoming "oriental fatalism" and leading to a newfound drive and ambition to change, the British saw radio's dominant contribution as linking segregated islands of culture into a network.

The erection of a radio system in Nigeria was part of the wider political and cultural role infrastructures were expected to play in Nigeria. Radio was indeed a powerful infrastructural presence. In 1946 Kano had 70 European subscribers to 430 African ones,[18] but by 1951 the total number of subscribers had risen to 1,222,[19] with Africans vastly outnumbering Europeans (and this did not count public loudspeakers). There were constant demands for more public boxes to be erected in the old city and the Sabon Gari, and with these increases came a call for more locally produced programming. The programming itself, under the control of a broadcasting officer housed in the Public Relations Department, made constant meta-reference to the infrastructural project of colonialism. In a series of talks, different government departments got their chance to introduce listeners to their work and achievements. Ostensibly educational, these talks on subjects such as "Water Supply and Electricity Provision" by the provincial engineer;[20] "How Trains Are Moved on the Railways," given by the traffic superintendent; and "On Infectious Diseases and Their Prevention," given by the health officer,[21] publicized the administration's infrastructural achievements. These are classic examples of technopolitics, the operation of political rule through the technical workings of social infrastructures.

10. Advertisement from the magazine *Drum* (Nigeria) emphasizing the centrifugal cultural force of radio. Image courtesy of Arewa House Centre for Historical Documentation.

The infrastructural work of radio diffusion was embodied in its antennae and loudspeakers and studios, and also in its programming on infrastructures. One gave publicity to the other. Bridges, roads, health initiatives, and radio sets were combined into concrete, material expressions of the developmentalist work of the colonial regime and its continual aim of progress.

UNINTENDED CONSEQUENCES AND BREAKDOWN

On 25 May 1951, at a meeting of the Kano RDS Advisory Committee, Bello Dandago, the broadcasting officer, advised the committee that following previous discussion, letters had been addressed to the provincial engineer and the electrical engineer to give radio talks on electricity and water supply, respectively.[22] This was part of a wider series of technical talks introducing the work of various government departments to the populace at large. Ahamdu Trader, a notable Kano business figure and the representative of the *birni* (Kano's Muslim old city) on the RDS Advisory Committee, maliciously responded to the idea by asking whether these talks could be supplemented with others on electricity failure and water shortages. His provocation points to the fact that while radio diffusion, infrastructures, and technology were invested with ideologies of progress and colonial supremacy, their reality in Nigeria was one of frequent breakdown and disrepair. Colonial rule was established physically through the grid of infrastructures that overlaid existing ones, refiguring territories and the political, economic, and social connections that went with them. But this rule was also embodied symbolically by the claims of science, progress, and power embedded in these infrastructures' technology. What happened when these ideologies of rule and symbolic power were subject to the everyday reality of failure?

Imperial rule produced the sublime as a powerful emotion evoked by immense transformations of colonialism and the spectacle of new machines and structures through which that rule was made manifest. But the sublime, while undoubtedly powerful, is vulnerable because it rests not in the thing itself but in the mind of the viewing subject and thus is constantly subject to change, always in motion. What may be incredible and terrifying at one point in history can become everyday and banal soon after. Reliance on technology for the production of sublime feelings works well in their moments of introduction when their technical properties are being established and their meanings still in flux. But soon the excitement, fear, and uncertainty diminish as the spectacular fades into the everyday. In Kano, debates about whether male voices could be heard in domestic female arenas quickly subsided; the fear that radio was magic, and that the bodiless voices emerging from speakers were diabolical passed on. Perhaps nothing reduces the grandeur and majesty of technological achievement more than its breakdown and failure. The plane that cannot take off, the bridge that sways and cannot be crossed, the distorted radio signal all evoke laughter or frustration, not fear and awe. It points to the gap between the fantasy of technology and its all too real operation. When Ahamdu Trader punctured the pretension of colonial public relations by suggesting talks on why electricity breaks down and why water supply dries up, his idea was rejected by another African representative from Sabon Gari. There was no point in having these talks, he argued, because these things happen all the time and everyone knows all about them already.[23]

In a letter to the *Nigerian Citizen*, the main paper of Northern Nigeria, one Nigerian reader wrote politely, "Sir, we all know that the position of a radio loudspeaker in the home is assuming an important part in present day civilization," before lamenting the fact that he signed up on a waiting list to receive the loudspeaker in April and had yet to receive it six months later.[24] Indeed the British inability to provide radio sets to meet demand was a problem that lasted for years. At one point the reason given was the waiting list for sets. When sets were available, there were problems in securing the necessary amount of copper wire to install them. One colonial officer argued that there was more than enough equipment to meet these needs but that it was all reserved for Lagos (where demand was higher)[25] and outside the North's control.

Whatever the reason, the reality was that the popularity of radio diffusion brought with it two immediate problems. By 1950 more than seven hundred people were waiting for boxes to be supplied to their houses. Three years later that number remained as high as six hundred, indicating the fundamental inability to repair failures in supply nearly a decade after the opening of RDS.[26] Additionally, the system had been built with only a small number of subscribers in mind, and the number of amplifiers available reflected that number. Every listener added to the service resulted in a progressive lessening of signal quality,[27] so the more successful radio was, the poorer it became. The lack of loudspeaker boxes, amplifiers, wire, and technical personnel meant that almost as soon as the service was up and running, listening to it was difficult, and service often unintelligible (even for those who understood English). Even when all were working in tandem there was an endemic problem with electricity supply, which "is subject to frequent breakdowns," the regional engineer pointed out, so that voltage continually varied causing the signal to fade in and out.[28] "My own experience was that it [the broadcast] was intelligible," wrote another officer in a defensive response to the engineer, but only "when the set was at full volume" (no doubt causing its own vibration and distortion) and that even then there was often "deep fading."[29] By 1950, only six years after RDS opened, the public relations officer (at that point in charge of all programming content) recommended that all broadcasts be suspended until repairs could be made, supplies received, and the signal made audible.[30] This advice was not followed.

The fantasy that media would provide a smooth aural channel connecting Nigeria to the wider world and making Northern Nigerians modern through this exposure and circulation was constantly undermined by the material conditions of existence for radio in the postwar period. In this case, the space of circulation itself was marked by disrepair and distortion, and if the deep mythologies of Enlightenment modernization rest on a neutral, invisible space of circulation, what does this do for the idea of modernity itself? Media like radio in the colonial era not only represent infrastructures (through talks and news broadcasts about the infrastructural achievements of the administration), they are infrastructures and, like all infrastructures, representational events. So what happens when what they represent is failure and breakdown or distortion and unintelligibility? Media still do the work of representing modernity, circulating information, generating new consumption practices, mediating urban space, and organizing new modes of leisure for individuals and groups. Yet at the same time they signify a lack. The connection is there but slowed; the new listening publics are formed but often dealing with media and technology in a condition of distortion or failure. In Nigeria, breakdown was as much a part of RDS as its connectivity and smooth operation, and technical disrepair produced sensorial and experiential conditions of distortion as much as regular functioning. Not surprisingly, disrepair had great consequences for colonialists' ability to produce a sense of sublime—the greatness of British technological achievement—in conditions of disrepair. Technological success was often threatened by the specter of failure, and as this success was intimately linked to concepts of progress, hierarchy, modernity, and subjugation, technology's failure could open spaces from which these concepts could be challenged. The operation of technologies threatened colonial rule by setting in motion unintended consequences.

WIRED VERSUS WIRELESS

By the early 1950s the poor functioning of radio diffusion was contrasted with the rise of a new, cheap wireless set—the saucepan special—made expressly for African listeners (Spitulnik 1998–99). While still much more expensive than renting a loudspeaker box, the saucepan special and the potential it represented emerged at the same time as an intense debate within colonial administration on the future of radio. Should radio be wired or wireless? Should it be controlled by the Nigerian state, commercial, or run by a foreign nonprofit (such as the BBC)? Should programming be geared to international, national, regional, or local needs? In terms of technical operation, institutional organization, and content, the entire organization of radio was being rethought with no necessary outcome. The intensity of this debate, in which the basic capacities of what this technology would become were discussed, and the passion of adherents on all sides reveal, the instability of radio as a set of institutional arrangements and even as an object itself. At the heart of this discussion was the question of Nigerians' political identity. Were they to be constituted locally, as *Kanawa* (Kano people); regionally, as Northern Nigerians; nationally, as Nigerians; or globally, as subjects of Empire? Given the tensions between the provincial and regional levels of government, and the even tenser relations between the regions and the national government in Lagos, these decisions were fraught with controversy. The outcome was the formation of the Nigerian Broadcasting Service (NBS) in 1952 and the switch to wireless broadcasting.[31] Broadcasts were to be based on a national program with substantial regional content. Gone was the International Service of the BBC, and gone, more controversially, were local programs at the level of the provinces (see figure 11). The debate over wired versus wireless service reminds us of technologies' instability. It interrupts their taken-for-granted status, recalling forgotten histories, and potential paths that objects could have taken. We are reminded that the technological order of reality a medium like radio brings about is a processual event. It emerges in specific circumstances from the interplay of material technologies with social and political contexts. Exploring why decisions are made in favor of one future for radio versus another makes palpable how these dynamics play with and against each other. This is all abundantly clear in the decision of whether to fund, build, and use wired or wireless radio.

The choice between radio diffusion and wireless came down two issues: technical questions of function and cost, on the one hand, and political

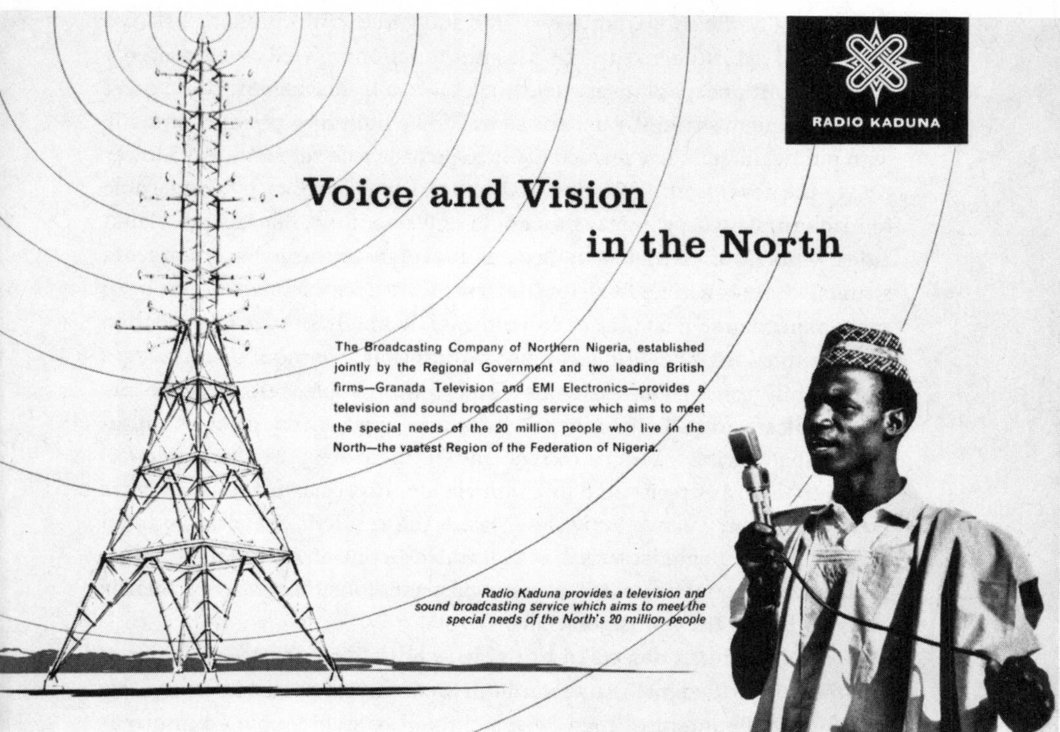

RADIO KADUNA
Voice and Vision
in the North
The Broadcasting Company of Northern Nigeria, established jointly by the Regional Government and two leading British firms—Granada Television and EMI Electronics—provides a television and sound broadcasting service which aims to meet the special needs of the 20 million people who live in the North—the vastest Region of the Federation of Nigeria.
Radio Kaduna provides a television and sound broadcasting service which aims to meet the special needs of the North's 20 million people

11. Detail from the brochure, *Northern Approach,* produced at independence to highlight the work of the Northern Region Ministry of Information. Image courtesy of Arewa House Centre for Historical Documentation.

control, on the other. Politically, the decision to switch to broadcast entailed reorganizing Nigerian radio and creating the NBS, with a national program based in Lagos and regional programs based in the capitals of the various regions: Enugu in the East, Ibadan in the West, and Kaduna in the North. The aim was to centralize news and use radio to create a greater sense of regional identity and national belonging. Producing a "Northern" identity became a major political goal in the North. Residents in the provinces, however, were altogether unsure of this aim. From their point of view, the change cut out the local programming tailored specifically to local ethnic and linguistic groups under their control. Politically, however, the greatest fear was that wireless introduced choice, and that no government would be able to control what station people listened to.

Technically, the choice between wired and wireless was pressing because with increased listeners the RDS was not functioning well and required a huge amount of capital investment to get it to a level where it would meet the government's needs. As wireless was to be built by a private company with public financing, it seemed likely to provide a better service at a lower cost to the government. Wireless also had the huge advantage of being able to reach rural areas, whereas RDS could only operate in densely populated cities. In its favor, though, RDS provided revenue to the government from rentals, whereas wireless did not (unless a license fee was levied). As cheap as the saucepan special was, at £6.10 it was still much more expensive than the £3 annual fee for renting a loudspeaker (payable in monthly rental fees of five shillings).[32] Wireless could reach more people, but those people could not afford it. Politically, the urban areas that RDS reached represented the crucible of social change and, in the run-up to independence, the likely locus of resistance to colonial rule. RDS "has obvious scope as a counter to subversive activities," wrote the resident of Adamawa in a minute arguing against wireless. "Need," he continued, cannot "be assessed from the technical broadcasting aspect alone [but] . . . is primarily dictated by political considerations."[33]

"One of the main objects of bringing radio to Nigeria," the resident of Kano was informed by the secretariat in Kaduna, "is to assist in the orderly and full development of the country through suitably planned informational and cultural programmes."[34] "Orderly" and "suitably planned" are key terms here, highlighting the politically charged role of radio in stimulating change and directing it in ways amenable to British policy. The great technical beauty of RDS, from a colonialist point of view, was that government bureaucrats could control exactly what information listeners had access to without fear that they might tune in elsewhere. At the height of the debate in the early 1950s, one broadcasting officer stated the argument for RDS succinctly.

> I said that I regarded rediffusion as being of great importance in the development of this country. It seemed to me unlikely that large numbers of people, especially of the poorer classes, would buy wireless sets of their own. It is these people that the government wishes to reach with propaganda and instruction. If they did have their own wireless sets, they would be unlikely to tune them in to reasonable stations. Rediffusion supplies an almost impregnable method of communicating rapidly with masses of people.[35]

For this officer, the technical function of rediffusion dovetailed with the political and developmental needs of a colonial government. Wireless loosens control by making available information outside the imperial circuit of the British Empire (from Russia, Egypt, and other challengers to British power). This was also a problem at the local level, as the effort to create a Northern identity was inspired precisely by the recognition that many areas geographically in the North refused to respond to this identity. Those bordering the Southern region were often oriented toward Southern Nigeria. Chief among these was the province of Ilorin, physically in the "North" but Yoruba-speaking and oriented far more toward Lagos and Ibadan than to Kaduna, capital of the North. By "reasonable stations," the NBS officer above undoubtedly is referring to the fact that sets in Ilorin would be tuned to Yoruba-language broadcasts from the Western Region, recapitulating the old tension between Southern and Northern colonialists.

Underlying the technical decision between wired versus wireless was a political controversy leading to the formation of the first independent broadcasting system in all of sub-Saharan Africa. In 1952, after the governor of the Western Region went on the NBS to criticize the proindependence Action Party. Its leader, Obafeni Awolowo, one of the dominant figures of Nigerian independence, asked for a right of reply. He was refused and responded to this by forming the Western Region Broadcasting Company, contracting with an outside private company to set up independent radio. This radio reached few people in the first few years, but its political effect was electric. It inspired Nigerians in all three regions to want their own broadcast services; it confirmed for the British the unruly, uncontrollable nature of Southern nationalism (spurring the desire for radio to counter this in the North); and it made clear the difficulty the British would have in controlling radio.

From the beginning of radio, Northern colonialists were worried about Ilorin. The decision to switch to wireless coincided with a reorganization of programming so that broadcasts would be initiated at the regional rather than the local level. Kano News and Zaria News were replaced with a single "Northern Region" broadcast in Hausa, a decision that had great consequences for non-Hausa-speaking areas of the North. Minority languages like Tiv, Igala, and Nupe would now receive a news broadcast in their language once a week instead of every day. The resident of Ilorin sent an immediate telegram on receiving this news, arguing that "for political reasons" alone there should be full regional news in Yoruba.[36] Writing at the same time, the head of programming for the Northern Region reported back from a tour of Ilorin arguing, "It is up to us here in Kaduna to do all we can to provide programmes that will keep the Northern Yoruba tuned to the North Regional rather than the West Regional Programme." The "very dangerous probability" he noted, is that "it will be difficult to stop listeners with private wireless sets from listening to Ibadan."[37]

The British were right to be worried by wireless. Northerners in Ilorin often did tune in to Ibadan rather than to Kaduna, facilitating what was seen as secessionist tendencies precisely at the time of maximum pressure to realize a new "Northern Nigerian" identity. This retarded the development of the community listening facilities that existed elsewhere, because to make radio widely available "might have a boomerang effect," as the program officer noted, and listeners "might listen more frequently to Ibadan than Kaduna and the intention of the exercise [the use of radio to produce a Northern identity] would be thwarted."[38] Hausa Northerners, presumably the focus of Hausa broadcasting, also began to listen to broadcasts from other African and Islamic countries. The emir of Gusau, for instance, asked that the frequencies of "Egypt, the Gold Coast, Saudi Arabia and Pakistan" be published in the *Nigerian Radio Times*.[39] The emir of Kano in the 1950s was rumored to drive quietly to Dala Hill in his Rolls-Royce so he could get good reception to tune in to broadcasts from Nasser's Egypt (Kukah 1993). The attempt at using radio to produce a new regional identity was contested by the ability of wireless—as opposed to RDS—to make possible the more intense engagement of Nigerians with other sorts of political identities.

CONCLUSION

RDS lost and wireless won out. In 1952 the Nigerian Broadcasting Service was formed and wired loudspeakers made way for saucepan specials and the more luxurious wooden cabinets that made radio a new sort of object—one of consumption. The historian Rudolf Mrázek (2002: 166), writing about Indonesia, argued that radio appeared as a new kind of "electric furniture," "without which, soon, no modern house was thought to be complete. As the design of the car had to suit the image of the fast motion along a modern road . . . so the design of the radio set became . . . a significant organizing principle of a modern colonial house."

The role of the radio set in African domestic life was not simply as a conduit for news and music but as a prestigious object of consumption that represented the transformation of a whole way of life (see figure 12). As late as 1994, when being taken around the house of an elderly Kano royal official, ostensibly to see the ornate mud carvings on the wall, we stopped so I could be shown a beautiful (but nonworking) teak radio cabi-

12. Advertisement from the magazine *Drum* (Nigeria) showing the modern African home. Image courtesy of Bodleian Library, University of Oxford.

net which for this owner still inspired pride and a sense of prestige decades after it was bought and years after it probably ceased to function. Those Africans wealthy enough to afford a radio were often those who were the most Westernized. As Debra Spitulnik (1998–99) has pointed out, radio was part of a larger advertising project to address Africans as modern, consuming subjects. Examining advertisements for radios published in Northern Rhodesia's *Radio Listener* magazine, she notes that those who bought radios were shown in photographs in a nuclear family, not an extended one (with one wife, not several). They placed the radio on a table, not on the floor, and sat in chairs to listen, not on mats on the ground. "Listening" to the radio, she argues, was not a simple act but involved a whole cultural complex designed to produce a new sort of modern African citizen.

The great difference between RDS and wireless was, of course, mobility. Mobility was greatly aided by the arrival of cheaper, lighter, transistor radios in the 1960s. If, in its early years, RDS was for most Nigerians a public event, the arrival of wireless began to move sound into the domestic arena and locate it in the ornamental space of the wireless cabinet and the unaesthetic but functional space of the saucepan special. Transistors in Nigeria took radios outside again, making them mobile, hand-held units. This time however, the public sound was privatized—not broadcast by the state over the urban space at large, but controlled by individuals, with the sound kept low, usually for one person or groups of three or four.

What was integral to the mobility of radio, and what became central to its function in the developing world, was the autonomous power supply of the battery. Electricity centralized urban areas. The more technologized a house became—the more it used lights, refrigerators, and radios—the less it was an independent island and the more it was a node tied to a grid by series of cables. This grid was also a public utility; it was in a real sense the material expression of the state entering each and every house, lighting each and every bulb. Batteries were immediately crucial in Nigeria, however, because the technological excellence that wireless relied on proved difficult to achieve. Electricity supply, in those areas lucky enough to have it, was patchy, and radio sets that relied on mains supply were often decorative objects unable to transmit sound. Because of this absence of supply nearly all radios marketed in Nigeria were sold in battery versions as well as mains supply, and the saucepan special was designed with batteries only in mind. In the 1950s this battery was so large that the radio was nicknamed woman with a baby on her back. Spitulnik (1998–99) has written insightfully on the symbolic and material importance of batteries in Zambia (Northern Rhodesia) and the way that batteries have given rise to a language and conceptual frame for ideas of power and independence. In an even more innovative essay Spitulnik (2002) tracks the material life of batteries in contemporary Zambia. There, where batteries are expensive relative to peoples' incomes, a world of battery conservation and use has been manufactured. Radio owners warm exhausted batteries on hot coals to excite a small charge; they string batteries together, tying old batteries together with cable, taping them to the radio, to extract what little power is left. Listening practices are tied firmly to the battery's life, so volume and time of listening are carefully controlled.

From RDS to the advent of the saucepan special, to the vibrant following that new FM stations have all over urban Africa, the mechanics of radio have been tied to the material conditions of its existence. Spitulnik's parsing of the life of a battery reveals that contemporary Zambians still have to deal with the culture of breakdown experienced by colonial Nigerians. When wireless came to Nigeria (its greater technical efficiency overwhelming fears about its cost and loss of political control), service was improved but was still marked by inconsistency and failure. The saucepan special, reliant on batteries, solved the problem of inconsistent mains supply. But it opened up the new difficulty of obtaining replacement batteries. "The battery service is still deplorable," wrote the controller of broadcasting for the Northern Region. "When I went into Kano recently, G. B. Ollivants [the main supplier of radios in Nigeria] had not a single battery in stock and Kano is reported to be their main radio station in the North."[40] If they were available these batteries were extremely expensive, and even when all equipment was working perfectly the radio signal was erratic and subject to deep fading. Wireless emerged to solve the technical problems of RDS, but as with many technophiliac solutions in modern African history, its promise outweighed its performance. While certain problems were fixed, others were initiated, creating the deep ambivalence that technology inspires in current African societies.

In Nigeria, and indeed in most of the developing world, radio in its early years was a public not a private phenomenon. Radio was not solely located inside domestic interiors where it created a listening community in the precise social locale of the family. Instead it was owned by the state and based in community listening centers or broadcast out of loudspeakers over the streets and open spaces of the city. What radio is now is something whose very constitution as an object and as an institutional practice is intimately tied to the necessities of colonial rule. Those necessities, however, resulted in a series of decisions and accommodations that were not fully understood. They created material objects—antennae, wires, receiving sets, and loudspeakers—that had their own material agency and were subject to physical limitations creating experiential conditions of existence sometimes wholly outside the imagination of British technocrats. This link between the ideology behind radio, its technological existence, and the practices it created I wish to trace also in the workings of the mobile film units that traversed the countryside and urban areas of colonial Nigeria.

PROGRESS AND INFORMATION
are inseparably connected. The African and Asian are on the March! They strive for economic and educational development.

They are engaged with nation building, literacy campaigns and health instruction. Fire signs and the tom tom are no longer considered good enough means of mass communication. Their place has been taken by the
MOBILE CINE CAR AND CINE VAN
which is equipped with modern projector and public address equipment to spread easily intelligible information to the remotest corners of the country. . . .

The cine car will shorten the development of your country too!

—Publicity brochure for Mobilwerbung GMBH Volkswagen Cine Car, from a brochure included in NAK/MOI, 3rd collection, vol. 1, OFF/82, vol. 1, Move of Cinema Section to Zaria.

3

Majigi, Colonial Film, State Publicity, and the Political Form of Cinema

IN 1932, ON EMPIRE DAY, the governor of Nigeria traveled north to open a railway bridge spanning the Benue River. At this point Nigeria was still a young nation formed through the amalgamation of two separate territories: Southern and Northern Nigeria. The Benue was one of the rivers splitting North from South, and spanning the river physically and symbolically represented the unification of the two territories into a new nation. It was, as one can imagine, a significant event. The governor of Nigeria traveled from Lagos, as did both lieutenant governors (of the Northern Region and Southern Region) as well as all the Europeans in the town of Makurdi and a large contingent of native aristocracy: fifteen Idoma and Egedde chiefs as well as the Tiv chiefs of Abinsi and Wukari. After the governor declared the bridge open, a Nigerian driver, Alhaji Baba Ehuembe Osuman, steered the first locomotive across. The native and European dignitaries then ate a feast and enjoyed a series of displays by native and European troops. In the evening the dignitaries were brought together to watch a fireworks display from the central span of the bridge and, most novel, a series of cinematograph films.[1]

The film screening that followed the opening of the Benue Bridge was one of the early film screenings shown to African audiences in Northern Nigeria. While cinema came sooner to other parts of the country, in the North the technology still carried that thrill of novelty and innovation in the early 1930s. The bridge opening presented the cinematograph as a spectacle, less important for the films screened (whose titles are not recorded for posterity) than as a scientific wonder. Cinematograph, bridge, and railway engine formed a technological complex, the signification of one bleeding into the other. As machines they served technical functions—transporting goods and people across a river, projecting moving images on a screen—but they also represented the magical, sublime world of scientific achievement. In the years to come, as government-sponsored mobile cinema units developed in Nigeria, this momentary link between film and railroad would be renewed, and the machinic complex uniting film projectors with technological infrastructures would be replayed countless times. Cinema vans drove across the highways and dirt roads of Nigeria projecting films that showed the building of railways, dams, factories, roads, and houses to millions of Nigerians. The opening of the Benue Bridge was one of the first times this link between railroad, cinema, and government was made manifest. It ties an early moment of cinema's entry to the North to the spectacle and bombast of government ritual, a political context that has haunted Nigerian film for many decades.

The central narrative tension in David Lean's *The Bridge on the River Kwai* (1957) revolves around the decision of the main character, Colonel Nicholson (Alec Guinness), to build a bridge that will aid the Japanese war effort in the Second World War. Nicholson takes over the organization of the work from the Japanese commander, Colonel Saito (Sessue Hayakawa). In a significant scene, he calls a meeting where his assistants inform Saito that the site for the bridge will not hold its weight and that the distribution of work is poorly managed and inefficient. Shot from a tripod in wide-angle, the scene reveals a table with Nicholson at its center, British officers on one side and Japanese on the other. Saito, emasculated as Nicholson dictates the agenda and usurps all authority, is filmed with his back to the camera. Nicholson calls on his engineering officer, who has run "tests" on pressure and soil resistance to prove "in black and white" that the site for the bridge should be moved farther down the river. Next, he announces that the work rate of the soldiers needs to be increased and that this is possible because Major Hughes has performed a time study proving that "the available forces have been badly distributed." Lean's fixed camera, preserving the spatial configuration of the meeting—that arch form of corporate capitalism—emphasizes that while *The Bridge on the River Kwai* is ostensibly a war film, what is really at stake are the workplace practices and the forms of time, order, and technical ability that mark Western industrial capitalism and from which non-Westerners are excluded. The film represents a conflict waged not through military force, as one might expect in a war film, but through meetings, time-motion studies, soil-resistance tests, and engineering expertise. Imperial rule is the constitutive outside of the film. Indeed, the only reason Nicholson can build what he calls a "proper" bridge is that Major Reeves, his engineering officer, has experience building five similar bridges in Madras and Bengal for the colonial service and can draw on this to avoid the technical mistakes of the Japanese.[2] For Nicholson, the bridge is more than just a technical object. It becomes a civilizational project, a chance to prove the superiority of British technical achievement and British society over non-Western peoples. "We can teach these barbarians a lesson in Western methods and efficiency," he tells his engineering officer, "that will put them to shame." What animates the bridge, giving it force, are the forces of order and rationality engineered into it. When one officer remarks that the trees they are using are like the elms that held up London Bridge for six hundred years, Nicholson replies wistfully, "Six hundred years, that would be quite something."

Since Wolfgang Schivelbusch's (1986) powerful study of the railroad, it has been well established that cinema found its technological double in the railway. Both are quintessential apparatuses of modernity that reshape our experience of space, time, movement, and speed (Kirby 1997). Like the railroad, cinema transports people to places they have not experienced before. Like cinema, the railroad creates new perceptual experiences, the paradox of moving while remaining still. But this takes on a whole new dimension in the colonial context, where the link between cinema and railroad is mediated through the logic of rule. Lean's film highlights a political relation between technology, infrastructure, and rule that I have discussed in the previous two chapters. It is a relationship brought into being in events such as the ceremonial opening of Benue Bridge, maintained through the colonial and postcolonial eras, and reinforced through the constant publicity of film screenings, radio broadcasts, and, later, television news. The history of film in Nigeria has something to tell us about the relationship between

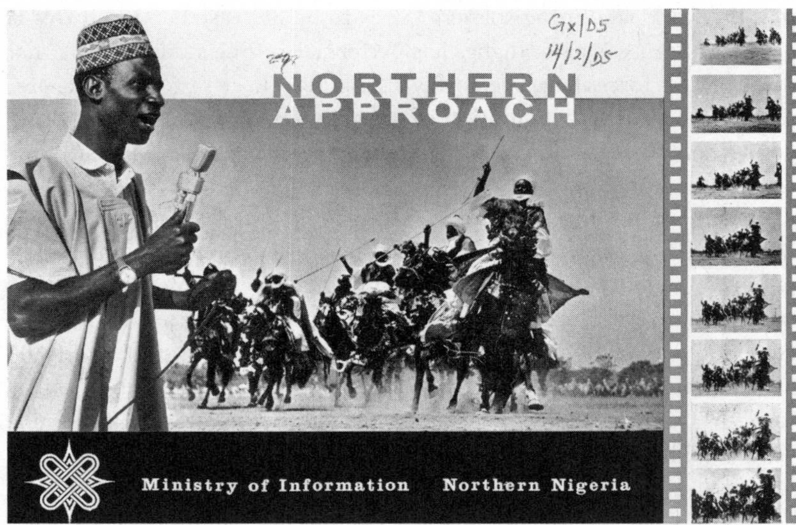

13. Cover of the brochure, *Northern Approach*, depicting a mobile film commentator narrating a *jahi* charge—a traditional royal salute. Image courtesy of Arewa House Centre for Historical Documentation.

film and political rule. On one level it helps us to think about the relation between technology and society and how this has played out in colonial and postcolonial Nigeria. On another level, it offers us a chance to rethink mainstream histories of cinema itself, by taking a marginal example of film history and using it to rethink processes central to the constitution of cinema and its role in the production of twentieth-century modernity.

During World War II, the British government established the Colonial Film Unit (CFU), which consisted of mobile cinemas that traveled to urban and rural areas screening short films, documentaries, and newsreels (figure 13). The unit was headed by William Sellers, a health officer in the Nigerian government, who had used magic lanterns and film screenings as early as the 1920s to instruct colonial audiences about the danger of plague. The organization established its own magazine, *Colonial Cinema* (figure 14), with a quarterly print run of one thousand, distributed to professionals and enthusiasts all over the British Empire. Sellers had made some of the first films shot in Africa for African consumption and had been campaigning for more educational cinema for years. Funding finally came because of the need to inspire the war effort among African audiences.

Colonial Cinema
JUNE 1953
COLONIAL FILM UNIT
COLONIAL OFFICE
VOL. XI NO. 2
PUBLISHED QUARTERLY BY THE COLONIAL FILM UNIT

14. Cover of *Colonial Cinema*, June 1953. Courtesy of British Film Institute Library.

In Nigeria, the history of cinema is split into two very different institutional practices, each with a distinctive film form, mode of distribution, and exhibition. Commercial cinema theaters screened entertainment films from the United States and the United Kingdom to urban viewers who paid for the privilege of entrance. This was an institutional practice familiar all over the world (though it played out very differently in a colonized Muslim society; see chapters 4 and 5). Mobile film units, however, offered something very different. These were educational teams created by the government to show a mix of documentaries, newsreels, and pedagogical dramas intended to instruct audiences about the achievements of the state and educate them in modes of health, farming, and civic participation. These units represent an alternative history of cinema that, in Nigeria, paralleled that of mainstream commercial films. Traveling all over the nation, mobile cinema vans would arrive in rural and urban areas, set up a screen and, once the sun had set, project programs of short films, usually accompanied by a short lecture. The address of these films was political, aimed at educating a mutable, developmentalist citizen, yet its practice created a highly popular event, and its influence far exceeded the intentions of its organizers. For millions of Nigerians, and for millions more all over the colonial world, mobile cinema units showing educational films were their first regular experience of cinema. While these programs originated in the 1930s and were only regularized in the 1940s and 1950s—hardly "early" in cinema history—because they represent the first experience of watching film for many African audiences, they overlap with features of what has come to be called "early cinema"—the cinematic and spectatorial practices established in the early years of cinema before the hegemony of feature-length narrative films (Elsaesser and Barker eds. 1990; Gunning 1986; M. Hansen 1991). This is because in both cases films were often short, screened as part of a diverse program mixing travelogues with scientific films, short comedy sketches, and so on. Key to both early cinema and mobile film was the emphasis on the spectacle and novelty of film technology and the way this new technology helped shaped subjects for modern life. But unlike the modern member of a salaried mass in urban centers in the West, the address of mobile film was to an ideal colonial subject—progressive, mutable, and politically quiescent. What separates mobile cinema from its commercial cousin is the dominance of this political exchange.

THE CINEMA OBJECT

In the last decade or so, theorists of early cinema have drawn on the Frankfurt school to push film analysis into a broader social and cultural context, forcing a theoretical examination of film's role in constituting the physical and conceptual transformations of twentieth-century modernity (Doane 2002; Elsaesser and Barker eds. 1990; Gunning 1986, 1994, 2004; M. Hansen 1991). The intellectual effort here has been to examine critically cinema's role in the standardization of ideas of time, the reorganization of the experience of space, and the imposition of a new sense of perception, stimulation, leisure, and desire, all part of a fundamental reorganization of life for new industrial and white-collar workers. The writing of Walter Benjamin and Siegfried Kracauer in particular offered scholars in cinema studies a means to theorize cinema through its role in a much wider complex of urban change and transformation. But following the logic of much of this scholarship—that cinema emerges in specific social formations that shape its ontology and influence—a natural question arises: If those social formations change, does this change our understanding of cinema itself? Does cinema have a stable ontology that simply reproduces itself in different contexts over time and across space or, if we wish to examine the role of cinema outside of the experience of Berlin in the 1920s or New York in the 1910s, does that force us to rethink our conception of cinema? Recent work on cinema in contexts outside that of the mainstream United States and Europe has begun to ask these questions (Amladi 1997; Carbine 1990; Himpele 1996; Hughes 1996, 2006; Jaikumar 2005; Lopez 2000; Zhen 2006), but this remains conceptually difficult as the link between the particular social formation of advanced industrial cities in the West and cinema is so tight it is often hard to separate what is particular to those social spaces from what is a constitutive feature of cinema itself.

If cinema is a product of historical circumstances, if its shaping of ideas of perception and the experience of movement and shock is tied to historical and cultural formations, how do we theoretically reconceive cinema when these formations change? Film theorists have analyzed the mutability of cinema and the contingency of forms of cinematic address and spectatorial relations, but this contingency is most often examined across time rather than space. This is clearly seen in the separation of "early" from "late" cinema (M. Hansen 1995), of the gaze from the glance (Friedberg 1993), of analog from digital media, and so on. Such work examines the nature of the film forms that characterize these different periods, the modes of perception they bring into being, and the sorts of publics they create, arguing that different moments in cinema history are separated because of the divergent social configurations on which they depend. I want to argue in this chapter that we also need to rethink ideas about film across space and time, that historical formations are formed by other dynamics, by different epistemic structures that shape what cinema is. I want to examine how we might reframe the debate about the origins of cinema if we look at its emergence in sites outside of the West and use that context to rethink some classical ideas about the nature of cinema. Perhaps this will become clearest when we question one of the bedrock assumptions of cinema theory, central to both mainstream and alternative versions of film history: the relation between cinema and that ur-form of modernity, the commodity.

The idea that the development of cinema is intimately linked to the commodity form is such an established part of film history and film theory that it hardly needs repeating. Cinema's pioneers were entrepreneurs, patenting new technologies to create monopoly control and exploit their new commodities. They wandered the globe as itinerant showmen recording and exhibiting fantastic images, drawing on older forms of spectacle such as the panorama and the magic lantern. In this light, the invention and history of cinema is wholly immanent in its history as a commodity. More recently, scholars have drawn on the work of Benjamin, Kracauer, and others to examine cinema's role in an emergent commodity culture (Charney and Schwartz 1996; Friedberg 1993; M. Hansen 1991; Singer 2001). According to these theorists, film emerges as part of a complex of changes associated with urban modernity: mass transportation, the rise of assembly lines and white-collar corporate workers, the emergence of department stores and new forms of fashion, consumption, and display (M. Hansen 1991). Jonathan Beller (1994) has pushed this line of argument to claim that the commodity form is woven into the very ontology of cinema itself. Cinema creates value, Beller argues, by simulating desire. It seeks to seduce and hold attention through the production of affect, and the more successful it is, the more value it creates. Seen in this light, cinema is an important part of a massive transformation in the nature of the economy and society in twentieth-century modernity, where the creation of value has shifted from production and the making of goods to consumption and the stimulation of desire. This is what accounts for cinema's special place in the history of twentieth-century commodification. "Cinematic time is inseparable from the matrix of the commodity," the film theorist Sean Cubitt (2005: 51) tells us, "because film became, already in the 1890s, the cutting edge of the commodity's reorientation as spectacle." As Beller and Cubitt argue, the commodity moves from being an historical a priori for the cinema—an integral part of the historic conjuncture from which cinema emerged—to being a fundamental part of the ontology of cinema itself. Any attempt to inquire into or study the object of film, Cubitt (2005: 2) concludes, "is also a study of the commodity form." There is, in this, no outside of the ruling idea of the commodity.

Commercial cinema in Nigeria is part of the history of the rise of urban modernity and the new forms of leisure and spectacle that accompanied that rise. But in this chapter I wish to examine a very different film practice. I will touch on many of the classic themes that have preoccupied theorists of early cinema: the link between cinema and the railroad, "first-contact" stories of audiences amazed by cinema, foregrounding of technological spectacle, exhibition of film programs made up of series of short films rather than feature-length dramas, the use of commentators, and so on. But in Nigeria these elements combined in mobile cinema to provide a very different mode of exchange between image and spectator—one governed more by politics than by the commodity. Early cinema screenings in

Nigeria, and the mobile film units that developed from them, offer a way of nuancing our histories of cinema by foregrounding the importance of what might be seen as a marginal film form. The film pioneers in Nigeria were not wandering entrepreneurs but government-paid civil servants; most films were not made to elicit affect as a means of generating value but were produced by the government to train citizens; all screenings were free; audiences did not travel to the theater, rather the theater came to them, in the cities, towns, and villages. Cinema, in colonial Nigeria, emerged in a sociopolitical configuration where the commodity form articulated with colonial rule, Islamic and Christian religious orders, and sustained animist practice. This is a profoundly different discursive context from 1920s Berlin or 1930s New York, and in this mode of exchange between audience, film, and film producer, the political achieved suzerainty over the economic. Mobile cinema in Nigeria did train modern subjectivities, but these subjects were progressive, developmentally oriented, modern colonial subjects split, to some degree, from their religious background. Analyzing mobile film units in Nigeria helps foreground the presence of different genealogies for the emergence of cinema, with resonance beyond Nigeria itself. In these genealogies, the relation between commodity and film is contingent rather than immanent, and the power and role of commodity culture is one element among several making up the social configuration of society. In other societies, the commodity form competed with alternate modes of constituting order, from state socialism in Russia to religious nationalism in India. In this light, mobile film units in Nigeria are interesting not because they offer peculiar circumstances wholly without precedent in the West, but because they bring to the foreground film practices common to the emergence of cinema but often relegated to the margins of normative film history: "The first films photographed in Mexico," Ana Lopez (2000: 61) has argued, "were not landscapes or street scenes but carefully orchestrated views of [the president] Porfirio Diaz." When cinema traveled to Mexico, Lopez points out, it was incorporated into a state nationalist project as well as into a commodity one. She argues that state elites wished to ally the prestige of these machineries of modernity to the power of those who ruled the nation. The complex association of early cinema with political projects is even clearer in the famous example of the "invention" of Indian cinema by the nationalist Dadasaheb Phalke. Because of Phalke's commitment to *swadeshi* (the nationalist effort to replace imported foreign goods with Indian made ones), it is impossible to separate the emergence of Indian cinema from the political project of anticolonialism (Amladi 1997; Barnouw and Krishnaswamy 1980; Cubitt 2005; Rajadhyaksha 1993). Here, technology was not a neutral object, tied to the needs of an emerging commodity culture, but a foreign invention that had to be appropriated and harnessed to a quite different political project. To give one more example, Paul Virilio's (1984) famous study of the relation between war and cinema takes this connection further in that he sees military and political power not just as a necessary precondition for the emergence of cinema but as constitutive of the technology and ontology of cinema itself (see also Kittler 1994). Virilio traces the origins of cinema not to photography or to precinematic spectacles such as the panorama, but to the machineries of war. Cinematic optics, he argues, have their roots in sighting devices used to facilitate shelling, just as Étienne-Jules Marey's famous chronophotographic rifle, which combined the repeater gun with the recording camera, was both a precursor of the Lumière brothers' camera and a direct descendant of the Colt brothers' cylindrical revolver.

There are other archaeologies for cinema in which the commodity form is significant but not dominant. Science has always been acknowledged as an important part of the origin of cinema (in the work of Étienne-Jules Marey and Eadweard Muybridge), but it is only recently that the interest in scientific film—its forms, modes of exhibition, and epistemic context—has been traced in any detail (Cartwright 1995; Griffiths 2001). Another important discursive context that shaped the introduction of cinema and is yet to be fully explored is religion. In an essay on the gnostic power of cinema, Tom Gunning (1997) makes the intriguing argument that one of cinema's primary functions is not to record reality but to reveal (a suggestive term with deep religious underpinnings; see also Cosander, Gaudreault, and Gunning 1992). But Gunning's main interest is how the religious register of revelation is secularized and used as a mode of displaying scientific evidence. His evocation of cinema's Gnosticism, however, indicates how even in the disenchanted world of Western modernity cinema occupied an unruly crossroads where science and religion, magic and rationality mixed. Cubitt similarly insists on Phalke's place in film history precisely to challenge normative narratives of the origins of cinema. He provides an insightful analysis of Phalke's early work, but while he acknowledges that Phalke's first films were religious, his main interest is in Phalke's anticolonial nationalism and his pioneering of special effects. For Cubitt, Phalke is a subaltern figure whose development of special effects *before* Georges Méliès upstages mainstream narratives of cinema (where Méliès stands as one of the great pioneers of cinema history). Religion exists for Cubitt to be secularized as nationalism or as the reason Phalke developed magical effects. But Cubitt avoids having to take seriously the role of religion-as-religion, and he finds it hard to feed Phalke's revelatory use of cinema back into his wider discussion of film's philosophical status and its effects on experiences of movement, time, and space. For Cubitt, the commodity is fundamental to the constitution of cinema. Other traditions might be brought into consideration but only *after* cinema has been constituted as an object; they are not part of the constitution itself. In India, as in many societies, religion is as important a part of the discursive precondition of cinema as the commodity, and it plays as great a role in shaping ideas of space and time, in training bodies and their modes of perception, and in regulating the experience of cinema (Amladi 1997; Hughes 2006; Rajadhyaksha 1993). In mainstream film history, religion emerges as something represented in films, or as the censorious order that chastises films, but not as part of the ontology of film itself.

Recent work has begun to address this lacuna by examining religious traditions as discursive preconditions for the emergence of media systems. Rachel Moore (2000) and Stefan Andriopoulos (2005; and 2006) have examined how intellectuals' efforts to understand and define cinema's seeming ability to operate outside of human mediation, and its power to split images from their owners and circulate them over space, drew on concepts of magic, animism, and soul theft. Recent work in media and anthropology has taken this further by examining how media technologies function as religious objects, bringing religious experience into being as well as pointing out the religious underbody to the seemingly rational world of scientific modernity (Hirschkind 2006; Meyer and Pels 2003; Meyer 2003a, 2003b; Morris 2000; Pemberton forthcoming; Pinney 2004; Taussig 1993).

If cinema works to produce subjects by intervening in the physical and cognitive ways people understand and live in the world, it does so in a social field. By extending our conception of the social field to include different sorts of discursive contexts we create a variegated picture of cinema's emergence and its social consequence. My effort is simply to create an analytic space where media such as cinema can be seen as being produced in different discursive traditions. In some societies the state will be paramount, in others the commodity, in still others religion, and so on. In this chapter, while I take the religious field seriously as a determinant of the evolution of what cinema does, my primary focus will be elsewhere—on the nature of the colonial state and the political form of cinema. I deal with many phenomena central to the study of early cinema, but I read these through the analytic of a colonial society. My aim is that the resulting analysis be read not simply as a marginal history of a marginal cinema but as having theoretical ramifications for how we understand cinema as a whole.

A POLITICAL CINEMA

In 1937 the medical officer William Sellers brought his traveling propaganda unit to Kano for three days to screen films and provide education about health. Sellers had been to Kano several times before, and this journey was part of a wider tour taking in nearly all the major provinces of Northern Nigeria. In Kano his aim was to give lectures and demonstrations during the day to health and education officials and in the evening to screen documentaries about health to emirs, councilors, and "prominent people." Each lecture lasted three hours and, while less spectacular than the evening film screenings, was deemed important because it trained those on the front line of health care and education. Over thirteen hundred people attended the daytime lectures. While the talks were primarily aimed at bureaucrats, Sellers was gratified to find that "there were frequently Emirs and their councilors in the audience. . . . There can be no mistaking the definite desire for knowledge of the subject from this class of influential Africans."[4]

In the evening the truly spectacular event began when a cinema van rolled into the emir's compound, a large sprawling palace in the heart of Kano's old city, and set up projection and sound facilities for a nighttime, open-air screening. This was a performance directed at the indigenous traditional elite. Because it was held in the prestigious space of the emir's palace, not only the emir attended but so did his councilors, district heads,[5] teachers, students, and elder members of the community. Even *mallams*—religious leaders who might be expected to be the most vocal opponents of colonial technological innovations—turned up, making the audience a mix of the traditional and modernizing elements of Hausa society. The British presence was headed by the resident, the senior British colonial administrator in the province, and his presence, combined with the general excitement of the occasion, brought out the European elite. In all, over thirty thousand people filled the emir's compound over the three nights. There they listened to a talk followed by a series of health films. One was about the breeding of mosquito larvae and the transmission of malaria.

Other films detailed the work of sanitary inspectresses in Lagos and demonstrated "proper" ways to care for infants.

Sellers's exhibition represents the prehistory of the colonial film unit in Nigeria (and, indeed, all over the Empire). Exhibitions like these, tied to wider public health campaigns, oriented toward training in new medical practices, represent some of the first film productions in Africa for African audiences. The film on the lifecycle of the mosquito has a place in Africa akin to the Lumière brothers' *Train Arriving at a Station*; screenings of it are the context for stories of audiences mistaking cinematic image for reality. African audiences were supposedly terrified of the giant mosquitoes, or else they dismissed the images as irrelevant because "our mosquitoes are not so big" (Burke 2002). In Kano in 1937, however, there is no indication of any such fascination. Here, in the careful context of the emir's compound, shaped by the daytime lectures and demonstrations that preceded the screening, no such misunderstandings were reported. The resident praised the event in his annual end-of-the-year report, stating particularly that the "significance of the very impressive sequence showing the development of the mosquito was . . . fully appreciated."[6]

Five years after the film screening at Benue Bridge, the performance at the Emir of Kano's compound reveals how ad hoc governmental film screenings were beginning to be regularized into a pattern of film distribution with discrete exhibitional and aesthetic characteristics with a political character. The spectators at these events were addressed not as consumers but as citizens, and what was exchanged was not money but political education. Emirs were expected to patronize events like these as a demonstration of their "progressiveness" and modernity, and attendance in itself became a sign of colonial development. Because emirs were required to attend, their presence brought out councilors and other Native Authority personnel. As part of wider campaigns to improve health or promote better farming, these screenings exemplify Michel Foucault's (1991) argument that in modern liberal states, citizens are incorporated into a state project through welfare and the provision of better housing, improved health care, and education. State control is exercised not through repression but by increasing "the welfare of the population, the improvement of its condition, the increase of its wealth, longevity, health" (100). This is not to deny that the audience enjoyed the evening, that they came of their own accord, or that the lessons in health practices were not of interest. But even if this was the case what they were attending was first of all a political event, and it created a tight link between the mobile cinema and political rule. At the end of the evening, the emir came to the mobile cinema and was projected in silhouette onto the screen. Taking a microphone he urged the audience to take seriously the advice they had been given. Exhorting the audience to act on the advice, the emir publicly performed a series of colonial claims: his support of the British administration, his acceptance of modern health practices, his belief in the desirability of modernization, and his commitment to cinema as a mode of education and transformation. Projecting his silhouette onto the screen condensed the representation of his political and religious authority into the technological performance of a political cinema.

The political nature of the screening was also implicit because European technologies were often a symbolic focus around which Hausa opposition to colonial rule was expressed (see chapter 1). The British resident of Kano, who praised the screenings in his annual report as a great success, ascribed activities like these as important "in overcoming native prejudice against European methods."[7] Attendance at the film screenings was restricted to "influential" and "prominent" people in order to use the authority of the Hausa elite to invest the new technology with an imprimatur of acceptability in a society deeply suspicious of colonial innovations. Sellers's mobile film vans were unusual (compared to those that came after) because they were equipped for production as well as exhibition. Indeed, while he was in the North of Nigeria he shot a short film, *Machi Gaba*, that contrasted the dirty habits of a farmer with the clean ones of a weaver, an early example of the division that came to define colonial dramas splitting backward from modern, African from Western, bad subject from good. The CFU and mobile cinema in Nigeria emerged from exhibition sites such as these. Cinema, in the health screenings pioneered by Sellers, was wholly outside of a commodity structure; instead, film was constituted as an object through which political relations between colonizer and colonized were constituted.

WHAT WAS MAJIGI?

By 1946 over two and a half million Nigerians were attending mobile cinema shows each year, and this was when the practice was still in its infancy.[8] Organization of the cinemas shifted from the CFU to national (the Nigerian Film Unit), then regional units (Northern Region Film Unit, Western Region Film Unit, and so on) as more Africans were brought into the production process and methods of production and exhibition were expanded and standardized. In Northern Nigeria, mobile film units were known by the term *majigi*, derived from *magic lantern*. Majigi traveled all over the North to both cosmopolitan urban and rural areas. The unit consisted of a driver and a projectionist/commentator. The two made arrangements for a tour and traveled from place to place, often staying in the guest house of the local hakimi, who was their official host. If possible they would appear on market days and arrive in the afternoon, after which they traveled around in the cinema van using the loudspeaker to announce that there would be a majigi performance that evening. Often they would also use the *mai roka*, a traditional town crier, to walk around announcing the performance.[9] In urban areas the majigi was often set up outside key municipal buildings, either traditional ones such as the Kano emir's palace or the city mosque, or newer colonial ones such as the administrative offices in Kaduna (see figures 15, 16, and 17).

Performances were open air, beginning after evening prayer and lasting for one to two hours. People gathered in front of the white sheet against which the film was projected (later cinema vans had screens). Children would sit at the front, men at the back or on the sides, with women in the middle.[10] Nearly all of the crowds numbered in the hundreds and frequently in the thousands. The program consisted of a series of short films, ranging in length from seven minutes to thirty-five minutes or more. The film program was mixed, including films made in the Northern Region for a Hausa public, others aimed at all of Nigeria, and films made in London for an imperial audience. Early on, however, the Public Relations Department realized it needed to vary educational documentaries with news and entertainment, so it alternated films about farming and health with ones of sporting events, newsreels, and cowboy or Charlie Chaplin movies. On 23 July 1959 in the village of Soba in Zaria Province, for example, some eight hundred adults and six hundred children turned out to see a program that opened with a British newsreel, followed by a thirty-minute film, *Nigeria's Constitutional Conference 1958*, then *Ride-Em, Cowboy* and a documentary, *Cotton Story* (1953, Nigerian Film Unit), and finishing with another newsreel from Britain that included scenes of a Northern Nigerian durbar. In his report after screening, Musa Zaria, the commentator detailed reactions to each film, noting that each was greeted with cheers and that *Ride-Em Cowboy* "carried the greatest cheers of all."[11]

When majigi arrived in town it was clearly an event (figure 18). In rural areas, one person told me, "everybody would come, *everybody*: adults, children, big men, *talakawa* [poor people]"; even women, as this was a period

The latest type of cinema van

15, 16, and 17. Different generations of cinema van during the colonial and post-colonial periods. Figures 15 and 16 from the magazine Colonial Cinema. Figure 17 courtesy of the Kaduna State Ministry of Information.

18. Audience gathered around a majigi van in Northern Nigeria. From the brochure *Northern Approach*. Image courtesy of Arewa House Centre for Historical Documentation.

where female seclusion in rural areas was much less common.[12] People walked from surrounding towns and made arrangements to stay for the evening, with the result that screenings were large and often full of energy. For example, in Kano city during the month of September 1957 over thirty thousand people attended majigi performances with audiences ranging from fifty to more than three thousand.[13] Outside the city, sixty thousand were seeing films every month (if the province like Kano had two cinema vans) though the size of the territory meant that for some areas a film showing remained a relatively novel and exciting event while for others it was common. The shows were popular (one commentator found them "even better than those of the Paradise and Rex theatres"),[14] and touring reports in the 1950s and 1960s were full of demands that majigi come more regularly. Screenings were noisy, filled with clapping and cheering, and occasions of genuine excitement:

> Penbeguwa, 7/10/58: "There was a huge crowd [900] . . . and all admired the films. The people exclaimed that they have never enjoyed film shows like

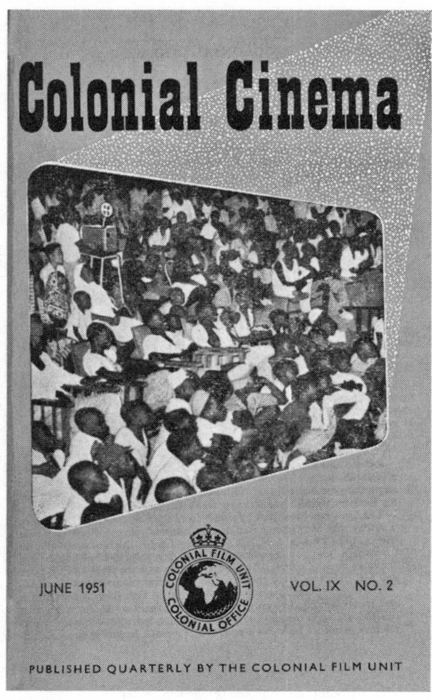

19. Cover of *Colonial Cinema*, June 1951. Courtesy of British Film Institute Library.

this one and refused to disperse after the last film until all the equipment was packed away."

Wusasa, 7/9/59: "The audience were smiling with cheers [while] they watched the films. Throughout the show of the film they kept cheering till the end. . . . Laughing and smiling as well as clapping of hands continued."

Kafanchan, 3/2/58: "The audience was nearly double the previous day [1,300 people] and admired the films but the children were too rough. They continued shouting and disturbing people's attention." (figure 19)

In all areas, the coming of majigi disrupted the steady flow of everyday life, especially in rural villages where, as one man said to me, it was like the city coming to town.[15] Children got to stay up late; people congregated in public spaces; friends got to chat and hang out; and the entertainment provided an excuse for larger groups to gather. While individual films were popular and well received, much of the audience response was to the event as a whole. For the vast majority of these rural audiences, majigi was their only experience of film and constituted their entire film world. For some animist peoples, as Peter Morton-Williams (1954) makes clear, this was their first contact with electronic visual technologies.

In urban areas the great difference was that mobile film units existed alongside commercial cinema, against which they were defined as a cinematic and a social practice. As I will discuss fully in the next chapter, the emergence of commercial film in Northern Nigeria was a contested, controversial process, with many condemning cinema on both religious and social grounds. The result was that commercial cinemas were seen as socially disreputable, the place where profligates, idlers, and bad Muslims went. The emerging moral order surrounding cinema meant that no "serious" people or women should ever attend. Because of the intensity of such reactions mobile cinema worked hard to be seen as educational and socially licit. Sellers's effort to project films in the emir's palace, and to encourage the participation of powerful royal authorities, was part of a wider attempt to generate a patina of respectability that would radically separate majigi from its commercial cousin. Majigi appeared in urban areas with greater regularity, and despite the existence of commercial cinema, reactions were similar to those of rural audiences. The famous Hausa actor Qasimu Jero, who grew up in the political center of Kaduna city, remembered majigi fondly. Initially, as with many British innovations, he said, the more conservative elements in society rejected mobile cinema as a form of evil, but in a cosmopolitan city like Kaduna such voices were relatively few. Instead, he said, majigi was how people like him "developed an interest in film."[16] Young people would start their cinema-going attending majigi performances. Where commercial cinema was condemned as *iskanci* (dissoluteness), majigi was felt to be "more respectable, educational and serious."[17]

SCREENING MOBILE FILMS

When mobile units came to town in Nigeria, the vans would drive around announcing that night's performance from their loudspeakers. In Northern Rhodesia, the cinema operator "attracted a crowd of people by playing gramophone records" before handing out leaflets and posters on malaria control.[18] Public lectures on health, farming, and political administration were integral parts of the performances. One African commentator, writing in the magazine *Colonial Cinema*, explained that he started every show by saying to the audience, "I am sure you think this is magic," before giving a detailed lecture on how the camera worked, how film stock moved through the projector, even how film rested on the physiological illusion of the persistence of vision.[19] In the Gold Coast, mobile cinemas brought along wireless sets; before the film programs began the operator would explain the wireless set to the audience and tune in to the national news from Accra,[20] making the cinema screening as much about the technology itself as it was about the films.

In 1954, Sellers detailed the ideal way to organize a mobile cinema show in *Colonial Cinema* with the idea of creating a standardized system of exhibition. Drawing on his experience giving film demonstrations to more than two million Africans, Sellers (1954: 76) cautioned that the key was to hold people's attention, and the "success of film demonstrations depends on showmanship and stage-management." The officer in charge, Sellers continued, should combine the qualities of the teacher, the orator, and the showman. Timing and organization was key. To this end, Sellers laid out a comprehensive guide of how to stage a film show. The driver and film officer should arrive in a town early and assemble a meeting of town notables under the eye of the colonial administrative officer (likely the highest British officer locally). "All local influential people, including the local chief and his council, headmasters, teachers, court clerk, and other enlightened Africans, are invited to attend" (77). At these meetings the main theme of that evening's exhibition was made clear. Sellers was aware that once the film crew left, any questions about smallpox, cocoa farming, or administration would be left to local elites to answer, so he wanted to make sure they were prepared. Clearly, film for Sellers was not a discrete event but part of a wider communicative effort. He recommended that in the afternoon, the projectionist should tape-record a local influential leader praising the information the cinema unit was about to impart. This would then be played back over the loudspeakers as part of the film show itself. He then explained how the cinema show should be organized. Because of the likelihood of large crowds, a sizeable open space should be selected. The cinema van should be set up facing toward the town, not away from it. Seating should be provided for elites only, about thirty feet from the screen. In front of them, children should be assembled sitting close together. Other adults should stand behind the elites. Before the performance began, "a rousing march" should be played over the loudspeakers—Sellers recommended "Empire Builders" or "Under Freedom's Flag," though he also found that rumbas worked well (79). Once the crowd grew, the commentator should go through the program "*without a moment's pause*" (80; his emphasis) in order to keep everyone's attention fixed. If attention did wander, the commentator should employ music hall tricks, such as saying to the crowd, "Are you all well?" and when the answer came, ask them to say it again louder until the answer came back with a roar. Finally, Sellers laid out his ideal staging of the program itself.

(1) Music	4 mins.
(2) Introductory Talk	3 "
(3) Film	8 "
(4) Talk	4 "
(5) Film	20 "
(6) Talk by influential local	5 "
(7) Film	15 "
(8) Talk	4 "
(9) Short entertainment film	8 "
(10) God Save the Queen	1 "
	72 mins.

Heike Behrend (2003, 2005) has written of how British colonialists self-consciously presented electrical technologies like cinema to East African audiences as a form of magic and wonder, a mode of power that could compete with indigenous supernatural force. Certainly many missionaries did the same, first using the magic lantern and later the cinema to publicly perform a complex set of connections linking the power of God, science, and the missionaries through these new forms of visuality (see Landau 1994). But Sellers was meticulously planning something else, carefully composing seating arrangements, attempting to regulate audiences' attention to create a hybrid of the music hall and the lecture room. He brilliantly incorporated local elites into both the audience and the performance at a time when Muslim distrust of new colonial technologies was often high. By positioning elites at the front of all spectators, seated on chairs, he made them highly visible to the audience and increased the sense that these performances had the royal imprimatur. Tape recordings pushed this farther, incorporating royal leaders into the mediated nature of the performance and conflating the traditional royal authority with the modern power of the cinema show. By giving short talks about the issues addressed in the films, and by handing out brochures for further information, the mobile film event never let film stand by itself but constantly incorporated it into a wider pedagogical initiative.

Mobile cinema performances were geared toward the regulation and

20. Painting of a majigi screening by Abdulhamid Yusuf Jigawa. Collection of the author.

production of new forms of perception and attention in a political economy where the political predominated over the economic. Unlike commercial films, people did not come to the cinema; it came to them. While it is true that knowledge of film screenings motivated some to walk miles from other towns and villages, most people present were highly local, often known to each other, and rarely anonymous. As the projectionist and driver had to contact local officials ahead of time to arrange to stay with them, cinema was hosted by the community and remained a somewhat evanescent presence, its impact all the more forcible for its relative scarcity. Performances took place on public grounds—open spaces used for all sorts of public events and festivals—rather than in theaters built for the purpose. Even the timing of the performance—starting after evening prayer—points to the way cinema fit into existing forms of temporal and religious life rather than expressing the new leisure time of industrial society (see figure 20).

Unintended Consequences While British colonialists and the independent Nigerian governments that followed them attempted to harness new visual technologies for political education, in practice mobile film exhibitions were domains where the political intentions of government ran up against the actual lives of Nigerians. It was also where the autonomous technical qualities of mobile films themselves created affective and intellectual experiences sometimes wholly at variance with their aims. For instance, interviews indicate that the decision to include entertainment along with educational cinema created huge tensions between cowboy and Chaplin films that were highly popular and educational documentaries that could look insipid by comparison. The anthropologist Peter Morton-Williams, who conducted research into audience reaction to mobile films in the 1950s, found that documentaries were often greeted with shouts of "Where's Charlie!"[21] And the touring reports regularly indicate that the cowboy films and Chaplin were the most popular. Colonial documentaries often presented solutions to what the British saw as key "problems" in Nigerian society—such as how to farm more efficiently and how to protect oneself from disease—but Nigerians did not grant these issues the same importance. One Yoruba farmer, after sitting through a documentary on how to farm cocoa, tuned to Morton-Williams and said, "We know how to farm cocoa, we've been doing it for years." Morton-Williams also recounted how the logic of colonial education ran up against indigenous systems of belief. Certain Nigerians believe disease is brought about as much by supernatural forces as by physical ones, so films conceived solely around biomedical etiology and therapy were inherently partial and incomplete. In his book *Cinema in Rural Nigeria* (1954), Morton-Williams gives the example of a film on smallpox shown to the Birom—at that time a largely animist people in central Nigeria. The Birom believed smallpox to be a disease brought about through sorcery and the anger of spirits; they sought to protect themselves from it by sacrificing animals, thus creating an invisible barrier over which spirits could not travel. "To people who are so afraid of smallpox that they never mention it by its proper name for fear the spirits may overhear them and visit them," Morton-Williams concluded, "the portrayal of the disease on the screen seems very dangerous." Ignoring spiritual causation meant that all the health films were greeted with "great skepticism" (54).

Morton-Williams's work makes clear the gap between British and Nigerian conceptual universes and potential that the meaning of films could always spin out of control. Commentators were often a source of problems: despite Sellers's great efforts to lay out how film programs should proceed down to the last detail, commentators often deviated from the script. There was often trouble when commentators from one ethnic group spoke to another, as there was a tendency for them to be condescending and patronizing in their commentary.[22] Southerners who spoke Hausa were often seen in this way when they played this role in the North. Hausa commentators were often greeted the same way among animist peoples, where Morton-Williams (1954) noted they could be rude and overbearing. If commentators thought the audience was too "backward" to understand the information, they would simply leave it out; if a written commentary forced them to say something that no local person would see as sensible, they would translate it into terms that made sense locally, partly to save themselves from ridicule. Films themselves could produce problems. One acting resident commented on a series of shorts depicting the harvesting and export of agricultural crops by saying that it contrasted the "harvesting, packing and shipment of produce by sweating natives, clothed, if at all, in rags" with a shot of "a very large vessel taking the cocoa, groundnuts, sisal, cotton . . . etc off to England and a shot of the Union Jack in high wind. . . . The total effect on any smart *Pilot*[23] reader must be to 'prove' to him all that Zik and the communists have been alleging about Imperialist Exploitation."[24]

Mobile film units, Sellers (1948: 9) argued, would "break tradition bound ground so that the seeds of progress in health, industry and agriculture could be planted" making them a smoothly modern technology for education and progress (see figures 21, 22, and 23). But for Nigerians involved, the technologies also had other uses. Mobile film unit teams were frequently caught using their trucks as taxis, charging for taking large numbers of people from one city to the next on the film team's tour. On one occasion a van traveling from Dambatta to Kano broke down just as a special duties officer was passing. He alighted to discover twenty-one people crammed into the van on top of the delicate film equipment. The van, "practically a new vehicle" had already been repaired for accident damage three times, its springs, shock absorbers, and steering had required constant maintenance, and the floor was nearly broken. And this despite the fact it had only covered fifty-six hundred miles. This problem, constantly mentioned by bureaucrats, in a small way reveals how the material existence of technology creates the space for all sorts of unexpected activities as it is put into social use. In a minute accompanying the letter, the resident Kano observed that "unless we exercise close and continual supervision, the NA will not get their money's worth of these two [cinema] units" (ibid). Unsurprisingly, it was after this, and in response to stories about the waywardness of mobile unit teams that he required the maintenance of touring reports—to be filled out in triplicate.

With Mercedes Unimog
approx £7000

FILMWAGEN CINECAR CINEVAN

MOBILWERBUNG GMBH

AUSLANDSABTEILUNG
STADTBURO BONN
Hohenzollernstraße 12
Bundesrepublik Deutschland
Telefon 53718/53735 · Telex 08/86433

21. Brochure for Mobilwerbung GMBH, a company selling mobile Volkswagen cinema unit vans to colonial governments. Courtesy, Nigerian National Archives, Kaduna.

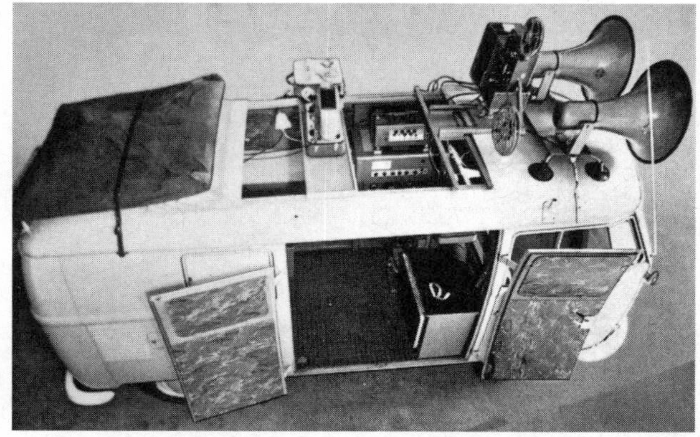

22 and 23. Volkswagen cinema vans. Courtesy, Nigerian National Archives, Kaduna.

MOBILE FILMS

Mobile cinema units innovated a film language and a series of genres particular to the situation of a colonized, developing nation. These genres eschew many of the narrative features of conventional Hollywood dramas. Newsreels were dedicated to providing publicity for the state, revealing its infrastructural achievements and projecting, in repetitive detail, the pomp and ceremony of official occasions. Pedagogical documentaries were divided into several genres. Infrastructure films projected the openings of factories, the inauguration of power plants, and the building of bridges as part of the visual repetition of the surfaces of colonial development. Imperial-spectacle films depicted royal tours of Nigeria, the inaugurations of governors general, the turbaning of emirs, and the installation of chiefs. These films became such a ubiquitous part of the regalia of government authority that by independence every aspiring royal figure in Northern Nigeria wanted his installation filmed and screened to the nation at large. Educational documentaries were designed to instruct audiences about health, farming, and citizenship. These differed from the other genres because they were aimed at transforming the individual spectator. What linked infrastructure and imperial-spectacle films was the near absence of dramatic narrative based on the spectator's investment in the psychology and emotions of the dominant characters of the film. These films simply displayed the objects of colonial power before an audience. Educational documentaries, by contrast, sought to intervene in intimate matters of hygiene, welfare, and health by stigmatizing traditional practices and modeling new ones. To do so necessitated splitting Nigerian subjects into the traditional and the modern, conflating these tendencies into two discrete and sharply demarcated practices rather than the hybrid continuum they actually were in Nigerian society. This splitting was a feature of Manichean drama, perhaps the most famous genre of colonial films—short narratives that contrasted the habits of two protagonists in order to drive home a pedagogical point. A classic example is *Mr. Wise and Foolish Go to Town,* which contrasts the behavior of two brothers who contract syphilis while working as migrant laborers (see Vaughan 1991). Mr. Wise treats his condition at a hospital, is cured, and goes on to run a successful farm and raise healthy children, while his brother visits a traditional healer ("witch-doctor") and remains diseased and poor.

Both documentaries and fiction films exhibit similar structural features, particularly in how they split African life into a traditional past and a modern future and in the way they refuse emotional storylines that would promote psychological identification. Even fictional dramas, because they present protagonists as types who represent divergent social possibilities, reify Manichean divisions rather than portray the sort of individual complexities that promote emotional identification by audiences. I will discuss the consequence of these divisions by focusing on two of the dominant forms of colonial cinema: infrastructure and imperial-spectacle films.

Infrastructure Films The stylistic roots of infrastructure films appear as early as 1935, before the formation of the Colonial Film Unit, in the films Sellers made as a health officer in Nigeria. *Slum Clearance and Town Planning: Lagos, 1930–1935* (1935, dir. W. Sellers), for instance, details the destruction of a "slum" neighborhood of Lagos and its rebuilding, ostensibly as a means of controlling plague. The film opens with the title stating that in Lagos between 1924 and 1931, 1,828 people died of plague and most of these in "unhealthy, congested areas." It then cuts to a bird's-eye shot of the roofs and narrow streets of the Oko Awo neighborhood, providing visual confirmation of this congestion. While this opening is ostensibly about the need to control plague, what unfolds is a film that details the work of colonial urban redevelopment. In a series of edits, white planners are shown in an office with a Nigerian assistant drawing up plans; workers are shown destroying informal ("slum") housing; others are digging ditches and laying sand for the new roads. The new roads are wider, allowing a freer circulation of air and light (see Curtin 1992; and Mitchell 1991). Unlike later Sellers films that address individual cultivation of proper hygiene habits, *Slum Clearance* is aimed at demonstrating the infrastructural work of colonial government. The film cuts from images of houses being demolished, to the laying of new roads, to building modern concrete houses in their stead. In a sequence on the new "garden suburb" of Yaba, Sellers pans across the wide streets and the large new houses, creating a vista of the clean lines of colonial modernity. Cutaways of wires stringing together telegraph poles and of streetlights reinforce the streamlined sensibility of colonial modernity—spacious, electrified, light. Sellers then cuts from an image of children using a stand pipe of running water to an establishing shot of a new school followed by an interior of a modern classroom. Again, one has to remind oneself that the ostensible subject of the film is controlling plague. What is actually screened is a stitched-together, futuristic urban fantasy of colonial rule. Electrification, running water, newly equipped educational facilities, tarred roads, and concrete houses reveal the brightly imagined world of tomorrow's Nigeria, hard, clean, and full of promise.

The film presents a spectacle of surfaces, an accumulation of details, repetitively depicting the various modernizing projects in which the state has invested. This accumulation of details piled one on the other, bereft of any emotional or psychological depth, makes little attempt to draw out the viewer's sympathies. Identification is largely absent. *Slum Clearance* prefigures mobile cinema's visual preoccupation with colonial infrastructural projects, turning these edifices of colonial success into spectacles. What distinguishes these films becomes clear when one thinks of Hollywood films of the era or documentaries about Africa made for European viewers. Both of these genres stereotyped Africans as illiterate primitives living in a world far removed from the wired modern world of concrete and electricity. The colonial archives are littered with the complaints of

Nigerian intellectuals and elites about Western documentaries and their focus on the most rural and backward aspects of Nigerian life. They complained about these representations incessantly to colonial authorities, who were well aware of the depth of feeling and who frequently had to ban documentaries made about Nigeria for fear the films would stir up unrest. The superintendent of education who wondered why a BBC camera team took a class out of school to sit under a tree because it was "more typically Africa"[25] is one classic example.[26] Against this backdrop, colonial cinema's visual repetition of a technological, electrified future full of dams, railways, tarred roads, and new factories is starkly dissonant, revealing the radically different imaginations presented in British (colonial) films made about Nigeria for Nigerian audiences and in films of Nigeria made for British ones.

Our Land Our People (1958, dir. Sidney Samuelson) was produced by the Northern Nigeria Information Service in the waning days of the Empire. It belongs to a genre of films that seems aimed at introducing Northern Nigeria to an unfamiliar expatriate audience. But its main use was for domestic consumption at mobile cinema shows.[27] Like other films in this genre, such as *Northern Progress* (1962, Northern Nigeria Information Service) and *Northern Horizon* (1965, Northern Nigeria Information Service), *Our Land Our People* provided a series of scenes revealing the modernizing achievements of the Northern Nigerian government, turning infrastructural projects into representational objects. The film opens with a high, wide-angle shot taken from the minaret of the central mosque in Kano. The camera depicts mud buildings in the background and thousands of people praying in the open air before cutting to a sequence of shots of new government buildings in the regional capital, Kaduna. The praying masses and the modern buildings are metaphors for the utopian ideal of a modern, yet still religious, Northern Nigeria. "The modern administrative offices typify the advances toward self-government in the British colonies," a voice-over tells us. To make this progress clear, the next shot is of Ahmadu Bello, the *Sardauna* of Sokoto and the Premier of the Northern Region,[28] sitting in full traditional dress behind a large desk in a new modern office. The sardauna looks straight at the camera: "Africans are emerging into the future," he tells us. "We want modern science to strengthen and not displace our well-tried traditions."

This theme is repeated in the sequence following the sardauna's speech, where the infrastructural logic of the film is made manifest. A shot of a person walking down a dirt road past mud buildings cuts to one of a large, tarred road with cars rushing by; an image of a decorated mud house jumps to one of a grand, concrete municipal building; a shot of people drawing water from a well is replaced by a close-up of a hand turning a tap to release running water; a farmer pulling a hand plow is spliced next to one driving a tractor; a sequence showing a camel caravan (the infrastructural backbone of precolonial trade) is replaced by a shot of a train. The voice-over announces that in Nigeria, "there is also pride in the achievements of the twentieth century. The new is replacing the old in industry, in education and in health and in all the other fields where development is necessary to further the advancement of the region and its people."

Lila Abu-Lughod (2004) uses the concept of "developmental realism" to describe the aesthetic forms that accompany state projects in Egypt. She refers to a specific genre, soap-opera-style melodramas, which use dramatic realism to encode pedagogical state messages about state-led development. The sequence described above could be termed developmental realism, but it is one of a very different sort. Here the techniques of drama are rejected in favor of an accumulation of details whose very longevity threatens to overwhelm any semblance of narrative and turn the film into a database. The sequence contrasting old Nigeria with new Nigeria lasts for a full eight minutes. After it finishes, the film shows workers at a boatbuilding yard, followed by shots of a railroad extension, before cutting to a wide shot of the tin mines of Jos, one of the largest infrastructural projects in Northern Nigeria. Next another sequence, lasting for more than six minutes, shows nothing but modern factories: a machine pressing ground nuts to make oil; a cosmetics plant staffed by Nigerian women; factories making soap, shoes, pharmaceuticals, a tannery, a bottling factory, and a cannery. People are learning new jobs, the voice-over tells us, "in order to move with the progress and the rapid industrialization of their country."

With the exception of the cannery, there is no narrative movement in these sequences. Instead of unfolding the working of the factory, displaying the transformation of raw materials into finished goods, we are presented with an accumulation of images that seem to take place in a constant present, their purpose not to reveal information but to spectacularize through the repetition of surface details. Images of the state's infrastructural achievements recur in countless newsreels and in nearly all major documentaries of Northern Nigeria in the 1950s and 1960s. Cumulatively, they create a visual mantra, tying the construction of industry and infrastructure to the politics of national development. It is no wonder that the district head of Soba, in comments written on a touring report, requested

24. Ahmadu Bello, Premier of the Northern Region, opening the Gusau Electricity Supply, 1959. Courtesy of the Kaduna State Ministry of Information.

more film screenings because they would "help develop the nation," since the repetition of these documentaries trained audiences to have the expected reaction.

After independence the use of cinema for state publicity was wholly adopted from the British by the postcolonial state. Northern Nigerian newsreels relentlessly depicted the Sardauna of Sokoto, Ahmadu Bello, the Premier of the Northern Region at independence. He is shown inaugurating a telephone exchange, turning the valves to open a new waterworks, visiting a soft drinks factory, cutting the tape for a new road, laying the foundation stone for a luxury hotel, attending installations, visiting polling stations, and monitoring the new dam at Kainji as well as a host of other infrastructural projects through which his persona as a modern, progressive leader is represented in the quintessentially progressive technology of cinema (figure 24). The sardauna also used mobile cinemas for the quite different project of projecting himself as a new type of religious as well as political leader. While most colonialists and indeed most intellectuals saw media technologies as inherently antireligious, the sardauna was adept at siphoning this supposedly secularizing power to heighten his sacred persona. The same newsreels that showed him in a modernist role visiting dams and factories also recorded his pilgrimage to Mecca and to the tomb of Sultan Bello (one of his ancestors and a key personage in the history of Islam in Nigeria). *The Premier Tours North West Africa* (1963, Northern Nigeria Film Unit), documenting the sardauna's trip to Guinea, Senegal, Morocco, and Libya, is a good example of the new sort of identity the sardauna was projecting as both a political representative of Northern Nigeria and a major Muslim figure. In Libya, the film cuts from a scene of his visiting a tomato canning factory to shots of him inside the mosque at Sidi Margout rubbing a relic of a hair of the Prophet Mohammed over his face. In Senegal he meets Léopold Sédar Senghor but also goes to visit the Grand Mosque at Touba. The film is essentially a record of his carefully mixing his political and religious status. In the binary logic of modernization theory, Islam represents the disappearing past contrasted with a developmentalist future. In complex ways this dichotomy was often repeated in mobile cinema even after independence. For instance, despite the legion of newsreels and documentaries showing the spectacle of colonial and nationalist figures, *ulama* are largely absent from colonial films. The films' Manichean logic represents progress as the result of education, voting, and infrastructural projects, not religion. But Ahmadu Bello's attempt to meld religious authority with the secular technology of cinema indicates his desire to forge a new sort of Muslim identity that rejected the artificial split between tradition and modernity. It would come to prominence in the years after Bello's death (Gumi 1992; Paden 1986).

Imperial Spectacle Perhaps the only subject as prominent in newsreels as infrastructural achievements was the pomp and majesty of imperial and postcolonial ritual. The installation of royal leaders, the appointment of colonial officials, the comings and goings of important personages, the marching bands that saluted them, the charging natives that hailed them. All of these visual elements were endlessly repeated beginning early on.[29] Andrew Apter (2005) has analyzed such rituals in some depth, arguing that political hierarchy was built into the visual logic of the event itself, with viewing stands erected for British and Nigerian elites. Colonial films re-mediated these rituals, expanding their political range and turning ceremonies into media events that necessitated the presence of a recording team. For Northern rulers, having one's installation filmed became part of the symbolic repertoire of royal authority. By 1960, to not have one's installation filmed was almost an insult. The *Sarkin Dekina*, member for Igala North in the House of Chiefs, submitted a motion in 1960 that asked: "Is the Minister [of Internal Affairs] aware that during the installation ceremony of the Attah of Igala in April 1959 no film unit was sent to cover the ceremony? . . . If the Minister is aware may I please know what arrangements he had made to publicize this particular ceremony . . . similar to those of other Chiefs we are used to see [*sic*] in the Cinema?"[30] The minister replied that the installation could not be filmed as the crew was filming the installation of the Emir of Lapai at the same time. Moreover, he argued, they had recently filmed the attah at a different ceremony. Filming, and the demand to be filmed, had become part of how elite status was constituted. It amplified the visual orchestration of political authority by creating new media on which these ceremonies could be replayed.

Film entered into the constitution of authority in colonial Nigeria by publicizing state infrastructural projects and turning them into political spectacle. It trained Nigerian elites in new forms of mediating power, new ways of constituting authority through dispersal and replication. The films allied British colonial projects of development to structures of royalty and at the same time created prestige for local elites. It is worth remembering, though, how evanescent this all could be. Occasions for dramatizing state power could also be occasions for mocking it. For instance, after the sardauna deposed the Kano emir following a bitter conflict, the ubiquitous newsreels of Bello took on a different valence. One commentator, screening films to five thousand adults and six thousand children in Kano noted, "All these films shown at Kano Emir's Palace are useless for them because they have seen the Premier in the films. NONE of them likes to see the Premier."[31] And this imperial spectacle, it must be remembered, has prominently continued in postcolonial television, where it has often exhausted its power to evoke any response beyond boredom.

A THOROUGHLY MODERN NORTHERN NIGERIA

In contrast to commercial cinema, the exhibition of majigi films is best seen as a political ritual through which the relation of subject to the state was negotiated. Mobile cinema had its roots in spectacular use of films at the opening of large infrastructural projects such as Benue Bridge, or in the traveling health displays of bureaucrats such as Sellers. Majigi was a machine of the state traveling away from the political center and into the

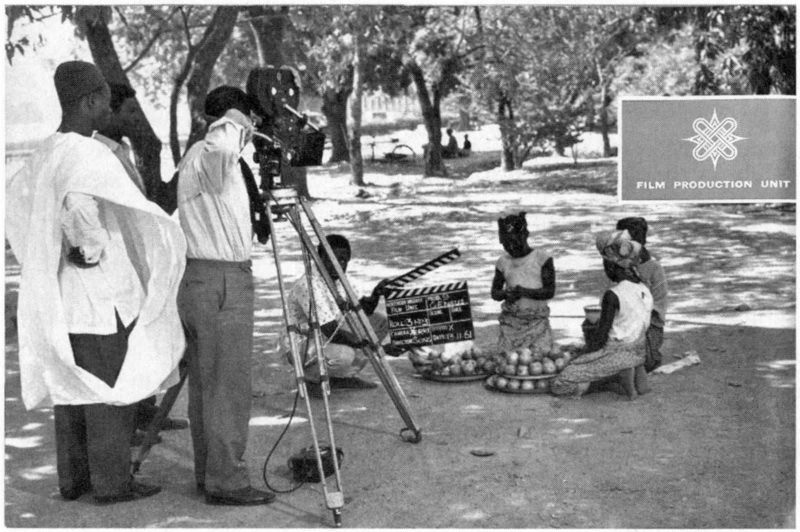

25. Northern Nigerian Film Unit shooting a scene for the film *Census*. From the brochure *Northern Approach*. Image courtesy of Arewa House Centre for Historical Documentation.

margins of the territory, pulling these margins into a state project. It was an institutional form of cinematic production that was, in essence, a bureaucratic instantiation of state power.

The screenwriters, filmmakers, commentators, projectionists, and drivers who comprised mobile film units were all salaried civil servants employed by provincial ministries of information (figure 25). To monitor their work, the regional government in Kaduna required each province to compile touring reports listing the place of exhibition, films showed, number of people in attendance, reaction of the audience, and comments by a local representative of the Native Administration or the colonial government. Three copies of each report were made: one for the Native Administration, one for the District Office, and one for the Ministry of Information. The forms were to be submitted monthly.[32] This is the effluvia of a bureaucratic order, the metareflexivity by which a bureaucracy constantly monitors and supervises the work carried out under its auspices. Its bureaucratic context places cinema in the context of other state initiatives such as education, public works, and tax collection, rather than popular visual culture. Each report had to be verified and signed by a local official—usually the district head—which had a number of effects. It guaranteed that the workers had shown up to screen the films; it helped counter accusations that films were *kafir* and un-Islamic by enforcing the presence of senior Muslim figures, a tactic that helped make majigi a socially legitimate cinematic event; and these leaders' presence as local representatives of the Native Administration confirmed cinema's role as an arm of the state.

According to the political scientist Lisa Wedeen (1999), states produce forms of language and modes of public ritual in their own image. She studies Syrian rituals surrounding the late president Hafez al-Assad, focusing on the performative statements made by states whose legitimacy relies on force. When Syrian rituals proclaim Assad to be the "Savior of Lebanon," she argues, or the "father of the country," or the nation's "premier pharmacist" (a reference to his early training), these are not referential statements intended to be taken seriously, but performative statements to be adhered to. Her argument is that the state is less interested in legitimacy—whether citizens believe the statements they are making or not—and more in subjection, forcing people to take part and mimic language even, or especially, when they do not believe it. Achille Mbembe (2001) makes a similar point about the simulacral language that was part of the aesthetics of power in African postcolonial dictatorships. He describes a simulacral language, one used by the state and accepted by its citizenry, but whose referential meaning has been evacuated. When African rulers state that they will develop the nation and bring progress, no one, neither the rulers nor the ruled, believes it to be true, but yet the performance continues. Both Mbembe and Wedeen argue that this system works not because it generates legitimacy but because it provides occasions that dramatize state power. The state offers a fantasy it demands to be taken as truth and creates occasions to force obedience (Wedeen 1999: 19).

The written comments by district heads and other notables on the touring reports of colonial film units exemplify the sort of simulacral language to which Wedeen and Mbembe refer. The mechanical, repetitive responses that mimic the overt developmentalist goal of the film screenings are revelatory precisely because their repetition manifests the political nature of the event. For instance, on 23 July 1959 the district head in charge of Soba signed off on a film program that included a cowboy film, a newsreel, a documentary about cotton, and one concerning Nigeria's constitutional conference by commenting, "The show was very good and everybody enjoyed it and they hope you will be coming at regular intervals because it will help develop the nation."[33] In the phrase "help develop the nation" lies the pastoral logic of colonial rule, fully mirrored in the speech of one of its subjects. Similarly, when the Sarkin Kagoro signed off on a program stating that, "It will be good next time to show the film pertaining to agriculture. I think that will encourage farmers to improve their farming,"[34] or when the Sarkin Kajuru stated that a film on farming was "helpful because people have seen the importance of fertilizer," what is being revealed is the fact that these lower-level figures in colonial hierarchy see film screenings as occasions to reproduce the received logic of colonialist development. Wedeen (1999: 78) argues that public rituals are occasions for a regime to present an idealized and untroubled presentation of itself which its citizens are required to adhere to not as a matter of belief but through public dissimulation. When the Sarkin Kubacca gives thanks for seeing an "impressive" program, "especially the Queen's visit and the film pertaining to fertilizer. . . . I hope you will be turning up at regular intervals,"[35] what is revealed is less the internalizing of state logic (though this may have been the case) than a recognition that the screening is a political event demanding a political response, one that might be monitored by higher-ups in the colonial hierarchy. Simply by attending and watching—no matter the reaction to the images—audiences at majigi screenings were constituted as communities subject to state messages.

THE LANGUAGE OF MOBILE FILM

One of the most remarkable aspects of mobile cinema was Sellers's attempt to create a standardized film practice that could be replicated all over the Empire. After becoming head of the CFU, Sellers (1948: 9; 1953) established a film language he saw as necessary given what he termed "the visual limitations of Nigerian peasants" and, by implication, all Africans. At its root was the evolutionist belief that the world's races were separated by fundamental physiological and mental differences and that variable standards of education and civilization led to wholly different cognitive abilities. This is not simply the idea that Africans new to watching cinema might mistake the image for reality—the classic modernist myth of the primitive and cinema. Sellers went further, questioning whether Africans could understand two-dimensional images, whether their vision had the same depth of field as Europeans', or whether they could see the same color palette. Difference was not just mental, but physical. To address this, Sellers (1948: 9), along with his collaborator, the film director George

Pearson, designed a filmmaking technique "specially designed for the inexperienced eyes and unsophisticated minds" of Nigerian audiences.[36] In a lecture to the British Film Institute Conference on Colonial Film, Pearson explained the language of this cinema. Africans, he argued, conflating vastly different peoples and social classes, were rooted in concrete reality, incapable of understanding abstract ideas, and because of this the formal conventions of cinema had to be thoroughly revised.

> All the conventional methods for short-circuiting time and place are utterly confusing to the illiterate, with the possible exception of the "fade." . . .
>
> Mixes and montages and wipes may suggest that something is wrong with the machinery. . . .
>
> Panning up and down, dollying backwards and forwards, amaze him. Trees seemingly running along the far horizon, buildings apparently rising or sinking, static objects seeming to move of their own volition, only divert his attention from the scene message to the mystery of seeming magic. (Pearson 1948: 25)

According to Pearson, visual continuity has to be maintained from scene to scene, as Africans would greet each new scene as if it were a new film. Scenes should take longer, because "the native mind needs longer time to absorb the picture content" (ibid.). All trick photography should be avoided, and even the subject matter should be strictly within the known, firsthand experience of the audience. For instance, for an inland African, images of the sea, ships, and ports are "beyond the comprehension of the illiterate" and effectively useless (ibid.).

Pearson here is ventriloquizing the ideas of Sellers, who became interested in the visual capacity of Africans when he was showing magic lantern slides and beginning to experiment with film. The historian James Burns (2002) writes that Sellers developed the idea of an African grammar of film watching from a screening in which audience members made reference to a chicken in the film. As he could not remember any chicken, Sellers screened the film again to discover it running off-center in one of the scenes. Burns (2002: 40) argues that Sellers drew a whole theory of African perception from this insight, arguing that Nigerians "'read' the screen from bottom to top, scrutinizing it as one would read a written page, rather than focusing on the projected image as a whole." "The eyes of illiterate people are not trained to see non-stereoscopic things," Sellers concluded, arguing that Africans "fasten their gaze on to any movement in the scene to the exclusion of everything else in the picture" (cited in

Burns: 40). Because of this, films made for Africans could only be based on strong central images, with little background movement that might distract. Sellers (1954: 80–81) reiterated this elsewhere, cautioning colonial filmmakers to remember that

> illiterate people, unaccustomed to seeing pictures of any kind, do not focus their eyes on the screen as educated people do. Educated people usually focus their eyes at a point a few feet from the screen and by doing so appreciate the entire screen at a glance. The illiterate, on the other hand, scans each scene and his eyes travel from one part of the picture to another. For this reason, films for illiterate people contain scenes which are much longer than is usual in film making.

Sellers thus reveals a specifically colonial theory of spectatorship, built into the language of mobile cinema. His ideas about cognitive differences in perception and mental faculties, in the ability to process sound and image (which was key to his arranging of the film commentary), constituted the way the majority of Nigerians first experienced cinema. Certainly they governed the language of CFU films despite powerful counterarguments from Africans[37] and other colonialists, and despite the clear popularity of commercial films filled with the sorts of cinematic techniques Africans supposedly could not understand. Pearson, in his directives on film commentary argued that it should never overlap the visual image but always come after the film has finished. This is because "the screen picture is a sense perception" and Africans need a longer time to comprehend that perception, making them unable to tolerate any other stimulation without losing the meaning. "Nothing must happen to disturb this absorption" (Pearson 1954: 29). Yet almost every report of actual film screenings suggests these were noisy, somewhat raucous events, far from the contemplative ideal Pearson imagined. G. B. Odunton (1950), an African member of the Gold Coast Film Unit writing in *Colonial Cinema*, scathingly dismissed the need for a "Specialized Technique," writing that the idea that uneducated Africans do not understand films led to a film style devoid of imagination or interest. The nail in the coffin of Sellers's theories was driven in by Morton-Williams, ironically hired at Sellers's behest to provide hard data on audience reactions to the CFU. In matters of vision, Morton-Williams (1954: 44) wrote, "it seems quite evident that the physiological aspect of the problem can be ignored," dismissing Sellers's belief that African vision had a different depth of focus. Using color cards and skeins of wool he observed that the "color vision of the different races of mankind seems not to differ" (ibid). "Mixes, fades, cuts, are all acceptable," he continued. "Audiences were not baffled by rapid changes of scene that took them over long distances or that compressed time" (45). "In general," he concluded, "all the apparatus of cinema was taken for granted" (ibid). Morton-Williams's report, based on two years of research, gave scientific authority to the rejection of Sellers's ideas.

Sellers translated his theory of film language into a film practice that introduced cinema to millions of colonial subjects. What gives his ideas depth is that his theory of cinema was ultimately tied to a political goal. The reason African perceptual abilities needed to be retrained was that this was a prerequisite to the possibility of cultural and economic advancement. Hygiene, modern farming, electoral participation, economic advancement, and political independence rested on the hope of transformation that started with the ability to comprehend the basic apparatus and grammar of film. Pearson (1949: 17) argued that the long-term aim of this work was not simply to help Africans read films better but to promote "cultural uplift that achieves a higher standard of living, ends illiteracy, and leads eventually to self-government." Here perceptual capability is tied firmly to the idea of a modern subject. For Pearson, Sellers, and other colonial officers, watching film seems almost a cognitive training for modern citizenship. This is what links Sellers to a theory of media with roots in the Frankfurt school but which transformed those ideas thoroughly to fit Cold War logic, thus becoming the dominant political ideology of its day: modernization theory.

MODERNIZATION

Sellers's theories of film language found a clear intellectual fit with the discipline of mass communications emerging in the United States in the 1950s, especially as it coalesced around the dynamic research of Paul Lazarsfeld and the Bureau of Applied Social Research (BASR) at Columbia University (see Wheatland 2002, 2005). The BASR was a quantitative research institute that pioneered the statistical study of communication to assess the effects of media on society. Unlike most academic departments, most of the bureau's funding for research came from outside sources, often federal agencies. In the early 1950s the BASR was hired by the Department of State to conduct a pilot survey for a large-scale program investigating the penetration of U.S. media in the Near East. The program began with Turkey and Greece and was later expanded to include Jordan, Syria, Iran, and Egypt. Government concern over the success of communist propaganda drove the funding, as did the desire to assess the effectiveness of U.S. media such as the Voice of America. The project was pioneered by the Program Evaluation Branch of the State Department under the directorship of the Frankfurt school scholar Leo Löwenthal. Löwenthal had been an active member of the Institute of Social Research (the Frankfurt school) and moved with the institute when it was housed at Columbia University in its years in exile during the war. After the institute returned to Frankfurt, Löwenthal stayed on, becoming director and sponsoring research related to the aims of the International Information Administration, a project established by President Harry S Truman in order to combat communist propaganda around the world. Löwenthal commissioned for each country a report based on extensive interviews that charted people's listening and viewing habits and assessed the penetration and influence of foreign media.[38] The political context of the research was clear. An internal BASR memo drawn up as part of the preparation for the project states that the studies should be directed so that they will be "of maximum use for the international propaganda activities of the State Department."[39] Lazarsfeld acknowledged this reality in the middle of the research, stating that "in various ways the United States has to exercise a considerable influence in far-flung parts of the world. . . . It can be predicted, therefore, that international communications research will be a natural concomitant of the current American situation in world politics."[40]

The eleven BASR country reports, which represent some of the most ambitious and in-depth studies on the influence of media in non-Western societies, were summarized and condensed in a secret report written for the State Department by the German critical theorist Siegfried Kracauer. Kracauer worked for the BASR in his later years as a qualitative social scientist while he wrote his classic study, *The Theory of Film* (1997 [1960]). Miriam Hansen has described the clash between Kracauer's early career as a Marxist critical theorist and journalist and his later work on film as a "violently fractured intellectual biography" brought about by his flight from Nazi Germany and his attempt to reconstruct stability as a refugee.[41] His work for the BASR must be seen in this light. Lazarsfeld, while a pioneer in quantitative methods, throughout his career stressed the need for skillful theoretical analysis (famously and disastrously trying to use Theodor Adorno in this role in his early years at Princeton; see Levin and Von der Lin 1994). Kracauer was enlisted to draft the final synthesis of this pioneering project. Kracauer's early work as a journalist in Weimar Germany explored the emerging mass culture of urban life—the dancing girls, photographs, cinemas, arcades, and hotel lobbies that made up the leisure practices of the new salaried masses. He was interested in how these new objects and the experiences they brought about worked on the bodies and subjectivities of urban workers, and how the new physical stimuli, the sounds and sights of mass culture, constituted the experience of urban life. Film broke down the perceptual standards of older forms of culture. It created modern subjects, distracted, mobile, mechanized, split from the more secure verities of a world fast disintegrating. As Miriam Hansen (1997) has pointed out, Kracauer and Benjamin's great insight was to analyze at length the role of media in producing this new urban subject.

Given this background, one can see why Kracauer was chosen to summarize the country reports on the role of media in transforming the Middle East. The BASR often operated with two objectives: (1) the narrow research interests of the corporation or government department it was working for and (2) the larger intellectual questions it used these projects to pursue. Kracauer fulfilled the mandate handed to him by Löwenthal, assessing the amount of anti-American feeling and procommunist leanings across the Middle East. In this he directly addressed the political aims of the project as is indicated by his subtitle, "Communications Studies along the Soviet Periphery," which suggests the Middle East was interesting not for its own dynamics, but for its strategic proximity to the Soviet Union and its vulnerability to communist infiltration. This singular document provides a concrete link between the Frankfurt school, through Löwenthal and Kracauer, and the emerging discipline of mass communication in the United States.

Kracauer's report defines the Middle East in the classic terms of modernization theory. Here was an area marked by the "inertia" of a people who, until recently, were frozen out of history because of "cultural and religious prejudice," but who were on the cusp of a period of violent change toward urbanization, industrialization, and secularization. Because of this, the political leanings of the newly educated peasants were about to become volatile. These ideas were current in the BASR, and Kracauer's work is the summation of an extended series of internal memoranda and preparatory papers that develop ideas of the "Arab mind" and the role of religion in mediating the reception of media.[42] Clearly this is a different Kracauer from the young Marxist intellectual of Weimar Berlin who was trying to understand a very different social field for media and culture. It is a world in which, as Kracauer points out, the cinema is seen as sinful, where messages from the mass media pass over peoples' heads and where there is "an ingrained aversion, strongest in rural areas, to let the doubtful blessings of civilization interfere with age-old traditions. The Bedouins reject wholesale the infidels and their devilish inventions" (Kracauer 1952a: 3). What Kracauer fails to see is that the media here emerge in a social formation as complex as Weimar Germany but that the elements making up this formation are different and need to be examined. Here the mechanized, electrified, modern world has a colonial genealogy, a political aura haunting its promise of modernity. Modernity, which Kracauer sees as secular (and thus neutral) appears in a religious register, as the work of "infidels and their devilish intentions" (ibid). Religion here needs to be analyzed not just because it is a barrier to the acceptance of secular modernity, but because it mediates peoples' understandings of that modernity and forms part of a complex of postcolonial rule, nationalist ambition, development, and modernity. The document does betray flashes of the old Kracauer, as when he notes the noisiness of coffeehouses, where radios are played, and their role in shaping the leisure of the "mobile" type of peasant who travels to the city for trade. But even here, while Kracauer's fine instinct for the detail of urban life surfaces, his aim—in the context of this unpublished report written for a specific audience—remains to determine how well the anti-communist propaganda of the United States is being communicated, what can be done to improve this, and how to "immunize the masses against the potential impact of Communist propaganda" (6).

Kracauer reveals familiarity with Sellers's work in Nigeria[43] and incorporates many of Sellers's ideas into his recommendations. He argues that "mobile film units are mental tractors conquering virgin territory" that might be used to great effect in transforming the traditional fatalism holding people back (Kracauer 1952a: 13). He also accepts Sellers's ideas of visual literacy: "Experience shows that people not yet adjusted to the cinema are unable to follow the events on the screen. Cinematic language is still unfamiliar to them. They may neglect the narrative proper in an unimportant incident reminiscent of their daily life; and they may be utterly confused by flashbacks, close-ups, and transitions which an ordinary moviegoer takes in his stride" (13). At first glance, it might be easy to assert that Kracauer was simply following Sellers wholesale. But Kracauer clearly was reworking Sellers's arguments to fit his own intellectual concerns. Kracauer's *Theory of Film* (1997 [1960]), defines a series of features that comprise film's distinctive capacity to record and reveal reality. Kracauer lists a series of film's unique properties: its ability to show movement, to estrange everyday objects through close-ups and camera angles, to record ephemeral and marginal phenomena, and so on. In this litany, Kracauer (ibid.: 53) cites Sellers's story of the fixation of African audiences on the marginal image of a chicken running in the corner of a film (ibid.: 53). For Sellers, this story is important because it reveals the structure of African visual and cognitive capacity. Kracauer retells it, however, to highlight distinctive features he sees at the core of film. He points out that after African audiences mentioned seeing a chicken, "the film-maker himself . . . attended several performances without being able to detect it. Had it been dreamed up by the natives? Only by scanning his film foot by foot did he [the filmmaker] eventually succeed in tracing the chicken: it appeared for a fleeting moment somewhere in the corner of a picture and then vanished forever" (ibid). For Kracauer, the story reveals the indexical nature of film as a storage medium. The presence of the chicken was clearly unintended by Sellers, who in fact had no idea it was there, and Kracauer uses the story to highlight the autonomy of film as a technical medium. At the same time, Kracauer sees the chicken story as illustrative of how film images are never just "seen" but are constantly interpreted and mediated through our cultural perceptions. Images that are overfamiliar to us, such as our house or the street on which we live, "cease to be objects of perception" (55), because we take them for granted. Elements of an image that are outside of our central concerns (such as Sellers's chicken) get seen but not noticed. In Sellers's use of the chicken story it is the African audience's cognitive abilities that are under discussion. In Kracauer's, it is those of Sellers himself. The former wishes to know why Africans see the chicken; the latter why Sellers cannot see it.

The significance of Kracauer's reading of Sellers and the presence of ideas developed by the CFU in the work of the BASR is that this shows the link between a seemingly marginal film practice and a colonial knowledge regime in Nigeria, the emergent discipline of mass communications in the United States, and the rise of modernization theory more generally. Kracauer's reworking of Sellers also forces us to rethink how African reactions to technology have been analyzed in African studies. Rejecting a racist history that has emphasized the primitiveness of African audiences, their fear of the "soul-stealing" properties of photographs, their propensity to mistake film images for reality, and so on, scholars in African studies have argued that stories of African wonder at new technologies are rooted in colonial racism. James Burns (2002), for instance, provides a fascinating overview of stories told *among colonialists* about African moviegoers who fled from a scene of a lion (or a snake, or a gun) because they mistook the image for reality, or who thought that time-lapse photography of maize growing meant that British colonialists had invented superfast crops.[44] Burns (2000: 208) concludes that, like many stories of the so-called primitive reactions of early audiences to film's uncanny power to re-create reality, these stories are important not for what they tell us about Africans but "because colonial observers found it intellectually comforting. It seemed to testify to the existence of innate intellectual differences separating Africans from Europeans." Similarly, Megan Vaughan (1991) has argued that stories of African credulity came about because colonialists failed to realize that African audiences were being ironic. Although I agree with many of these arguments, the early work of Kracauer, and more recent work on media and technology, forces us to pay greater attention to the destabilizing, terrifying effects of technology. Not because this is evidence of cognitive difference but because it is a feature of the introduction of technologies across all cultures. We must beware of an agentive theory of history that insists on the autonomy of human subjects who "indigenize" and "rework" technologies at will, as this denies the autonomous properties of technologies—the way technologies fashion subjects rather than the other way around. Fantastic reactions to the introduction of technologies such as cinema do not have to be dismissed in order to assert the modernity of non-Western audiences; they can also be analyzed for what they tell us about the destabilizing, sometimes terrifying work of technology itself.

In 1954 the eleven country reports of the BASR were analyzed again and a synthesis of their insights condensed into *The Passing of Traditional Society* by Daniel Lerner (1958), one of the major texts of modernization theory and a foundational text in international mass communications. Lerner had been one of the original country researchers on the project, but he stripped his book of all its political origins (the assessment of the relative power of U.S. and communist propaganda) and focused instead on the intellectual question of media's role in social change. His analysis drew heavily on Frankfurt school ideas about the role of mobility in modernity tying the materiality of media to psychological transformation. Developing societies, for Lerner, were in the midst of an inexorable shift from a traditional world of collective belonging, fatalism, and inertia to a modern one of individualism, rationality, and dynamic change. His most innovative assertion, and the one that shows the clearest trace of Frankfurt school thinking, came in his argument that modernization was not primarily located in economic development (*pace* Rostow 1960) or in political organization (D. Apter 1965) but in the mental faculties and psychic makeup of individuals. A modern society, for Lerner, is a mobile one, where people are prepared to move physically from villages to new urban areas but where a form of psychic mobility must first be formed. Psychic mobility involves empathy, which, for Lerner, referred to the mental capacity to contemplate a way of life different from one's own and the consequent ability to realize that there are alternative life paths one can pursue. It depends on a mental framework that understands the future as manipulable and open to change rather than preordained and fixed. Modernization, for Lerner (1958: 211), was thus a process, a "psychic course" that carried "people from the Traditional universe of fatalism, ignorance and apathy to the Modern world of self-reliance, learning and participation." To be modern was a complex of different attributes, of self-reliance, enterprise, rationality, but first among these was this power of empathy as economic and political change could only come about after psychic transformation. Media were the key institutions involved in disciplining and training sensory perception, thereby bringing about psychic mobility. Media taught "interior manipulation," Lerner argued. They "disciplined Western man in those empathic skills which spell modernity," and because of them "millions of people who have never left their native heath now are learning to imagine how life is organized in different lands and under different codes than their own" (54).

Lerner's work, along with modernization theory as a whole, was famously critiqued by dependency theorists, who saw the roots of underdevelopment not in the psychic structure of the individual but in the unequal trade relations forced on developing societies. Many also were uneasy about the development of a theory that saw U.S. democracy as the teleological endpoint to which all non-Western societies must necessarily progress. In many respects Lerner's theory of modernization is more theoretically sophisticated, but in essence it is the same as the ideas motivating British colonial officials in Northern Nigeria in the 1930s, 1940s, and 1950s (see chapters 1 and 2). British colonialists in Nigeria believed that development could only come about by breaking open the parochialism of Northern elites and "exposing" them to ideas from elsewhere. The belief that media—particularly radio but also mobile film units—were instrumental in this process undergirded state funding for media projects. In welding psychoanalytic ideas with the technological effects of modernity, in exploring the ways new technologies discipline the body, train mental faculties, and create new forms of mobility, and in his emphasis on the role of the imagination as a constitutive part of the experience of being modern,

Lerner both looked back to core ideas coming from the Frankfurt school and looked forward to contemporary analyses of the role of the imagination in globalization. The lineage of ideas from Sellers through Kracauer to Lerner makes us realize the complex interrelations between colonial conceptions of the role of film and technology and key ideas in media and film theory. It creates a more complex genealogy for media theory but at the same time helps explain how these ideas played into the everyday life of media in Nigerian society and the experience of social change for Nigerians.

CONCLUSION

The first newsreel made by the Northern Nigerian film unit in 1959 opens with the installation of Alhaji Mohammadu Aminu as Emir of Zaria attended by Ahamdu Bello, the Premier of the Northern Region, and the British governor of the Northern Region. Sequences show the arrival of the premier and governor, their inspection of the troops, the installation of the new emir by the governor, and a series of *jahi* charges in honor of the occasion, making visually coherent the sequence and hierarchy of power in the colony. This celebration of colonial authority in the guise of ancient tradition is followed by the opening of new law courts in the Northern capital of Kaduna, contrasting the continuance of tradition with the march toward progress and modernization. If the theories of William Sellers stressed the astonishment and magic of Nigerian audiences' "first contact" with the modernizing technology of cinema, by independence Nigerian elites had fully adopted this thoroughly modern form of political publicity (figure 26). The cut from Ahmadu Bello attending a traditional royal event to opening law courts stitches together worlds of tradition and modernity that are more often split and radically opposed in the logic of modernization theory. Indicative of how these domains blurred and fed off of each other, it created a political connection between the state and media that continued long into the nationalist period and up until today.

Historians and African film scholars who have looked at mobile colonial films have tended, with good reason, to focus on their paternalism and racism; scholars of African film have often sought to separate them discursively from what constitutes "African cinema" (see chapter 6). The normative narrative of African cinema acknowledges the role of Sellers and other colonial filmmakers in pioneering film production for Africans (Diawara 1992; Okome and Haynes 1995), but it regards mobile cinema as

26. Detail from the brochure *Northern Approach*. Image courtesy of Arewa House Centre for Historical Documentation.

largely foreign in inspiration and colonialist in intention and separates it firmly from the work of African filmmakers after independence. Both film scholars and historians have tended to treat mobile cinema as if it were historically bounded, beginning in the 1930s and finishing somewhere around the independence era (Burke 2002; Burns 2002; Diawara 1992; Okome and Haynes 1995; Smyth 1992). After independence, mobile film units were maintained by the independent state and in fact experienced a boom. Still largely educational, providing publicity for the (now postcolonial) state, majigi in Northern Nigeria continued until the rise of television. Newly independent governments were as committed to legitimating their rule through grand infrastructural projects as were colonial ones, and like their predecessors this legitimation occurred through publicity. Far from disappearing, mobile film units became an established part of the ministries of information of postcolonial regions and states. Moreover, the form and language of mobile film units continue to have a powerful presence in contemporary Nigeria. Television news still gives priority to the rituals and pageantry of the state. Wealthy individuals appointed to royal positions often pay television stations to broadcast their "turbaning" (their installation as a royal authority), publicly dramatizing not just their position but the networks of power and influence of which they are part (through coverage of other dignitaries attending the installation). Television dramas still ground many stories in a Manichean split between "backward" and "modern" practices and are geared toward public pedagogy. Mobile cinema units should be recognized for their patronizing and sometimes racist origins, but that should not obscure their deep influence on Nigerian media.

Another aspect of mobile cinema that complicates any easy dismissal is the fact that it was often highly popular. People's recollections of the cinema coming to town are highly nostalgic, and contemporary reports indicate the sense of excitement and enjoyment at these events (backed up by the number of requests from different regions for cinema visits). While many of the films are remembered fondly, one in particular, *Baban Larai* (1954, dir. Adamu Halilu), commanded immense respect. Perhaps the first genuinely popular Hausa film made by a Hausa director, but made in the colonial period and firmly in the Manichean drama tradition, it was sponsored by the British Cotton Growers Association and contrasted the good habits of a modern farmer growing cotton with the ineffectiveness of his opposite. The director, Halilu, is best known for his feature films in the 1970s and 1980s. Most famous is his adaptation, *Shehu Umar* (1976), taken from the book of the same name by Tafawa Balewa, the first prime minister of independent Nigeria (see Ukadike 1994). But Halilu began as a civil servant directing mobile films for the Northern Region Ministry of Information. His *Mama Learns a Lesson* (1964) tells the story of a woman, Fatima, who falls pregnant and on the advice of her mother consults with a traditional healer rather than go to a modern hospital. Her illness worsens and though she is finally rushed to hospital, treated, and her baby successfully delivered, she dies in childbirth. The film ends driving home the pedagogical point of this Manichean drama with her mother regretting the use of a traditional healer. Halilu's work clouds the binary separating the mobile film unit from "African cinema," and one could plausibly argue that for an older generation *Baban Larai* was far more popular and successful than his later feature films. It indicates some of the complex ways that colonial media has fed into postcolonial visual culture and cannot be so neatly separated off. When mobile cinema units finally did draw to a halt, this was only because its aesthetic forms and political functions were taken over by the rise of television in the 1960s and 1970s. Dramas depicting the good farmer who uses new agricultural techniques versus the lazy one who refuses to modernize now became television soap operas. Iconic images of governors and heads of state opening factories, making pilgrimages, and being cheered on by crowds of supporters migrated from newsreels to nightly news broadcasts.[45]

The concurrent rise of mobile film units and commercial cinema theaters makes the history of cinema in Nigeria really the history of two cinemas. Majigi operated within the bureaucracy of the colonial civil service and was geared toward education and uplift. By bringing in social elites and using the status of Northern aristocracy to confer legitimacy, majigi became socially acceptable and legitimized to a far greater degree than commercial cinema ever did. As we shall see in the next chapter, commercial film is an entirely different structure of exhibition, content, and audience. *Sinima,* as it was called, was marked by entertainment not education, by illicitness not respectability, by a young and socially marginal audience not elites. Where majigi focused on documentaries, newsreels, and short dramas, commercial cinema showed feature films that ran the gamut from love stories to the ubiquitous cowboy films. While mobile cinema films showed images of Africans and Nigerians, commercial cinema projected Indian, American, and Europeans faces to Nigerian audiences. Fundamentally, majigi was a political medium, outside the traffic of capital and commercialism that characterized urban mainstream cinema, its form of leisure tied to the prerogatives of colonial and postcolonial rule.

The rise of mobile cinema in Northern Nigeria is an example of the emergence of a cinema dominated by a political form. It suggests that the relation between cinema and the commodity form should be seen as contingent rather than necessary, prominent in those societies where a commodity culture was advanced, but less so where social formations were constituted differently. State nationalism, colonial rule, religious imaginaries, anticolonial agitation, and state socialism were all constitutive parts of the emergence of cinema on a global level, each cinema with its own discursive forms, own aesthetic modes, own practices of exhibition, influencing histories of perception, modes of leisure, and relations between technology and the self. My aim is not to claim that cinema outside of the West was *wholly* different or that the commodity form had no role to play in these societies; rather I argue that it intertwined with them, taking on greater importance in some cases, lesser significance in others. Realizing this helps us to understand that the role media technologies played in producing colonial and postcolonial Nigerian subjects is not simply a replay of a history of media that occurred first in the West; it is one with its own distinct trajectory, one that helps us return to and reexamine mainstream narratives of cinema history. This is perhaps especially the case when we turn toward the history of commercial cinema and its relation to the urban experience, a history that is more parallel to that of the West. But commercial cinema emerged in a social configuration tying together colonial rule, religion, and an expanding capitalism in complicated relations of mutual distrust. And it did so, of course, in a media environment where mobile cinemas represented a form of legitimacy and morality denied to commercial cinema, which was cast as immoral and deviant.

4

Colonialism and the Built Space of Cinema

THE HISTORY OF CINEMA IN NIGERIA is split between two overlapping but separate institutions. One is mobile cinema (*majigi*), traveling to communities physically, in the early days of itinerant cinema vans, and electronically, when the work of mobile cinemas was taken over by television. Majigi was a bureaucratic state institution. Mixing documentary with newsreel and fiction films advancing publicity for the state and its development projects, majigi addressed viewers as citizens, not consumers. It played films largely made by Nigerians about Nigerian issues. Commercial cinema, by contrast, was an entertainment medium designed to make money and existed largely outside of state control. It generated a new style of urban leisure and places where Northern youths gathered to see and be seen. Commercial cinema is based on the exchange of money for the promise of an experience, a thrill of excitement, romance, or comedy. *Si-*

nima, as it is known in Hausa, stands in distinction to majigi, showing fiction films[1] dominated (until recently) by Indian, American, and Chinese images. In the moral order of Northern Nigeria, mobile cinema was socially legitimate. Its origins lay in showings in the emir's palace or at colonial rituals that staged royal and colonial authority. Commercial cinema, by contrast, was, and remains, socially marginal, viewed by mainstream Hausa society as a lower class, un-Islamic activity. Commercial cinema is of a radically different sort from majigi, institutionally, textually, and in the modes of leisure it promotes. This chapter analyzes the origins of cinema in Kano, examining the built space of theaters to see how cinema came to be suffused with an illegitimate and immoral ambience.

The introduction of cinema theaters in colonial Kano inaugurated a series of controversies among urban Hausa. It upset gendered and racial divisions of public space by creating new modes of sociability and offered new, Western-derived forms of leisure based on a technological apparatus that was religiously questionable. These controversies can be seen as moments of struggle in the reterritorialization of urban space, the attempt to reassert Hausa moral values in the face of an encroaching colonial modernity. Cinema is a technology whose place in Hausa social life had to be defined. Its built form, the stories and rumors surrounding it, and the words used to refer to the technology itself all contain traces of the history of colonialism and the reaction of urban Hausa to the colonial experience. They tell us about the way that cinema as technology entered into Hausa space and took hold in the Hausa imagination.

Until recently, in African postcolonies like Nigeria, a trip to the cinema has always been translocal, a stepping outside of Africa to places elsewhere.[2] To move from the foyer into the dark night of the cinema hall was to be magically transported into a universe where American realities, Indian emotions, and Hong Kong choreography have long occupied Nigerian cinema screens. But cinema theaters are a peculiar kind of social space marked by a duality of presence and absence, rootedness, and transport, what Lynne Kirby (1997) refers to as the paradox of travel without movement. Cinema is made distinctively modern by this ability to destabilize and make mobile people, ideas, and commodities. This can be experienced as threatening, eroding "the cultural distinctiveness of place" (Watts 1996: 64), but it can also reaffirm and intensify forms of belonging by providing a cultural foil against which local identities may be hardened. While often seen as engines of mobility, cinema theaters are also deeply parochial, intimate parts of the urban landscape drawing around them social practices that make cinema-going an event that always exceeds (and sometimes has little to do with) the films that are shown on the screen. My focus here is on the materiality of the cinema theater, its sensuous and formal characteristics through which "we are able to unpick the more subtle connections with cultural lives and values" (Miller 1997: 9). Theaters, like radios or mobile projectors, have specific technical qualities that govern what they do in the world. These have origins in human intentions but in practice are relatively autonomous and can never quite be captured by them. Cinema theaters offer an emotional experience based on a sensory environment regulated by specific relations of lighting, vision, movement, and sociality.[3] In colonial Nigeria this emotional experience was mapped on to an urban landscape in rapid transformation and cinema was both shaped by and contributed to the remapping of the sensory experience of the city. By examining the interplay between the material qualities of the theater and the social practices they set in motion, we can gain insight into the experience of colonial urbanization in Kano.

PRODUCING THE CINEMATIC ENVIRONMENT: CINEMA, THE PHENOMENOLOGY OF THE SURFACE, AND COLONIAL MODERNITY

Objects that were once new and symbolized modern life but whose historical moment has passed become inadvertent but dense signifiers of transformations in social structure. Walter Benjamin built a powerful hermeneutics around these sorts of objects—those swollen with the force of history, but whose significance had ebbed with transformations in social and economic structure. According to his friend Theodor Adorno, Benjamin created a "petrified . . . or obsolete inventory of cultural fragments" that provided concrete embodiments of historical process or "manifestations of culture" (cited in Buck-Morss 1989: 58). Benjamin shared this evocative theorizing of material culture with Siegfried Kracauer, who also pioneered the historico-philosophical interrogation of the marginal, momentary, and concrete. Like Benjamin, Kracauer was interested in surface phenomena and argued that their marginal, mass-produced nature revealed the social order. "The position that an epoch occupies in the historical process can be determined . . . from an analysis of its unconscious surface-level expressions," he wrote in his essay "The Mass Ornament," arguing that these "expressions . . . by virtue of their unconscious nature, provide unmediated access to the fundamental substance of the state of things" (Kracauer 1995: 75).

For Kracauer and Benjamin, the quotidian landscapes of life—posters on the walls, shop signs, dancing girls, bestsellers, panoramas, the shape, style, and circulation of city buses—are all surface representations of the fantasy energy by which the collective perceives the social order. This structure creates an interpenetrated analysis of urban culture in modernity, one in which strikingly different phenomena are structurally linked. The stained concrete of Nigerian cinema theaters, the open-air screens, and their proximity to markets reveal knowledge of "the state of things" which in Kano refers to the imposition of a colonial, capitalist modernity. Cinema theaters were part of a much wider transformation of the restructuring of urban space and leisure practices under colonial urbanism (Martin 1995; Mitchell 1991; Thompson 2000). Like the beer parlors, theaters, railways and buses, public gardens, libraries, and commercial streets that preceded them, cinema theaters created new modes of public association that had to be regulated—officially by the colonial administration and unofficially in local Hausa norms.

The ambivalent place of cinema theaters and the social uncertainty around how to understand them is something that plagued cinema's rise in Europe and the United States. Miriam Hansen (1991) argues that cinemagoing emerged as a leisure practice in the United States by catering to young women who were entering into the new industrial workplace and who had for the first time disposable income outside the control of fathers or husbands. She argues that the rise of cinema is part of a wider transformation in the gendered construction of public space and that, as in Nigeria, this transformation was highly controversial (see also Chanan 1996 [1982]; Friedberg 1993; Kuhn 1988; and Tsivian 1994). The ambivalence of many Nigerians to the social space of the cinema is simply part of the common anxiety produced as societies come to terms with the new political and social possibilities that technologies bring. Reactions by local Arab, African, or Asian populations against the introduction of cinema cannot be glossed as the antimodern stance of traditional societies toward modernity but more properly should be studied as a common reaction by all societies to the epistemic uncertainty produced by new technologies.

THE EVOLUTION OF URBAN KANO

The spatial arrangement of cinema theaters in urban Kano was mapped onto a terrain that was already the site of intense confrontation. This tension began in 1903, when, after conquest, the British began to construct a modern city outside the mud walls of Kano. Administratively and symbolically, the British divided Kano in two: the walled *birni* (old city) and the modern *Waje* ("Outside") or township. The birni was dominated by the political rule of the emir and the economic importance of the trading families based around the Kurmi market, one of the major precolonial nodes in the trans-Saharan trade. In the birni, pre-British custom remained strong and, under the principles of indirect rule, was actively protected from the transformations of colonialism. Missionization and Western education were restricted; families still lived in domestic compounds which were largely passed down through inheritance rather than rented or sold; female seclusion and strict sexual segregation were the norm to be aspired to; prostitution and the sale of alcohol were forbidden and the values of conservative Islam upheld.

Economically, ethnically, and culturally, the township provided a strong contrast to this pattern. It was divided into several different areas: a commercial area, "Asiatic" quarters for Syrians and Lebanese, the Sabon Gari for non-Hausa Nigerians, and a European section, the GRA (Government Residential Area). As Kano grew under colonial rule it did so steadily in the birni and explosively in the township. In this latter area the new banks, companies, and businesses were established that connected Northern Nigeria to the economies of Europe and the United States, and this area became the motor of the Kano economy. Alongside its factories and businesses stood social clubs and restaurants, beer parlors and dance halls.

Erecting this new city entailed hardening a series of ethnic, architectural, and symbolic cleavages in Kano. The red and brown ochre of the birni contrasted greatly with the lush greenery of the European sections of the township. The broad, sweeping crescents and star-shaped intersections of the European residential areas were based on the garden city designs of Ebenezer Howard (Frishman 1977). There, residences were set back from the road by large green gardens (an innovation in a climate as arid as Northern Nigeria) and were well ventilated, according to sanitary rules aimed at preventing the spread of disease. The openness of the European area was predicated on its opposition to the congested and, to Europeans, chaotic and disease-ridden interior of the birni.[4] When the British came to lay out the design for Kano's development, the fear of contamination was encoded into the built environment. According to colonial planning regulations, Europeans were to be separated from Africans by buffer zones of at least 440 yards.[5] All Africans except for domestic servants were prevented from residing in any European area, and servants' quarters were required to be at least 150 feet from European residences.

Waje was separated from the birni more than just physically and aesthetically. Waje contained the companies, banks, railway station, and post office that were the economic and communication engines of the new colonial economy. It quickly eclipsed the economic importance of the birni, which in precolonial times had been one of the most important trading centers in West Africa. As Southern Nigerians began migrating in numbers to fill the positions made available by the new economy, they brought with them their religious and cultural values, many of which were at odds with those of their Hausa neighbors. As this urban development took place, *Kanawa* (Kano Hausa) saw the birni as the repository of traditional Muslim Hausa values, while the modern Waje became defined by as an area marked by *kafirci* (paganism). The physical segregation instituted by the British reinforced the sense of cultural and ethnic distinction.

AN ENCLAVE OF DISREPUTE

In 1975, the Hausa scholar Ibrahim Tahir (1975: 110) described Sabon Gari as "the home of strangers, on their way to assimilation, Nigerian and foreign Christians, the European Christian, *Nasara* or Nazarene, the urban drifter, the wage worker, the prostitute, and the pimp. It contains churches, beer houses and dance halls, hotels and brothels. There deviant conduct prevails and custom does not have a stronghold."

His opinion does not much differ from the 1926 view of the British resident of Kano, who described Sabon Gari as "an enclave of disrepute"[6] full of "dissolute characters." Arjun Appadurai (1996) has written that the symbolic definition of what constitutes a locality is the outcome of a deliberate set of actions. The production of a neighborhood, he argues, "is inherently the exercise of power over some form of hostile, or recalcitrant environment, which may take the form of another neighborhood" (184). For colonized Hausa, whose ability to define urban space had been decisively taken from them by the British, the emergence of an economically aggressive, physically expansive township over which they had little or no control was a tremendous challenge to their own ability to shape the nature of urban life.

Sabon Gari, literally "New Town," was created in 1913 after the establishment of the Lagos-Kano railway led to large migration from Southern Nigeria. In 1914, the British incorporated the area into the township (the area administratively under British control), a seemingly commonsense idea that was to have profound ramifications for ethnic relations in the city. The idea stemmed from F. D. Lugard's (1922) principle of indirect rule, whereby, in return for political allegiance, the British promised to preserve Hausa political, religious, and cultural structures and protect them from alien influences, especially Westernization. In keeping with this policy, European companies were not allowed to trade in the birni, Christian missionaries were restricted in their activities in the North, and the Kano emir retained political control over the Northern Muslim areas of Kano (the old city and Fagge, a traditional trading area north of the city). Southerners were seen as necessary because they "spoke, read, and wrote the language of the colonizer" (Ubah 1982: 54), but while this made them useful to colonialists, there was a fear that they would culturally influence their Northern compatriots. Segregation was intended to prevent this. "Controlled in this way," as the historian David Allyn (1976: 87) describes it, the aliens "would provide necessary services for the government and European firms but would have limited opportunity for contaminating the highly-regarded culture of their Hausa-speaking neighbors."

Sabon Gari was allowed to develop at a different rate and in a separate fashion from the old city because it was placed administratively under British, rather than native, rule. A few decades previously, in precolonial times, all migrants wishing to trade in the North would have been subject to the legal regimes and cultural norms of Hausa society. Instead, Sabon Garis, which existed in all major Northern cities, had little reason to conform to or even respect Hausa institutions. The Nigerian historian C. N. Ubah argues that this administrative division estranged and opposed Southern and Northern Nigerians, a state of affairs which continues until this day. Consequently, the physical space of the city mirrored the philosophical prerogatives of indirect rule. Kano developed as a city split into discrete, separable areas. Each area was built according to its own cultural logic so that the progressive liberal values of the garden city movement were objectified in the spacious, aerated homes of the GRA, while the multiple-occupant tenements and the grid streets of the Sabon Gari stood in contrast to the high mud walls and narrow alleys surrounding the traditional Northern family house. Each area had its own ethnic group, often its own economic base, and, after time, its own moral ambience. The intensity of this separation can be seen in the fact that Southern migrants were officially known by the oxymorons of "native foreigner" or "alien native," a vivid example of Georg Simmel's (1950: 402) argument that the stranger embodies the contradictory principles of nearness and remoteness, that while being outside, he or she is always "an element of the group itself."

Urban Kano developed in this segregated, politically charged way, in which tensions between colonizer and colonized were mediated through interethnic conflicts and found their expression in the atmospheres and reputations which came to mark different areas of the city. For Hausa, the emergence of a Kano city outside of their control, free from the religious and social limits by which Hausa space is produced, and existing alongside the traditional boundaries of the birni was unruly, ambivalent, and threatening. Intensely negative stereotypes were one of the few means available of asserting some sort of moral control over it. Yet inevitably for others, probably because of that stereotyping, cinema became deeply attractive, a source of economic and recreational life that remained illegitimate yet seductive. Waje, and Sabon Gari in particular, became the moral antithesis of proper Hausa space. It was the home of *iskanci* (dissoluteness) and *bariki* culture (see chapter 5), a complex that refers to a mix of overlapping immoral behavior such as drinking alcohol, consorting with prostitutes, and, over time, attending cinema. The historian Bawuro Barkindo (1993: 94) describes life in Sabon Gari as "permissive," that for "the majority of *Kanawa*, birni was home, and one only ventured to waje out of necessity. Its life was an evil which was tolerated because one had no choice." Onto this highly politicized grid cinema theaters were mapped. They became defined by the moral ambience of the areas in which they were situated, and over time, their own charged atmosphere was used to define the areas in which they were housed. If, initially, Hausa Muslims ventured to Waje out of necessity, as Barkindo asserts, then we must analyze the emergence of cinema-going in the light of this taboo, examining cinema as a space of illegitimacy and attendance as a leisure practice that is transgressive.

THE MORAL AURA OF CINEMATIC SPACE

The first commercial film screenings in Kano took place in Sabon Gari, as one-time showings set up in dance halls, such as the Elsiepat, where they were sandwiched between dances and prize-giving.[7] By 1934, however, cinema had become popular enough that the British resident of Kano could report that films were being shown "with considerable frequency,"[8] and within three years the first cinema built for the purpose, the Rex, opened. Funded by a Christian Lebanese businessman, Frederick George, the Rex was built as an open-air or "garden" cinema and consisted of two rooms as well as a bar which the businessman proposed "to build quite decently and with stones."[9] While the colonial government rejected the application for a bar, it did issue a series of temporary liquor licenses so that like the Elsiepat, the Rex linked the recreation of watching films with that of drinking alcohol. This exhibition format was repeated two years later when J. Green Mbadiwe, a hotel owner in Kaduna, the capital of Northern Nigeria, applied for a license to build a more formal and elaborate hotel and cinema complex in Kano. It was to include "all the latest amenities usually associated with first-class Hotels and Cinemas in the aristocratic world."[10] His application was denied but his proposal shows the conceptual construct of what people in Nigeria expected the space of cinema to be. Mbadiwe's proud insistence on the quality of construction material, and his boast that Kano cinemas would be like "first-class" cinemas in "the aristocratic world" reveals not only the elite, foreign nature of cinema but also conveys cinema-going as a standardizing practice of modernity, the presence of which could bring a city into a cosmopolitan urban world. Cinema, from the point of view of its Lebanese innovators, was both a place and a practice from which Africans were to be excluded and which was beyond the pale for Muslim Africans with a religious prohibition on alcohol.

One reason that cinema was such an unruly space is that it challenged the existing hierarchies of public space in colonial Northern Nigeria. Could white and black people attend? Could different ethnicities intermix? Were women, expected to be in seclusion, to be allowed? Mbadiwe attempted to address this by proposing to divide his cinema into two discrete compartments, one for Europeans (with alcohol served) and one for Africans. These would be approached through separate entrances and connected by a fire door but this, he assured the authorities, "will be always locked."[11] For the British, however, overt racial segregation was potentially controversial. They rejected Mbadiwe's application and informed Frederick George that his cinema must be open to all and that no liquor license could be issued. Alcohol was a problem for the British because Hausa viewers would inevitably attend. George responded by reasserting his aim informally rather than formally. He reserved two nights a week for Europeans and Syrians (Lebanese) and imposed this by a differential pricing policy. "It is fair to say," wrote the acting resident of Kano, "that if an African sought admission on one of these nights and was prepared to pay 3/6d he would not be refused admission but the number of Africans who would pay 3/6d admission, when they can attend exactly the same performance on another night for 2/-, 1/- or 6d is very small."[12] George then applied for temporary liquor licenses for one night only (the nights when Europeans attended) and received temporary licenses regularly for a number of months, assuring that the opening of the first cinema theater in Kano yoked the un-Islamic presence of alcohol to the transgressive space of the cinema.[13]

Mbadiwe's plan to segregate the audience in separate auditoriums reveals how the physical space of the cinema can be the outcome of local ideologies of hierarchy. The spacing of seats in Nigeria, for instance, came after the secretary of the Northern provinces wrote to the chief secretary in Lagos about his concern for fire safety regulations; the physical arrangement of the cinema thus incorporated colonialist conceptions of African mentality: "As regards seating: In view of the natural tendency of some Africans when in a crowd to be seized by panic at the mere rumor of danger it is thought that in Cinema halls in Nigeria much wider spaces should be allowed between fixed seats, wider alleyways and more and wider means of exit than is obligatory in England."[14]

In many parts of the British Empire the regulations surrounding cinema construction were imported from cinematograph laws established in Britain. But as the debate about segregation underscores, how cinemas were built was often shaped by racial ideologies and political and cultural relations. Out of these bureaucratic battles between colonialists and Lebanese entrepreneurs cinematic space emerged, located in particular areas, built to certain specifications, and open to prescribed audiences. For Muslim Hausa, a foundational link was secured between cinema and a complex of activities that were deeply antithetical to ideal Muslim values. This made the introduction of theaters so controversial and their presence a lightning conductor around which the Hausa critique of colonialism could be levied.

CINEMA AND TRANSLOCAL SPACE

While cinema may seem strikingly modern in its capability to transport people's imaginations and transform local identities, these attributes also define some of the most historically important public spaces in Kano, most especially the mosque and the market. These arenas can be defined as threshold spaces that mediate the boundaries and construct continuities between indigenous place and the wider world. As open, public spaces and the sites of ethnic and gender interaction, markets and cinemas are inherently unstable. Their publicness necessitates the coming together of strangers, potentially cutting across class, religious, ethnic, and gender boundaries. In the (racially, ethnically, and sexually) segregated environment of colonial Northern Nigeria, this took on added significance, and it is no surprise that most markets (and cinemas) were located on the boundaries separating the segregated areas of urban Kano. Cinema may be modern in providing a space for a new mode of commodified leisure, creating new arenas for public association, but this new space was defined by its association and linkage with the older spaces of the mosque and market, with which it shared significant symbolic similarities.

In Kano mosques are often defined by their locality, by association with the individual who paid for their construction. Attending a particular mosque can be a mark of loyalty, reinforcing relations of hierarchy, class, and religious ideology. As religious institutions, mosques erase their local significance by creating an experience of transnational religious affiliation. As Michael Gilsenan (1992: 176) argues, the mosque produces a "field in which certain social forms and relationships that are vital to the identity of groups in the ordinary [local] world are neutralized by forces defined as religious [translocal]."

Mosques are spatially oriented toward Mecca, the sacred center of Islam. This translocal orientation is physically inscribed in the mosque in the form of the *mihrâb*, the recess that signifies worshipers are praying in the direction of Mecca. It is also reinforced through everyday Muslim practice. Religious prayer is based on Arabic, a foreign language for most Muslims in the world and one identified with the religious centers of the Middle East. The translocal orientation of Islam is demonstrated most famously in the directive that all Muslims, as a matter of faith, should try to make the pilgrimage to Mecca at least once in their life.

The public spaces of prayer and ritual in Kano oscillate between emphasizing local (Hausa) relations of space and power while imaginatively transporting worshipers to sacred places in the wider Muslim world. Because of the mosque's complex range of meanings as a public space (religious, social, economic, and political), Gilsenan compares it to the other important public space in Muslim life, the market, arguing against the view of the market as the secular antithesis of the mosque. He points out that all major religious sites in the Middle East also have been market towns. Just as the mosque is not solely a religious space, neither is the market solely economic since it also provides an arena for personal, social, and even religious interaction.

Where Gilsenan stresses the links between markets and mosques as public stages that reveal the divisions and separations between people in a village society, I wish to emphasize the links between markets and cinema theaters. This is because for *Kanawa* (Kano Hausa) both places are socially ambiguous and potentially dangerous. A market is a public, open space, which, as Adeline Masquelier (1993) has discussed, makes it socially unbounded, a place where strangers, spirits, and witches mix. This unboundedness contrasts with the ideal of domestic female seclusion (*kulle*, in Hausa), and Masquelier cites the proverb, *kasuwa bai gidan kowa ba*, the market is anyone's home, highlighting the distinction between the unsafe public space of the market and the secure, private environment of home.[15] The fundamental spatial duality of the market makes it most homologous to the mosque and the cinema. While rooted in a particular place, it is the site for the international exchange of commodities and information.

Cinema theaters mimic the symbolic and spatial qualities of markets in Kano. Nearly all theaters are located adjacent to, or near, major markets, usually on the spatial boundaries between different areas. The Rex, the first cinema in Kano (since demolished), was built next to the Sabon Gari market, separating Sabon Gari (Southern Nigerians), Fagge (non-Hausa Northerners and Arabs), Bompai (Europeans), and the commercial district. The Orion and Plaza were built just outside the gates of the birni, one near the Kofar Wambai market, the other near the Kantin Kwari market, on the boundary between the birni and Fagge. The El Dorado, located on the edge of Sabon Gari, a short walk from the market, marked off that area from Bompai, as did the Queens a mile or so to the north. El Duniya was also located close to Sabon Gari market, but a little to the south, separating it from Fagge and Fagge from the commercial district.

Cinemas are linked to markets for obvious economic reasons. Markets are centrally located, with good transport, and they are hosts to large numbers of potential audience members. Yet the consequence of this is that cinema theaters and markets share the symbolic work of defining the moral division of urban space, emphasizing boundaries between different areas and thus different ways of living in the world. The Rex, for instance, separated the winding alleys of Fagge from the grid system of Sabon Gari and the open crescents of the township, culturally mediating between Christian Southern Nigerians, Northern Muslims, and Europeans. Like the morally legitimate space of the mosque, cinema theaters define local social relations of space, marking the gendered, ethnic, and moral attributes that delimit who is allowed to move where. Urban spaces such as markets, cinema theaters, and mosques are not just given entities but comprise sets of social and political relations, moral ideas of what it is to live in the world, that are internalized into the routines and habits of everyday life.

HAUSA RESPONSE TO CINEMA

Layered on top of these conflicts and substantially adding to them was a sustained religious critique of both the ontology of cinema and the structure of cinema exhibition. According to Lawan Abddullahi, an older Hausa man I spoke with who went regularly to the cinema in the early 1950s, cinema was universally condemned by religious authorities and elders. For the religious, because cinema appeared to take for itself the power to create life by showing a dead person walking, it was effectively usurping a prerogative reserved for Allah and was a form of *shirk* (a denial of the oneness of God) and magic. The result was that a series of *fatwas* (advisory, but not compulsory, legal opinions) condemned cinema as un-Islamic.[16] Abdullahi's opinions were echoed almost verbatim by Sheikh Nasiru Kabara, one of the most important religious authorities in postwar Nigeria, a key figure allied with the Native Administration, and himself a sometime member of the cinematic censorship board.[17] Kabara recounted the accusations of shirk and magic. "Local mallams," by which Kabara meant poorly educated neighborhood Islamic teachers, posed the question, "If someone is killed in a film did he die? If not, then this is magic," and cited the Qur'anic story of the fight between Musa (Moses) and the pharoah. In this story, Musa is attacked by the cream of the pharoah's sorcerors, and his victory over them is proof of the superiority of the power of Allah over the power of magic. These local mallams, Kabara recounted, also questioned the Islamic legality of watching images. In all of these instances it is the technology itself, irrespective of content, that is essentially un-Islamic. The early Hausa names for cinema—*majigi*, derived from the word *magic*,[18] and *dodon bango*, literally, "evil spirits on the wall"[19]—indicate how deeply this sense of enchantment and magic was felt.

Religious critiques of modern technologies are the result of specific historic conjunctures and must be understood as situational rather than as inherent "antimodernism." Barry Flood (2002), in his discussion of the history of Islamic iconoclasm (written after the destruction of the Bamiyan temples by the Taliban government in Afghanistan), argues that Islamic societies have veered between using representational iconography and rejecting it, and he ties the moments when certain societies become iconophobic to specific political conflicts in which these societies were engaged. Talal Asad argues similarly that the rejection of Western technologies (by Saudi society) has to be understood in the context of Islamic tradition. He defines tradition not as an essentialized repudiation of change but as a socially organized mode of transmitting knowledge and power. Islam consists of a discursive tradition made up of sets of texts (foremost among them the Qur'an and *hadith*) and established bodies of practices that scholars draw on to legitimize and enforce conduct in the present. He counters simplistic arguments of Islamic antimodernism by pointing out that while Saudi *ulama* (religious authorities) reacted strongly against many forms of modern technology, innumerable other forms—new modes of transport, electricity, medicine, building, and so on—were accepted with little or no objection. "What the ulama are doing [when appearing to resist "everything modern"] is to attempt a definition of orthodoxy—a reordering of knowledge that governs the 'correct' form of Islamic practice. . . . That is, like all practical criticism, orthodox criticism seeks to construct a relation of discursive dominance" (Asad 1993: 210). Resistance to change is not a knee-jerk reaction, according to Asad, but a deliberative and selectively invoked tradition of criticism of innovation that is *internal* to Islamic practice and not simply a reaction to the spread of modernity. The rejection of cinema among certain elements of Hausa society in the 1940s and 1950s must be seen in this context as intimately involved with the wider symbolic conflict over the nature of technology and its role in colonization in Northern Nigeria.

Conservative reactions to new technologies are not limited to Islam, as scholarship in early cinema has abundantly shown, though the essentialized linkage between Islam and antimodernism often requires this to be restated. Africanist scholars (e.g., Burke 1996, 2002) have argued that stories of African wonder at technologies were a form of oral culture among Europeans, rather than Africans, fostered by rumor and exaggeration that spread widely among Europeans in different African colonies. These stories can be analyzed as examples of the colonial sublime, of investment in technology overwhelming African senses with the experience of European greatness. But, as Timothy Burke (2002) also argues, we must take seriously these stories and how they reveal the strangeness of technologies. Miriam Hansen has pointed out that cinema as a cultural practice—the proper relations between viewer, projector, and screen—had to be learned and that early audiences in the United States effectively had to be trained in practices of what cinema, and being an audience, meant. How these technical capabilities come to be regularized is an often highly unstable process that is important precisely because it highlights the interaction of technology with society. Charles Ambler (2001) is right to assert that the popularity of cowboy movies with Copperbelt audiences and their vibrant reactions to them demonstrated "little evidence of 'primitive' machine terror," but the fact that audiences quickly became habituated to such films should not forbid analysis of the period when none of this could be taken for granted. The Copperbelt audiences he describes were clearly familiar with cinema-going as a practice. They had learned appropriate modes of viewing film (cheering, mimicking actions on the screen) and were trained in bodily modes of reception (talking like cowboys, having a "cowboy attitude"; see De Boeck 2006; Gondola forthcoming). But these practices take time and discipline before they are internalized and reproduced as natural. In Nigeria, the difference of opinion between Kabara and "local mallams" over the acceptability of film, or between sections of Hausa society bitterly opposed to cinema and others whose members attended regularly are precisely the data we can draw on to see how this process of incorporation took place in the dance between technics, religion, and society in colonial Northern Nigeria.

When Sheikh Nasiru Kabara criticized the Islamic reaction against cinema as due to ignorance, he is not referring simply to "primitive" ignorance of modern technologies (though this is probably partly responsible) but also to the ignorance of "local mallams" as to the proper application of Islamic law. He poses himself in contrast, as someone better educated religiously and also cosmopolitan in that he can draw on a range of Islamic learning from across the Muslim world. His defense of cinema is a good example of how Islamic tradition (in this case Islamic law) is mobilized to achieve discursive dominance over other Muslims authorities that Asad describes. This is particularly important because Kabara was implicated by the controversy in potentially unsettling ways. As a major religious figure, he was closely allied to Hausa royal elites, and while he was relatively independent of the British—certainly compared to the emirs and aristocracy who took part in colonial government—his closeness to the aristocracy placed limits on his ability to critique their positions. As the British placed sustained pressure on the emir of Kano and other elites to allow and to visibly support cinematic projection in colonial mobile cinema units, to declare all film un-Islamic potentially placed those elites in the untenable position of being against Islam. Kabara's support of cinema projection was no doubt part of his wider acceptance of new scientific and technological innovations in Hausa society, but it also created a religious legitimation for those Muslims walking the ambiguous line of preserving Islamic faith while incorporating the aggressive new changes brought about by colonial society. But his support only extended so far. While Kabara legitimized projection, he condemned commercial cinema itself as un-Islamic, distinguishing between the (acceptable) ontology of film technology and the un-Islamic social arena of cinema houses themselves. The reason commercial cinema was un-Islamic, he argued to me, was first because of content. Cinemas mainly played Indian films whose actresses were so beautiful they aroused audiences and corrupted their hearts. Moreover, the non-Islamic origins of many actresses ("they worship cows") could lead Muslim men astray.[20] Second, and decisively, the fact that cinema houses were open to both men and women fundamentally contravened the Islamic separation of sexes and meant that cinemas could only attract *'yan iska* (dissolute layabouts), who consorted with prostitutes and were involved in other illicit activities. "There is nothing Islamic in cinema houses," Kabara concluded after a long defense of cinema itself. His critique of cinema was not its colonial origins. Nor was it the nature of iconic cinematic representation. Rather (and in this reflecting the dominant opinion of Hausa society), he condemned the moral ambience that surrounded cinema houses because of the way these sites have evolved in Hausa society. As illicit moral spaces, commercial cinemas repelled respectable people, attracting only the marginal, the young, or the rebellious. Commercial cinema, as a social space and a mode of leisure, was neither universalizing nor standardizing in any simple way but emerged, over time, as a result of the interaction of the material qualities of the apparatus and its modes of exhibition and the particular social context in which they evolved.

YOUNG TURKS

For all of its controversy, and perhaps because of its rejection by religious elites and elders, cinema-going quickly became established among Hausa youth. This is significant given the colonial intent to impose cinema as an elite, white-only, form of leisure, and the wider Hausa rejection of cinema. "The local outlook is as follows," wrote one colonial official in the early 1950s. "The intelligent and educated malams[21] simply do not go. . . . They disapprove of the sort of low-type Hausa that revels in the cinema."[22] Its disreputable nature meant that women who attended were seen as *karuwai* (independent women/prostitutes), and their presence added significantly to the illicit nature of the arena. Sexual availability and sexual activity in the cinema meant that pleasure and desire were to be found on and off the screen, the eroticism of one context feeding into the other. Despite the best of intentions of Frederick George of the Rex, cinema went from being elite to marginal at an impressive speed. As early as 1948, the resident of Kano could write, "Among a large youthful class of Kano City, Fagge and Sabon Gari which has money to spare in its pockets it has become the thing to do to go to the Cinema quite regardless of whether they understand what they see and hear or not."[23] This statement is interesting for several reasons. It depicts a mixed ethnic clientele for cinema at this time (Kano city was wholly Hausa Muslim, Sabon Gari was dominantly Southern Christian, and Fagge was a mixed-ethnic area comprised mainly of non-Hausa Muslim Northerners). It also indicates the emergence of a leisure class (see Akyeampong and Ambler 2002; and Martin 1995) of people working largely in and around the new colonial economy. The emergence of leisure, as Phyllis Martin (1995) has pointed out, involves the reordering of categories of time and space brought about by the new economy but at the same time involves the emergence of new practices of self-expression. Resident Featherstone's comment about audience members' lack of understanding misses the importance of cinema-going as a social, as well as a visual, event. One viewer told Featherstone that although he did not always understand the films being shown, "he went regularly to the cinema to be seen and to see his friends."[24] Cinema-going was becoming established as a social activity, an experience that was always much more than the viewing of the film itself.

Alhaji Lawan Adamu, one of the young Turks going to the cinema regularly in the early 1950s, certainly saw cinema in this light. Adamu was a well-educated, young colonial bureaucrat, part of the emerging class of Western-educated Hausa Muslims (called *'yan boko* in Hausa).[25] He said cinema was *very* popular with Hausa youth at the time precisely because it did not require any education. He characterized the audience as a few "rebels" like himself and mostly *'yan daba* (hooligans) who were organized into "hunting groups" and would go around with dogs.[26] Adamu also argued a commonly held belief in Kano that cinema acts for these youths as a safety valve, a way of relieving tension and boredom without resorting to violence. He also said that by the mid-1950s there were many Hausa leaving the old city each night. To do this, in the context of contemporary Hausa society, was consciously to transgress from a moral to an immoral area. It put Adamu in touch with a cosmopolitan Western world he regarded with interest as well as suspicion, but more than this, it was a powerful mode of self-expression that defined him and his friends as confident, socially rebellious young Turks. As a social space and leisure activity, cinema theaters drew their moral aura from their social and moral place on an urban landscape in the process of transformation.

Chapter Four

THE PALACE, EL DUNIYA, AND THE MAINTENANCE OF HAUSA MORAL SPACE

The introduction of cinema theaters in Kano intervened in an ongoing conflict over the moral definition of urban space under colonialism.[27] How cinema theaters were to be built, what they were to show, and where they were to be located were all intensely debated issues whereby the transformative spatial and social ideologies of colonialism were debated and enacted. Conflicts in the Hausa community over the location of cinema theaters are an example of what Appadurai (1996) has referred to as the reterritorialization of urban space, one that was rapidly expanding outside of Hausa control. Specifically, the attempt to prevent the building of a cinema theater in the old city of Kano can be seen as an attempt to reassert the Muslim basis of Hausa life in opposition to the encroachment of non-Muslim (European and Southern Nigerian) cultural and religious values. Cinema theaters became markers of neighborhoods, embodying the moral qualities that allowed these neighborhoods to exist. For urban Hausa the cinematic experience was (and is) embedded in the history of ongoing debate over the nature and regulation of urban public space.

In 1949 Frederick George wrote the resident, Kano emirate, asking for permission to build a cinema, the Palace, in the birni, in Jakara quarters, next to Kurmi market. When the application for the Palace was received, cinema-going was well established in Kano; many Hausa regularly left the old city to travel to one of two cinemas located in Waje. The uniqueness of this application was that the Palace was to be the first cinema theater constructed in the confines of the birni. The application sparked off a firestorm of protest, rumors, and even rioting that directly probed the power of colonial authorities and the limits of Hausa authorities in relation to that power. I can date the application and the opening of the Palace from the colonial archives in Kaduna that contain copies of the application file. However the story of the Palace I engage with rests on rumors and prejudice, stories and memories that do not provide an objective history of the Palace as much as they reveal the social place that it and other cinemas occupy in the social imagination. Rumors about cinemas, stories that have come down from parent to child, are a form of local hermeneutics. They are quasi-religious allegories by which people divine the "real" motives underlying phenomenal events (Masquelier 2000; Stoler 1992; L. White 2000).

The decision of Emir Sanusi to allow the construction of the Palace cinema provoked a strong backlash in different sections of the Hausa community. Kano ulama were outraged by the penetration of this disruptive, sexual arena into the Islamic space of the birni. The more conservative among them issued fatwas forbidding the showing of films and citing the religious injunction against the creation of images as evidence that the technology itself was *kafirai* (pagan). As Emir Sanusi himself had authorized the construction of the theater, to attack it was tantamount to an attack on emirate authority and Sanusi himself. This was particularly the case as Sanusi's father, Emir Abdullahi, had refused to allow any cinemas to be built in the birni, citing their negative effect on women.[28] The conflict was seized on by politically active, Western-educated Hausa—the 'yan boko (see chapter 3)—who saw the dispute as a means of critiquing emirate authority. Perhaps because of this, when the fatwa came before the Emirate Council, the panel refused to endorse it, since this would be seen as supporting the challenge to the emir's authority. This refusal only widened the issue, allowing the young radicals to argue that the emir was in the control of colonial overlords and contemptuous of the will of the people. Lawan Abdullahi, who worked in colonial government during this period, told me that the British resident indeed placed great pressure on the emir to allow the Palace construction to go ahead.[29] Maitama Sule, an important Kano political figure and himself a young radical at the time, said that opposition to the Palace brought together and mobilized young, Western-educated Hausa active in education and politics (ironically, Lawan Abdullahi describes these as precisely the sort of "rebels" most likely to be attending cinema). The young men wrote in the press attacking the emir and organized petitions against the construction, infuriating the emir and his advisors.

In 1951, while the controversy over the Palace was raging, but before the cinema was actually open, matters were brought to a symbolic head when the El Duniya cinema burned down, killing 331 of the 600 people in the audience.[30] The government inquiry that followed established that the fire began in the projection room with flammable nitrate films. From there it rapidly spread along the ceiling as the insulation used for soundproofing began to burn. Fire doors were locked and people were trampled in the rush to exit at the back. Hausa complicity in the tragedy was reinforced by the fact that 82 percent of the cinema audience during the afternoon performance was Hausa, not Southern Nigerian or European. The youngest person to die was nine years old.

The colonial state's functional explanation was accepted by Hausa as explaining how but not why the disaster occurred. For a long time, rumors had been circulating about cinemas—that mosques would be torn down to make way for them; that one was to be built on the grounds used for the celebration of the Eid festival—rumors which posed this new "Christian" space as an aggressive attack on Islam. Many believed that the fire was direct divine retribution for Hausa participation in illicit and immoral activity, and for the growing Westernization of Hausa society. A series of rumors emerged to explain the tragedy. Most common, and still widely believed, was the accusation that the film being shown that night in the El Duniya contained the image of the Prophet Mohammed, harnessing the colonial technology of representation for blasphemous ends. Others believed that during construction of the theater people passing every day cursed (*tsine*) the theater, so that the theater was engulfed not just by flames but by these curses' combined magical force.[31]

In a religious society such as Kano, where God's intervention in the material world is a day-to-day occurrence, rumors and stories become part of a critical discourse in which everyday events are interrogated. Stories about the El Duniya represent conflict and ambivalence about the Western cultural arena that was infiltrating the Hausa moral world. They argue for the profane nature of cinematic representation, making it guilty of the heresy of representing Mohammed, and they do so for political reasons. These rumors grew so strong that the colonial government was forced to take official notice and counter them over the radio. Twice daily for two days in four different languages, the Radio Diffusion Service (RDS) announced that there was no truth to the stories that the people handling the bodies of El Duniya victims had died, or that Native Authority warders who helped victims of the tragedy had all gone mad, or that prisoners from Kano prison (who helped in handling the corpses) could not eat for days afterward.[32] The government used its technologically mediated information order to counter the swirl of oral rumors, but stories about the El Duniya became part of the folklore of Hausa society. They were an informal moral economy by which cinema was discussed and judged in Kano, and the enormity of the disaster lived long in the popular imagination. Two years after the event there was a complaint to the RDS that it should stop playing Hausa songs about El Duniya because parents still found it too upsetting; a year later, in 1954, that feeling remained so intense that the RDS agreed to a ban on playing songs about El Duniya altogether.[33]

On 2 July 1952, a year after the El Duniya burned down, the Palace finally opened after months of controversy. A small riot ensued. The emir called in police to quash the violence and to arrest youths demonstrating against the opening.[34] Three months later, the British superintendent of police reported that ever since the Palace opened, youths outside the open-air theater had been regularly stoning patrons inside. Worse, he complained, the *alkali* (Muslim judge) to whom the cases were being reported was letting the youths go free, making it difficult for the police to ensure "good order" during cinema performances.[35] For young radicals, the campaign against the Palace was about the undue British influence over the emir and whether the emir would stand up for Hausa cultural values or be an agent of colonial authority. They continued organizing meetings against the Palace, raising the matter as a public controversy and appealing against the cinema's license. Maitama Sule, active against the Palace when he was young, still remembers an anti-Palace song written by the poet Abdulƙadir Danjaje:

> Now that there's a cinema house in Jakara
> Soon there will be alcohol at Maɗataye
> Now that there's a cinema house in Jakara
> Soon there will be alcohol in Maɗataye[36]

Sule said that Emir Sanusi reacted to the controversy in two ways. First, he forbade any woman from attending the theater out of concern for proper morality. Second, outraged by the public challenge to his authority, he refused to even consider an appeal against the Palace license that came before him, prompting some of the more radical figures to suggest that the emir should be reported to the British regional governor for not following proper legal procedure. This appeal never happened as the "patricians" (Sule's term) among the radicals would not countenance bringing a case against the emir to the British authorities. As a result the group split for quite some time. When it came back together the matter of the Palace was effectively finished, but, according to Sule, the core of people mobilized by this issue went on to form the nucleus of the Northern Elements Progressive Union (NEPU), the dominant Northern progressive party of the independence era. This gives the conflict over the Palace a significant place in Nigerian political history.

CONCLUSION

Ironically, or perhaps inevitably, the Palace became the immoral social space that its opponents feared. It became a notorious place where, as one friend told me, men would go to drink alcohol, take drugs, and engage in sex with women and other men ("There! There! Right there in the seat next to you!"). In the early 1980s the governor of Kano state, Sabo Bakin Zuwo, who came from Kano's old city and was a veteran of the anti-Palace campaign, closed the cinema down and, in a grand populist gesture, converted it into a clinic. To this day hundreds of Hausa youths travel nightly through the mud gates marking the city's boundaries to cinemas that lie outside in Sabon Gari, Fagge, and Nassarawa.

The resistance to the construction of the Palace cinema was an effort by Hausa Muslims to reestablish the moral and spatial equilibrium of urban Kano society. The growth of a metropolis *outside* of what formerly constituted the city, the shift in economic and political balance from the birni to the township and Waje, and the rise of a substantial migrant population of "native foreigners" who owed little allegiance to existing political structures (some of whom openly mocked local religious and cultural practices) helped to create a situation where the assertion of Hausa control over a threatened political and social world became increasingly important. When the Palace as a foreign, immoral, and potentially irreligious institution was built in the birni, it threatened to erode the carefully produced social, religious, and political division between the birni and Waje, collapsing two very different moral spaces and making protest almost inevitable.

After the controversy over the Palace, Lebanese entrepreneurs never attempted to situate a theater in the birni again. As a compromise, two theaters were built *just* outside the city walls: the Orion in Kofar Wambai and the Plaza in Fagge. This construction is a testimonial to the fact that since the 1950s Hausa people have made up the dominant cinema-going population in Kano. Despite, or perhaps because of, the fact that cinema theaters occupy an ambiguous moral position in Hausa society, certainly much more than they do in Yoruba or Ibo society, cinema-going has never waned in popularity among Hausa youth.

Cinema theaters in Kano are not discrete buildings but integrated nodes in an urban environment from which they draw their significance and, indeed, which they help to define. As the site for screening fantastic texts of love and adventure, cinema theaters project Hausa audiences into the imagined realities of American, Indian, and British culture. Here my focus has been on the place of theaters as part of a wider urban materiality produced by, and thus expressive of, transformations in colonial modernity. Their social significance cannot be divorced from the other technologies and public spaces produced under colonial rule. Cinema theaters in Kano came into being only twenty years after the construction of the Kano-

Lagos railroad and were built in areas created for the masses of male migrants brought into Kano; they were sited alongside the new colonially constructed markets marking the borders and moral qualities of the new metropolis; and they formed part of the construction of new modes of sexual and ethnic interaction produced by the transformation in urban public space. Encoded in the physical space of the theater, in the dirty bricks and broken lights, and in the walls that divide the arena are traces of history of colonial rule and colonial urbanism.

J. Green Mbadiwe never received permission to build his hotel/cinema, and the Rex could never operate as a garden cinema serving gin and tonics in the cool evening to a film-watching audience, but these origins and the force of these intentions cast a long shadow over how cinema evolved in Hausa society. They call into question the assumption that cinema is a universal technology—a similar arrangement of tickets, seating, projection, and screen—that is the same everywhere, promoting similar modes of leisure and standard cultural experiences. In its place the cinema theater emerges as a hybrid, mixing the standardizing qualities of technology (as a mode of projection, seating, etc.) with the social and political singularities of Hausa society. Together they created the grounds from which the experience of cinema and cinema's larger place in the urban experience of Kano city was formed. I now wish to examine the consequences of this, to see how these ideas and conflicts matured over time to create the experience of "going to the movies" in contemporary Kano.

5

Immaterial Urbanism and the Cinematic Event

IN THE MID-1990S, when Garba Tarauni took me to the Marhaba cinema in Kano city, we climbed onto his scooter, rode to meet some other friends, and set off through the mud gates marking the boundaries of the Muslim old city and along to the Marhaba. The Marhaba is in a sort of no man's land, not marked specifically as either Muslim or Christian, convenient to nowhere. To get there one has to take a bus, ride, or drive. As we entered, the parking lot was already filling with hundreds of Vespas, motorbikes, and vans disgorging young people who began to chat, buy kola nuts and cigarettes from hawkers, and walk quickly to the long line at the ticket office. It was a Friday night, the busiest, and touts stood outside offering the impatient a quicker way in for a little more money, sprouting satellite lines all over the front of the cinema.

Inside, the two thousand seats were full. People stood at the back and squatted in the aisles so one had to squeeze past bodies to get anywhere.

The audience was dominantly male, and the women who did attend were seen as *karuwai* (prostitutes). Because it is illicit, though legal, the cinema had a bawdy, rowdy atmosphere. Men shouted lewd comments at the screen and at the karuwai or else bantered teasingly with them as they walked up and down the aisles (karuwai being well able to hold their own in verbal jousting). The film was an Indian one, *Gumrah* ("Ignorance," 1993, dir. Mahesh Bhatt) starring Sanjay Dutt, and the audience knew it well. They cheered at tense points, thumping the seats and stamping their feet. At other points they mimicked dialogue and shouted out responses to the hero and villains.

Like all Northern cinemas, the Marhaba is open air, and as we sat I noticed lightning in the distance. As the film progressed the lightning came closer, and members of the audience clearly wondered which was going to arrive first, the end of the film or the storm. Long before the final credits, rain fell down in heavy sheets, drenching the audience and forcing all who could to scramble into a small covered section at the back. Others, realizing the futility of this, sat calmly watching in their seats as the rain passed over, beating the ground, seats, screen, and people. After the climax, but before the dénouement, the audience rose en masse and began scrambling to leave, thereby starting a game. In Kano, parking lots are run by a guild of deaf attendants who arrange the bikes and look after them while patrons are inside watching. One leaves a half-empty parking lot and returns to a full one, with the hundreds of Vespas and scooters arranged neatly in rows next to one another. As the audience streamed to the parking lot people ran to their bikes, starting them quickly, each trying to see if he could get out without having to "dash" (pay) the attendants, who can never cover all the people leaving at the same time.

The only illumination in the lot came from the headlights of the bikes, slicing through the thick fog of exhaust fumes. We sped off down a side street and spilled out onto the main road with thirty or forty other scooters, everyone weaving in and out of the pack, some racing, shouting jokes and challenges, and sending sheets of water into the air as they ran through the huge puddles left by the storm. Sitting at the back of the theater, under cover, we had remained dry during the performance, but now were soaked by our own bike and by those of others racing past us. As we turned into the quiet neighborhoods of the old city, where most people had gone to bed long before, the event of the cinema was behind us, but the energy remained, and, laughing, we climbed off the bike and locked it up before going inside (see figure 27).

27. Painting of the outside of the Marhaba cinema, Kano. By Abdulhamid Yusuf Jigawa. Collection of the author.

Colonial urbanism provided public buildings and streets that created the skeleton of colonial and postcolonial urban life. But built form creates platforms for the making of everyday experience, and those streets and buildings give rise to a profusion of activities which overgrow and overwhelm the space and logic of earlier structures, reusing and redefining them for a postcolonial age. Cities like Kano are anchored in the mosques, video parlors, streetlights, houses, potholes, and markets that make up their physical presence. Along with these material objects come the immaterial urbanisms they provoke. These modes of affect suffuse the bricks and mortar of its streets and buildings: the tedium, fear, arousal, anger, awe, and excitement felt as one moves from one space to another or seeks out particular places at particular times. Moving through the city means moving through these emotions—praying in the morning, eating, traveling, working, dealing with petty bureaucracies, hanging out with neighbors, reading, and praying again—circumambulating the routes offered by the city and the forms of life that come with them. In *dabas* where hooligans hang out, mosques where adepts gather for prayers, or hairdressers where women swap stories, urban formations of recreation and business, sacred and secular, are continually being made and unmade. These routes depend on the material infrastructures that constitute them, but they take their characteristics from the immaterial experiences they provoke and which cast their spirit over the form and understanding of city life.

Going to the cinema in Kano is a visceral event, often charged with feelings of danger, illicitness, eroticism, and excitement. These emotions overcode the space of cinema in Kano, imbuing it with a moral aura that emerges from cinema's particular history in that area but which is continually being replayed and reexperienced in the present. This is why cinema is rejected by so many Hausa for being indecent and un-Islamic, while for others it is an important mode of public leisure, and a key way of learning how to live in the world (by inversion) as a Muslim Hausa. As quickly as cinema was banned after the introduction of shari'a law in 2001, it was reinstated—although altered so that women were prohibited until separate seating can be built. Because it is such a densely symbolic domain, cinema articulates the eclecticism of contemporary Hausa life. It is stereotyped as frequented by *'yan daba* (hooligans), who smoke hemp and whose presence at cinemas is key to the theaters' reputation as un-Islamic and full of *iskanci* (illicitness). Yet 'yan daba were themselves at the forefront of the popular class agitating violently for the introduction of shari'a law (see Casey 2002). For most Hausa, cinema is not serious, detracting youths from proper *tarbiyya* (religious training), yet many attend precisely because they feel they receive moral instruction, and there is no question that this instruction (and not just escapism) is one of the pleasures of cinema.[1] Cinema-going is stereotyped as un-Islamic yet remains a vibrant popular pastime during a period when Islam intensified in the North and cinema-going virtually disappeared in the South (where there were far fewer religious condemnations of it). Cinema stands both inside and outside the moral boundaries of Hausa society, a marginal space that transgresses orthodox norms yet strangely becomes a site where those norms can be intensified. It reminds us that Muslim societies like Northern Nigeria are variegated and made up of different interests. The place of cinema in Hausa life, and the practice of going to the cinema that this chapter is concerned with, draws out these contradictions.

Cinto Usman, who grew up in the heart of Kano's old city, in the Jakara neighborhood, told me he first started going to the cinema as a child in the 1970s. When I met him he was in his late thirties, married, and leaving "youth" behind for a respectable middle age. An independent trader, he was doing well enough to think about taking a second wife. Going to the cinema was part of his past, something he had loved to do when he was younger but socially beneath him now. When he was young, he said, his parents were against cinema. "They would beat me!" if they knew about it, he said, so to get there he had to sneak "10 kobo here, 10 kobo there" each time his mother sent him to fetch groceries. Even though this built up enough money for a ticket, it was still not easy to go, as evenings from Monday to Thursday were devoted to Qur'anic school. Weekends were the only time he could attend, and when he did he would come back late, yawning, and say he had fallen asleep at a friend's house. "My parents would answer, 'Where have you been! I hope you haven't been to the cinema!' and I would rub my eyes as if I had just woken up from sleeping and swear, 'No, I haven't been anywhere near there.' But they would be suspicious." He said his parents told him how immoral it was and how dangerous it could be "and these warnings would be in my head." Usman said he took these warnings seriously and they weighed on him. "But then your friends would come to you the next day and say, 'Kai! That was one fine Indian film last night,' and you would wish you had gone to see it."[2]

From a young age Hausa children in Kano are trained to internalize a series of prohibitions on "illicit" cinema. Jibrin Magashi, a bureaucrat in his early forties, was told when he was young that that the only people who go there are karuwai, "women who have left home,"[3] 'yan daba (hooligans), and *'yan gaye* (Westernized youths), who consort with the karuwai and smoke hemp.[4] This is because, his parents would say, cinemas show images of idols: they are against Islam, and God punishes boys who go to the cinema. Magashi was told that children who went to the cinema got burned to death just like the children who were caught in the El Duniya disaster (see chap. 4). Another Hausa man, who like Magashi grew up in the 1970s, was told by his father that if he went to the cinema seven times, he would go to hell.[5] When I asked Ado Ahmad, a Hausa novelist, what would happen to him if his parents caught him at the cinema, he laughed and replied, "*Suka za sun ji min,*" "They would beat me . . . They would say that we go there in order to see idols, that since it was brought by white men the thing is no good and is against our tradition [*ya sabawa al'ada*]," and that women who have run away from their families go there to smoke hemp and drink alcohol.[6]

Garba Tarauni, who rode with me to the Marhaba, was famous in his area for being an inveterate cinema-goer and huge Indian film fan. He was part of a group of friends, all in their twenties, who hung out together every night and gave their group the name (in English) "the live wires." One of Tarauni's close friends in the group was Lawan Ahmed. Ahmed, instead of going to university like some of his friends, or leaving for work (like Tarauni) attended a religious Islamiyya school. Despite the different choices members of this group made—between work, secular education, and religious education—all of them fundamentally shared the same religious and cultural outlook. Yet while Tarauni loved the cinema, Ahmed refused to attend at all on religious principles. He was a huge Indian film fan but he watched all of his films at home and argued that cinema was un-Islamic. "It is against my religion and my culture," he argued. "At the Marhaba," he explained, "there are all these people. They are drinking and smoking and there are women. It is very exciting. You see women hugging each other and you want to hug them. You feel that you can go there with a girlfriend and no one will know about it. . . . And this is against the religion."[7]

Ahmed's avoidance, Tarauni's attachment, and the threats of physical and spiritual punishment are all evidence of the complex disciplining that Hausa youth undergo in regards to the social space of cinema and the emotional effects it produces. One friend of mine, Bashir Ɗan Ladi, from a prominent trading family, had an elaborate story about his first evening at the cinema. Because his parents were expressly against it he told them he was going on a trip with a friend for the weekend. He packed his clothes, got some food and a little money from his mother, and then crossed the city to stay at his friend's house. All weekend he never left the compound because he was afraid someone would see him and mention it to his family. Finally, on Sunday evening he and his friend sneaked out to go to the cinema to see an Indian film. I asked him which film. "I can't remember," he said. "All I can remember is that my heart was pounding."[8]

THE LIVENESS OF CINEMA

If going to the cinema is an event, what marks this event is its temporal and spatial coding of excess. An event interrupts the flow of time, distinguishing itself from other moments by imposing a surplus experience.[9] In this way, events are temporal blocks of distinction and singularity. Spatially, cinema takes on meaning in a similar fashion, emerging as a space from its sets of relations with other places of the city with which it forms a syntagmatic chain (de Certeau 1986). Cinema can only be marked by excess, by its immoral aura, in comparison with the moral spaces of home and mosque, bureaucratic spaces of work and government, and educational places of school and university. Each of these is invested with its own atmosphere, hosting and producing the sorts of subjects who inhabit those areas. Cinema's excess draws its immoral charge from these connections. Roland Barthes (1980: 1) referred to it as a "festival of affects," a place marked by its opposition to the sedate domestic place of the home.

> Submerged in the darkness of the theater . . . we find the very source of the fascination exercised by film (any film). Consider, on the other hand, the opposite experience, the experience of TV . . . : nothing, no fascination; the darkness is dissolved, the anonymity repressed, the space is familiar, organized (by furniture and familiar objects), tamed. . . . The eroticisation of space is foreclosed. Television condemns us to the family whose household utensil it has become. (2)

Cinema famously creates a very different sort of space than the home: In Nigeria, the image can be fifteen feet high rather than the twenty inches of a television with its snowy, crackly reception; the sound is louder, shrill and distorted by old loudspeakers; and the attention one gives to the image towering above is more intense. By comparing cinema to television Barthes brings over the distinctiveness of the cinematic space but he does so in a search for generalities, in particular a universal psychoanalytic experience of the cinema. This isolation, loss, and passivity is unfamiliar in Kano, where, in the 1990s at least, desire and attention were often focused on the karuwai bantering along the aisles as well as on the screen image. Open-air showings prevent the isolation of the cinema from the surrounding area and indeed the surrounding area has to be understood as part of the cinematic space itself; its aura and the practices it sets in motion are not enclosed in the architectonics of a building but bleed out to take in the hawkers coming to sell food, the karuwai who never enter the cinema but rely on its customers for their support, and the clubs nearby soon to be filled when the cinema disgorges its patrons.

It is hard in Kano for cinema to be a banal domain. Its early use as a contested site over which debates about the nature of colonial urbanization were fought invested it with a particular ambience from which, in a sense, it has never recovered. As an object, it retains the history and identity of those early moments. To be sure, one of the reasons that cinema remains popular in the North, when it has relatively died out in the South, has to do with poverty, and with the fact that cinema remains cheaper than purchasing a television and video recorder. But while this explanation has some force, it cannot cover the whole. One can argue that it is precisely its marginality in the Hausa cultural imagination that provides the transgressive pleasure and the heightened affect of going to the cinema. If space is "practiced place" as de Certeau has it, a general abstract space that has been worked on by generations of people that inhabit, traverse, or avoid it, creating its singularity, then the pounding of Bashir Ɗan Ladi's heart is the affective evidence of those practices working on the heart and emotions of one who goes within.

Children in Kano are disciplined into understanding what the cinema is. Through instruction, threats, and cajolery Hausa children are made to understand the place of cinema in constituting the proper boundaries of Hausa society. Cinema is a place marked by an excess of affect. It is sensational in its literal meaning of working on the body to produce physical effects. Racing home on the bike, charging in to get a good seat, shouting, and thumping chairs, the cinema-goer's experience of the theater itself can be as melodramatic as that of the films it screens. As a technology, then, cinema congeals the social effort of those who attend it, investing it with illicitness. And like the tar on Nigerian roads that sucks up heat all day only to release it at night, cinema gives off aura, affecting the experiences of those who go there by quickening their blood and heightening their senses.

It should also be pointed out that parental warnings about the immorality of cinema and the potential consequences of attending are not necessarily given or taken at face value. These warnings represent both real religious injunctions but also more quotidian parental manipulation. Cinema is a dangerous place for many reasons beyond the spiritual and can teach children many lessons parents would rather they did not know. Parents are against cinema because they fear it will make children steal money from them; that it will stop them from attending Qur'anic school and expose them to foul-mouthed, violent hooligans. Children are warned off of cinema because of its idolatry in houses where the television is always on and the video recorder an important domestic item. Idolatry here is invoked like the bogeyman, less an example of an invariant religion unable to adapt to the modern world than an instance of parents using something at hand to get a child to do what they wish.

THUG LIFE

'Yan daba, as one commentator puts it, are "a social problem in Kano and a matter of concern to every resident" (Ɗan Asabe 1991: 85). They are local thugs, organized into gangs, hired out by political parties to rough up opposition rallies, and often accused of being paid to wreak violence during religious riots. 'Yan daba make money in various ways, from selling gasoline illegally on the black market, to buying and selling tickets at the cinema, to beating up and sometimes killing people for hire. They are often accused of other violent activities, from robbery to kidnapping and rape (Casey 2002; Ɗan Asabe 1991). 'Yan daba employ magic and medicines to protect themselves from harm and are believed to have links to the rural hunting groups (*mafarauta*) known for secrecy and magic (Casey 2002). They are poor, socially marginal, and they inspire fear and respect, annoyance and disgust.

'Yan daba claim, and some support the claim, that they uphold Hausa values by intimidating women who walk outside of the home unaccompanied by a male escort, and by publicly enforcing Muslim norms, making them a sort of inverted reflections of the Hisbah, the organization of youths established after the introduction of shari'a in 2001 that became responsible for enforcing Islamic law.[10] Complexly, 'yan daba are the objects of government campaigns and Islamic moralizing, and just as often they are used both by political parties and traditional elites for crowd control during major events and festivities (Casey 2002). In the urban arena, 'yan daba form gangs that hang out in particular neighborhoods; they are stereotyped as going around with hunting dogs, hanging out with prostitutes, and getting high. One of the places they are most associated with is the cinema.

'Yan daba are present at all cinemas—especially at busy ones—selling tickets outside. But it is the poorest, oldest, and cheapest cinemas that they dominate. In the 1950s and 1960s 'yan daba took nicknames from Indian film stars and, especially, cowboys, identifying with the violence and independence of Western film icons.[11] In recent years, 'yan daba have begun to dress like "niggaz," in baggy jeans, sunglasses, and gold chains, though they still take nicknames from Indian actors as well as rappers and other prominent figures in the black diasporic world (Casey 2002). Outside the theater, their presence is most visible in their buying and selling of tickets. Inside they shout and curse at the screen, make ribald comments about actresses, and banter with karuwai. Their presence is also obvious from the smell of Indian hemp (although only in the poorer cinemas). When cinemas were closed down as part of the moral cleansing that accompanied the introduction of Islamic law, the congregation of 'yan daba was one of the main reasons given. Ironically, 'yan daba also became one of the chief reasons for reopening theaters: the Kano state government was faced with the prospect of loosing hundreds if not thousands of 'yan daba onto city streets. According to Ishaq Agboola, the manager of Wapa cinema, when cinemas were first closed down the "crime rate increased. There was now no place to drink, no place to watch a film, and there was a lot of unoccupied youth."[12] Agboola was part of a group lobbying the commissioner of information, to whom he cheerfully held up a nightly scenario of hundreds of unoccupied, potentially violent, young men with nothing to do. With the cinema open, however, the evening of 'yan daba would be different: "After eating his dinner he will be thinking of what to do. He will sit here [Wapa cinema] for two or three hours and will leave feeling happy and sleepy and will go home" (ibid).

'Yan daba account for, at best, a fraction of the cinema audience, but, like the karuwai with which they are associated, their image looms large over the public imagination of cinematic space. Their noisy and vibrant presence—the scalpers outside, the cursing inside, the sense of danger and violence that moves with them—creates a more general atmosphere that exists whether they are there in numbers or not. This atmosphere gets translated into bodily experience, the sensate fear and excitement inspired by such individuals moving from one physical space of the city to another.

The presence of 'yan daba at the cinema is one reason why the movie theater gets defined by Hausa as part of *bariki* culture. *Bariki* is an ambivalent term that derives from the English "barracks." It refers to the leisure culture that grew up around male migrants, usually Christian, imported to the North from the South of Nigeria early in the twentieth century to work for the expanding colonial economy.[13] These young workers lived in male-only barracks, often in new areas built on the physical margins of Hausa cities. Around them new leisure spaces and practices grew to accommodate the different cultural lifestyles of migrants. Over time, as men brought new wives with them and began raising families, these "barracks" became amorphous parts of a larger urban landscape and *bariki* came to refer to a set of institutions and practices taking place in these areas as well as to the areas themselves. These practices include *bikis*, large parties organized by important karuwai featuring *'yan daudu* (men who sleep with men),[14] *bori* spirit possession, and the beer parlors which dot the landscape. Hausa people stereotype barikis as being full of *'yan iska*,[15] dissolute youth, who waste their time drinking and frolicking with women. Cinemas are most often located in these marginal spaces, physically separated from traditional Hausa Muslim neighborhoods and conceptually lumped together with the wider complex of bariki culture.

Public cinemas in Kano tend to show action and other violent films that reflect the tastes of the 'yan daba reputed to be filling the theaters. The Indian action star Dharmendra, or *Sarkin Karfi* (King of Strength) as he is known in Hausa, had enormous cult popularity at the cinema, especially with 'yan daba, so that years after his star had waned, his films continued to fill Hausa cinemas with devotees. This is in stark distinction with the Indian films popular on television and video, where pictures about love and familial tension (often stereotyped as "women's films") are dominant. In recent years the action genre has been dominated by the muscular figure of Sanjay Dutt, who often plays poor, hard-nosed, thug-with-honor characters. In Kano cinemas, where he is very popular, his persona mirrors the social persona of the audience, creating a feeling of identity acknowledged in his nickname, *'dan daba mai lasin* (licensed hooligan—in the way James Bond is licensed to kill). The presence of these stars creates a circular feedback where the films shown at cinemas help produce the audience as a moral object just as audience tastes help dictate which types of films are played.

While it would be easy to stereotype 'yan daba as the immoral heart of Hausa youth, there is a complicated relation between them and official Hausa values. Conerley Casey (2002) argues that "yan daba are considered "revolutionaries" who guard Muslim ideologies and traditions . . . (and) at the same time . . . are criticized for their non-Muslim moral aesthetics." She goes on to point out that 'yan daba often grow up with the Islamic youths involved in enforcing Islamic rule, and during confrontations between 'yan daba and the Hisbah the sides are often well known to each other. More complexly, 'yan daba were deeply involved in the street demonstrations and violence demanding the institution of Islamic law in Kano state in 2001, although since then they have become a focus of Islamic concern and a prime example of the sorts of anti-Islamic practices that shari'a must stamp out.[16] 'Yan daba support for shari'a and their strong identification as Hausa Muslims, as much a part of their subjectivity as "niggaz" clothes, Indian nicknames, and hemp smoking, suggests a wariness of adopting wholesale theories of Islamic revitalization that fail to recognize these complex sorts of heterogeneities.

THE CINEMA THEATER

The Marhaba cinema was built expressly to be different from the other cinemas in Kano. Before the Marhaba, cinema owners sought to build in areas of dense population, often adjacent to a market, and on the edge of several neighborhoods so that the cinema would be a border point where areas and ethnicities mixed. One could walk to the cinema, go there straight from work, and pass it every day, seeing announcements for which films were now playing and which were coming soon. The Marhaba, by contrast, is in a wholly different part of town, on the border of a well-to-do area, a quiet place that receives no through traffic. This was a conscious effort to try and create a more "upmarket" viewing experience, one with higher prices and better quality films. Inside the theater, attendants patrol, making sure that no one is smoking Indian hemp or starting a fight.

At night the place comes to life as patrons begin to roll up and hawkers and small shops set out their wares. To the right of the steps leading to the entrance of the Marhaba cinema, shoeshine stands supplement their business by selling postcards of Indian film actors. Vendors wander through the crowd selling sweets, cigarettes, and kola nuts. To the side, small stations roast and sell *tsuya* (pressed meat basted in ground nut and pepper) and chicken. Others sell oranges and fruit, or soft drinks. Most other cinemas in Kano are located at key transit points of the city, marking off one area from another, creating nodes where people meet, buses disgorge, and a world of social activity takes place, generated by the cinema but having little to do with the film itself. Next to the Marhaba a social club for journalists mutates after hours into a night club servicing the clients that pour out from the cinema—the space of one bleeding into the space of the other.

Because the structure of film distribution differs from that in Europe and the United States, the practice of attendance has a different configuration. In Nigeria, distributors purchase a single print of a film. After they show it in one city, they move the print on to another cinema they own, and then to another the next night. Weeks, sometimes months later, it will return to the original cinema for a second performance before resuming its peripatetic journey. Therefore, while regular cinema-goers get to see their favorite films many times, this can only be with gaps of several months in between. Every night each cinema shows a completely different film, charging particular days with particular meanings. In the 1990s, Friday was reserved for the newest and best films, followed by Saturday; Monday and Tuesday were for the cheapest and least popular. Tuesdays were for Hong Kong films, Thursdays for U.S. ones, and the other five nights for Indian movies. People chose to go to the cinema as much because of what day it was as for the film shown (often they might not know which film was being shown). As film showings were not advertised, the only way to know what film was playing was through word of mouth or by attending the cinema in the days running up to a showing. The pricing complexly reflected this differentiation, with Friday night costs approximately double those of Monday. Once I paid fifty naira on a Saturday to see the film *Aashiqui* (1990, dir. Mahesh Bhatt). The friend I saw it with told me that the first time he had seen it, he paid fifteen naira; when it returned it was thirty naira, and the fourth and fifth times he went it was seventy-five naira.

On the night I went with Shehu Alkali, the Marhaba was partly full, interest was desultory, and there was a great deal of wandering about and talking with other people (rather than the more usual talking at the film). The print was extremely poor, the subtitles, added in Dubai, often unreadable. Inattention was no doubt aided by the fact the film broke down four or five times during the performance. This was a regular occurrence and one of many interruptions to films' schedule. For Hausa viewers, films were regularly interrupted by the insertion of trailers for the following night's film. As the film program changes every night, and because there is no advertising in the newspapers or elsewhere as to what a cinema is playing, there are only four ways of knowing what film is coming next: (1) a small sign and a poster outside the cinema announcing that night's film; (2) posters inside the foyer that indicate the next five nights' movies in order; (3) viewers who see these posters telling their friends (word of mouth being by far the most important means of publicity); and, most dramatically, a reel of the coming night's film inserted in the middle of a showing, usually as the film is coming to a climax and interest is the most intense. In the film we were watching, as the hero was about to avenge the death of his parents by a wealthy landowner, the image abruptly jumped to a scene from a kung fu film. This was not an edited trailer highlighting main themes of the film, but simply several minutes of a reel from the next night's film—an extended narrative sequence—dropped right into the middle of the film we had paid to see, the jump cut all the more jarring by the scenery's shift from India to Hong Kong.

Shehu Alkali goes to the Marhaba three nights a week: on Wednesdays, Fridays, and Saturdays, a frequency that leads his friends to describe him as "addicted." Like that of others, his attendance is dictated not by which film is showing but by the day of the week, an indication of the genre and quality of film being shown. A huge fan of Indian movies, he only sporadically goes to see American and Hong Kong films. He told me he prefers the Marhaba because, unlike other cinemas, like the Wapa and the Plaza, there are far fewer 'yan daba. At the Marhaba he finds the quality of the cinema higher, the films newer, and the experience generally better. Also, nearly all films at the Marhaba are subtitled in English, a language Alkali can read somewhat well although he speaks it falteringly. Lawan Ibrahim, a friend of Alkali's who sometimes accompanies him, said that Hausa people go to the cinema because they like the films, they like to go and meet friends, they like to see girls in the audience, and because the sound and picture is so much better than on television.

At the Marhaba, Alkali and Ibrahim always sat in the same section, up front and to the right of the screen, where they could meet friends who always claimed the same space. If a girlfriend went, it was common to leave with her, but inside they would sit in their usual place with male friends. *Girlfriend* is a complicated term in Northern Nigeria. Lawan Ibrahim classified three different sorts of relationships: *budurwa*, *yarinya*, and *karuwa*. For Ibrahim, a *budurwa* is someone you wish to marry. This may be someone your parents arrange for you to wed but whom, possibly, you have never met. *Yarinya* refers to a girl you may be sleeping with, but there is not necessarily a deeper commitment. Inside the relationship you may call her a burdurwa as a term of endearment, but to others the distinction is clear. *Karuwa* is a prostitute, but, again, this does not simply refer to a cash for sex exchange; often the relationship can take on features of what in the West is covered by the term *girlfriend* (see Pittin 1979). So, for some karuwai, Ibrahim explained, one has to court them, buy them small presents to win their affection, and take them out. If you annoy them they will refuse to have anything to do with you; you must plead to get back in their good graces. Cinema-going plays into this complex set of moral rankings as attendance can be a defining feature separating burdurwa from yarinya and yarinya from karuwa. No one would take a budurwa to the cinema, as respectable women do not attend. All women who go are seen as karuwai. Some yarinya might go while some might refuse. These terms are widely recognized but not wholly fixed. Ibrahim himself was in the middle of a long and protracted conflict, as he wished to marry his yarinya—someone he had met at the Marhaba, in fact—but his parents were opposed. They kept presenting him with more respectable girls, and Ibrahim kept quietly refusing, hoping to wait out his parents so that over time they would relent and allow him to choose his partner.

Like 'yan daba, the presence of prostitutes helps produce cinema as a symbolic space in Hausa society. As I noted in chapter 4, the first cinemas in Kano were all built outside the old city, sited on the edges of several different areas where ethnicities and religions mixed. Many of the parental critiques of cinema-going had to do not with the films themselves but with the parents' suspicion that after the performance, their children would go to areas like Fagge (site of the Plaza and Orion cinemas, two of the oldest in Kano) to sleep with prostitutes.[17] Moreover, the illicit sexual activity seeped outside the cinema's walls and into the spaces beyond. In cinemas like Wapa and El Dorado, many prostitutes congregated nightly outside the cinema, never going in, bantering with men who also never attended, although both sides of this encounter were pulled there by the spatial order of the cinema. Prostitutes were an important reason that after the film's climax and before the dénouement, audience members rushed home as fast as they could. No man wanted to be caught with one at the roadblocks Nigerian police set up around the city at eleven o'clock each night, supposedly in order to protect residents and keep a watch out for armed robbers but in practice often to extract bribes during the many months police in Nigeria went without pay. Often, the police arrest the karuwai traveling home with their boyfriends for indecency, knowing that the boyfriends will then pay a bribe in order to have their girlfriends released. The Marhaba is a prime target for such roadblocks because few people walk there, so the clientele is a little more affluent, and the mad rush that comes at the end of a performance is partly that people can race back home before the roadblocks are established and the police can harass them.

For a cinema like the Marhaba, karuwai were also a key aspect in regulating attendance. While there were just as many prostitutes at the Wapa, the Wapa was rougher and appealed more to 'yan daba, so its selection of films was aimed primarily at this male audience. Higher quality cinemas such as the Marhaba chose films that could appeal to women as well as to men. As one Lebanese distributor argued, while women make up at best 15 percent of the audience, their presence is key to drawing in males.[18] When police raids intensify, and prostitutes are arrested in large numbers, cinema owners even send someone to the stations to bribe some of them out so that attendance will not dip.[19]

THE AFFECTUAL COMMODITY

The art historian Jonathan Crary (2000) has argued that one of the defining transformations of twentieth-century modernity was the emergence of attempts to regulate and control attention as a means of ordering society and economy. In the late nineteenth century, molding attention emerged as a means of producing stable and productive subjects for new urban, industrial societies. It also protected them against the fragmentation and constant stimuli of a growing leisure society, which threatened to dissipate and overwhelm workers' attention. Cinema, as one of the most important emerging visual cultures of the era, was significant in this process, a point argued forcefully by the film theorist Jonathan Beller (1994). Beller finds attention to be a key aspect of the commodity nature of film. What the dominant narrative structure of film offers, according to Beller, is a means of securing attention, an organization of narrative and spectacle in order to win over the viewer's identification and affective response. By regulating perception in this way, films train the senses. The commodity value of film lies in its ability to hold our attention, to turn viewing into the social production of value. For Crary and Beller, twentieth-century attention was something that could be bought or sold, a mode of economic exchange. Affect is the bodily reaction that holds attention, sustaining it over time.

For Crary and Beller, affect is the consequence of cinema's operation as a standardizing technology. But the production of affect and its role in defining the commodity nature of film cannot be reduced to the technological operation of the medium and the narrative form of Hollywood film. Cinemas in Nigeria represent a specific site of pleasure and transgression whose modalities are heavily indebted to the films shown there, but which are equally indebted to the systematic training youths go through that produces cinema as an experience. Starting from theorizing formal textual properties (but using this for a much more expansive theoretical discussion), both Crary and Beller examine how these works order vision as privileged examples of the senses' training in modernity. I am more interested in moving beyond film to the cinema as a total event,[20] a mode of association that includes flirting, bantering, hearing, and yelling. Attention is certainly elicited through spectacular images, arresting sounds, and narrative devices internal to the film itself, but that attention is regulated by encounters with the audience, the journey to and from the cinema, the bartering with hawkers outside, and the bantering with karuwai inside. Cinema is a site of urban pleasure. It emerges from a series of encounters between technology and people who are themselves subject to a deep training in the sort of social space and leisure practice they are enacting.

Film is a standardizing commodity, but in Nigeria, the variegated pricing system builds locality into the commodity structure of film itself. On a Thursday night, as I stood looking at a poster for the next evening's film, the man beside me asked if I had seen it. I replied no. He said, "It must be good, look at how much it costs," tying the pricing of the film into the construction of its aesthetic value. Each cinema has operatives—the manager and others—who survey the audience at film's end, measuring its responses, recognizing its attachments, in order to gauge how much entrance will cost the next time the film appears. If a film is popular, the price will rise, if not, it will fall. Film value here, has a dual character. One is tied to its nature as a standard homogenized commodity, deriving value from its circulation across space and time. The other comes precisely from the noncirculating locality of the cinema theater and the structure of feeling that suffuses that space and is complicit in generating the sense of transgression, excitement, and desire integral to the affective experience of cinema. The experience of a film is produced from an encounter with it that cannot be reduced solely to the apparatus of film technology, the narrative organization of film, or the world outside it, but is an assemblage of all three. In Kano, this reality is recognized in the structures of Nigerian cinema, where the pricing is not standard but mutable, constantly changing in accordance with the reactions and emotions displayed by the audience as it leaves the theater.

Cinema in Kano is marked by this play between the standardizing logic of the technology itself and the social practices that congregate around, constituting cinema as a "practiced place" (de Certeau 1986). Karin Barber (1997) has argued that the experience of a mass public is uncommon in Africa, where the full penetration of mass industrial or mass consumer society has rarely been achieved and where the tendency of African forms of popular culture has been to reinscribe and reorder these spaces. Isolation is one of the theoretical prerequisites for the cinematic theory of identification, but it is hard to determine how this isolation occurs in Kano. Barthes's theory of the cinema theater, where "slipping" into the cinema seat is like slipping into bed, a prehypnotic condition that prepares one for the dream state of cinema, is ideal and strips cinema of the historical relations key to the modes of affect it creates. The lack of a ceiling, as simple as it seems, makes clear that the cinema cannot be so easily isolated from the world outside.[21] The association with friends, the banter with prostitutes, the repetition of dialogue, and the running commentaries to the screen all restrain the technological and social mechanisms of isolation. Identification certainly occurs, but it is communal as well as personal and achieved, I would argue, without a state of reverie. It is an open question how widespread the ideal of cinema-going as a dream experience is in Western societies where the middle-class habits of silence, isolation, and attentive watching are complicated by class-based and queer-based practices of talking, interacting, and sexual play (see, e.g., Harper 1999; and Warner 2002). In Kano, this ideal cannot be maintained, as cinema-going represents a different kind of assemblage of technologies and social practices that shift the basis of the cinematic event.

INDIAN FILM

One Friday night at the Marhaba I went with Shehu Alkali to see *Gumrah*. As it was a Friday and *Gumrah* was a new Sanjay Dutt film, the cinema was packed. There were hundreds of people outside, so Alkali quickly bought tickets (for N70 instead of the N60 they officially cost) from a scalper and ran inside to save some seats. *Gumrah* follows the adventures of Roshini (played by the actress Sridevi), an innocent girl who becomes a famous singer. Sanjay Dutt plays Jaggu, a small-time street thug who fights for money. He becomes Roshini's biggest fan, falling in love with her from a distance, following her around to her concerts, and financing this by selling tickets illegally outside. He declares his love for her, but she is from a good family and refuses him. Roshini, meanwhile, is searching for her long-lost father and is helped by a rich family friend, Rahul (Rahul Roy). They find out that her father is in Hong Kong, and when they travel there Rahul slips some drugs into Roshini's suitcase, using her as a mule. Roshini is caught, arrested, and sentenced to death. Jaggu, meanwhile, has followed her to Hong Kong and now sets about trying to free her. When he cannot do this legally he has himself arrested so he can get inside the prison, find Roshini, and break free. They flee to India just in time to catch Rahul about to use another unwitting young girl as a drug mule.

Despite a modicum of fighting, *Gumrah's* story was primarily dictated by love and received an enthusiastic reaction in the Marhaba. When people found out that Jaggu was a scalper they started screaming in delight, as many had just bought (or sold) their own tickets outside. There was a huge identification with Jaggu, constant talking at the screen, and cheering during his fight sequences. Although the film's action progressed from one wealthy bungalow to another and was set primarily amid the sort of opulence few in the cinema had experienced, there was a strong sense of connection with Jaggu's experiences and his love for Roshini. On the way back Alkali could not stop talking about Sanjay Dutt, his favorite actor and one whom all Hausa liked "too much."

For the past forty years, cinema-going in Kano has been inextricably caught up with Indian films (see figure 28). Originally, Westerns were popu-

28. Painting of the inside of the Marhaba cinema. By Abdulhamid Yusuf Jigawa.

lar, and later other genres like gangster films and Roman epics had great followings. But almost from their inception in the 1950s, Indian movies emerged as by far the most vibrant and popular film form (see Adamu 2005a; and Larkin 1997, 2004). One older Hausa man who grew up in the city of Kaduna in the 1970s said that Indian films were the dominant influence on his popular culture. He and his friends gave themselves nicknames after Indian stars—Jitendra, Faroz Khan, Amitabh Bachchan. After the release of *Amar, Akbar, Anthony* (1977, dir. Manmohan Desai), he and his friends began to wear wide collared shirts, flared trousers, and headbands; even their *wando* trousers under the traditional Hausa *dogon riga* (a long collarless shirt) would be flared. Women, he said, were even more affected, wearing long gowns and trousers (like the Indian *salwar khameez*), gold rings in their noses, and even red *bindi* dots on their foreheads.

When I asked Michel Issa, a film distributor, why Indian films had taken off so powerfully in Kano, he replied that there was no reason, that Hausa people just liked them more. He said that people had tried importing Arabic films, but there was no real enthusiasm, yet as soon as Indian films came in they quickly surpassed those from Hollywood. "Their culture is the same," he told me, repeating an observation I had already heard many times. Lebanese distributors, Indian film importers, and Hausa audiences all explained the powerful attraction of Indian films in Nigeria with cultural similarity. As the novelist Ado Ahmad put it:

> Our tradition and . . . the Indian tradition [are] almost the same: they have capitalists and we also have them; there are smugglers and we also have smugglers; there are evil people and we also have evil people. But the only difference is that they used to follow their lovers singing a song to them but we don't . . . do this. . . . So our tradition and that of India is almost the same, the difference is only small.[22]

Ahmed picks up on some of the numerous reasons why Hausa recognized such an intimate connection to Indian film. Usman Bala, a friend of Lawan Ibrahim's, argued that Hausa men watched them "because our women like them." They have great songs, he told me, which people like to hear and besides, the women singing them were beautiful. Both he and Ibrahim agreed that one of the key features of Indian film was they had *kunya,* a Hausa term that refers to a proper sense of shame and respect. "Indian films do not show kissing," he told me, and the older ones show great respect (by which he means great separation) between the sexes. While enjoyed for the music and spectacle, Indian films are also widely respected for engaging real social problems and offering practical and moral lessons about them. These lessons are played out through themes that recur in Indian films: the stark dichotomies of poverty and wealth; the corruption of the postcolonial state embodied by politicians, police, judges, and so on; the primacy of family and kinship as a means of moralizing political economy and translating the tensions of society into the dramatic conflicts within the family. But by far the most important similarity for Hausa is the way Indian films play out the tension between arranged and love marriage.

Lawan Ahmed, who, as I mentioned before, refused to go to the cinema on religious grounds, was also a huge Indian film fan. When he was young, he said, boys watched the Indian film shown on Sunday morning and then in school on Monday vied to see who could mimic the dance sequences the best (copying Indian film dance routines is popular in Hausa schools). One day when Ahmed was explaining to me why he felt Hausa love stories were un-Islamic he did so by comparing them to Indian films. Indian films have traditions (*al-adun*—custom, or traditional culture) which are a lot like Hausa life. He gave the example of a woman who wanted to marry someone but whose parents forbade her. He said what was good about Indian film is that the men and women really loved each other, but they hardly touched and rarely kissed. He praised this by going into an extensive discussion of the Qur'anic basis for the separation of men and women in Islam.

The perceived closeness between Hausa and Indian culture results in one of the strongest pulls of Indian films in the North, their role in *tarbiyya*. Strictly defined, this Islamic term refers to religious training, the complex disciplining whereby adherents undergo modes of learning (see Mahmood 2004). One novelist told me he watched Indian films intensely as a boy: "I like the love stories. I like the emotions between a boy and a girl. I see how I should behave."[23] Indian films have been key in training the Hausa sexes in how to relate to each other. Novelists like Sani Bashir often argue that they play a key social function in revealing to parents the negative consequences of arranged marriage. They share the aim of "enlightening the entire youth" Bashir argued, as well as "most of our parents regarding forced marriages and early marriages[24] to make them understand the rights of the youth and the rights of their children."[25] Indeed it could be argued that the shifts in marriage practice away from full parental control to allowing children a right to refuse an arranged spouse have come as a result of the influence of Indian film in Hausa culture. Ado Ahmad, arguing that new ideas being introduced into Hausa culture challenged parent's total authority, saw Indian films as key to this movement. They also taught young men how to speak to women (a pedagogical feat cited by both those who admired and reviled Indian film): "Before you could not call a girl and say you love her," Ahmad said. "She would refuse to come and . . . talk to you . . . because of shyness." Even men who tried to speak to women would become tongue tied. Women who were addressed would hide in their head scarves and run away. "But now, there are films and through these films we take some peoples' ideas and traditions. In Indian film, you will see how two lovers express themselves to each other." This, Ahmed concluded, could allow young people to break free of the invisible wall that separated men from women.[26]

CONCLUSION

While in other parts of Nigeria the rise of video has decimated cinema attendance, distributors and commentators insist that in the North cinema remains well attended and continues to be a vibrant part of Hausa popular culture and leisure. Cinema provides a visual experience difficult to reproduce on a video screen and a social space of interaction impossible to recreate in a domestic arena. When government authorities in Kano closed cinemas down following the introduction of Islamic law in 2001, they were responding to the socially marginal, ambivalent place cinema occupies in Hausa society. But this is a performative act as well, one that constitutes cinema's marginality by referring and reacting to it. When authorities allowed cinemas to reopen, it is hard to know whether this merely added to the sense of illicitness and transgression that marks the experience of cinema as an event and thus added to the value of the venue itself. The immaterial experience of cinema in Kano throws into relief how media are made to have meaning and the extent of cinema's institutional, technical, and social variation over time and space. It points to cinema's contingency and historical variability. And it adds to the idea of cinema-going as an embodied practice.

Cinema in Nigeria is an event produced by the encounter of social subjects with the specific architecture of film distribution and exhibition in Nigeria and the technological ordering of projector, screen, and seating that occurs there. While the standard structure of cinema in the United States and Europe creates a model that is sometimes explicitly copied (and at other times explicitly avoided), one cannot presume the universality of cinema and must instead interrogate this constant tension between standardization and local difference. Even the audiences attending cinema have a relationship to film as a visual medium and cinema as a social institution that emerges from a long training specific to colonial and postcolonial history of a Muslim society. The immaterial experience of cinema emerges from this encounter.

6

Extravagant Aesthetics

INSTABILITY AND THE EXCESSIVE WORLD OF NIGERIAN FILM

IN THE LOGIC OF MODERNIZATION THEORY, media were expected to be the technologies that effected the labor of making Nigerians modern. Mobile film units were to be "mental tractors," to borrow Siegfried Kracauer's (1952a: 13) apposite agricultural metaphor, breaking the hard ground of tradition to plant the seeds of progress. The developmentalist task of colonial films was taken up by the new medium of television, where their generic forms and political prerogatives fed into the emergence of television dramas. In contrast to these media, commercial cinema rose in popularity along with an urban Nigerian leisure class that flocked to cinemas, imitating the cowboy swagger and gangster slang of Hollywood stars. In the 1990s, these two cinematic traditions collided and were mutu-

29. Hausa video films on sale at Kofar Wambai market, Kano. Photo by the author.

ally transformed by the rise of a wholly new genre of media called Nigerian video films or Nigerian film.[1] These are feature-length fiction films shot, distributed, and exhibited on video and home digital technologies. Standing outside of the existing structures of urban cinemas, on the one hand, and television, on the other, these filmmakers take advantage of the technical and cultural possibilities of videocassettes to create a film form and an institutional structure that is wholly new in Nigerian history. Video films collapse the divide between state and commercial media, between Nigerians and foreigners, and between uplift and escapism. The result has been the emergence of a series of quite distinctive generic forms rooted in the extravagant, inflated world of melodrama (see figure 29).

Contemporary Africa is marked by the erosion of accepted paths of progress and the recognition of a constant fight against the insecurity of everyday life. This insecurity is a generalized condition that drives a range of seemingly disparate domains of African life: the collapse of state economies and the rise of informal markets, the rapid spread of new religious movements such as Pentecostalism and Islamism, the powerful resurgence of religious and ethnic conflicts accompanied by frequent outbreaks of violent conflict, the deep concern in many societies with issues of witchcraft and ritual abuse, and more widespread social disruptions brought about by the presence of oil economies and the rise of "fast capitalism."[2] In African studies, these domains are often examined separately, sometimes split between different disciplines, so that the study of informal economies, for instance, commands a wholly different literature and set of concerns than analyses of Islamism and Pentecostalism. These can be seen though, as reactions to the disembedding of Africans from a world economy and the collapse of traditional routes to security such as education and the civil service. What links these disparate phenomena is the realization of the instability of everyday life, the need for new networks for advancement, new conceptual schemas that explain the suffering of people, that proffer a means for escape and represent a yearning for justice. AbdouMaliq Simone (2001) has argued that the need to provide security has led to a certain sensibility among urban Africans, one he describes as a constant state of preparedness, a willingness to experiment in situations of poverty to achieve some measure of stability and control. This insecurity is economic, social, and spiritual, and it is a world of instability and experimentation that provides the grounds on which Nigerian films feed and grow (see also Okome 2002).

At the same time, these films indicate urban Africans' skill at constantly innovating new forms of cultural production—much of it woven into the fabric of religious movements—that generate their own experiences of pleasure and play and are coterminous with this experience of insecurity. Each epoch generates aesthetic forms that are sites of symbolic intensity where peoples' experiences of political and economic life are brought into being and made vividly legible. Africans do not merely exist in a state of permanent crisis, the crises themselves generate modes of cultural production and forms of self-fashioning that address widespread feelings of vulnerability—sometimes proffering modes of escape, sometimes exaggerating and distorting these insecurities for dramatic effect, and sometimes ignoring insecurity altogether. In photography, fashion, music, and film, the constant invention and experimentation of urban Africans are played out in public and are as constitutive of urban experience as the forms of crisis they address.

Nigerian films evoke their world's constantly shifting sands. The doctor who murders his brother to prevent being revealed as a thief, the wife who betrays her husband for another man, the con man who pretends to be in love to steal money, the grandmother who is part of a coven and seeks to ensorcell her granddaughter, dramatize the predicaments of an unstable and ultimately unknowable world. Here people who appear to be one way are revealed to be completely different. In Nigeria, the family provides crucial economic support, the closest affective ties, and, for many people, the only means of advancement. Yet perhaps because of this, in Nigerian films the family is often the source of the deepest treachery, and family members are represented as corrupt, cheating people of money and betraying them as well as offering love and support. As much as the family offers security, it threatens destruction. These fears are refracted in the vivid, brightly imagined world of melodrama where the struggle for everyday survival is depicted in extravagant, fantastic form. They compress politics, wider social conflict, and material inequities into relations between people. In this way they "moralize political economy" (Marshall-Fratani 2002) and use the stark moral polarities of melodrama to explore and interrogate the inequities of everyday life. The Indian cultural theorist Ashis Nandy (1998), writing about popular cinema in his country but in ways directly relevant to Nigerian films, argues that the repetitive storylines, grandiloquent dialogue, and outrageous plots represent a world of fantasy and myth that was supposed to atrophy with the rise of a modern, rational world. To study them is to examine the part of Indian life supposedly rejected by modernity. It is "the disowned self of modern India returning in fantastic or monstrous form to haunt modern India" (7). While Nandy's evocation of a field of cultural and religious alterity unaffected by Westernization may be overstated, his observation that these "traditional" sides of life were often marginalized by the discourse of modernization and development is insightful. Nigerian films draw on the sides of African life that were downplayed in the colonial period, in the nationalist era of independence and in the discursive concept of African cinema. As independence loomed, both colonialist and colonial subject alike emphasized the modern, educated, developed aspects of Nigerian life. Nigerian films, however, draw on themes of corruption and betrayal, naked desire for material goods unrestrained by ties of loyalty or love. They dwell on the witchcraft and sorcery that were shameful to nationalist elites and, more than that, they examine them in lurid technicolor without a trace of cultural embarrassment. They take the sides of Nigerian life associated with tradition and backwardness and mix them with the Toyota Land Cruisers and mobile phones, bank managers and oil executives of contemporary Nigeria. In these films, crass consumer desire bumps up against a spiritual realm that is manifest in everyday life, and African alterity sits cheek by jowl with Western modernity. Through these fantastic desires and outrageous plots the utopias and dystopias that dramatize the struggle and experimentation of contemporary Nigeria are formed and aired.

Nigerian films are the unintended consequences of the stuttering evolution of cinema in Nigeria. They are unthinkable outside of the urban world of leisure and experience that cinema brought, but at the same time they could never be thought of through the institutional and conceptual terms that traditional theories of African cinema constructed. In this chapter, I analyze the melodrama of Nigerian films—both English-language films in the South and Hausa-language films in the North—as a fantastic response to the insecurity and vulnerability of everyday life. Northern and Southern films differ from each other and are themselves made up of varied genres, from comedy to romance, horror, and religious films. But all of them refract and magnify, sometimes in lurid terms, the experience of contemporary urban life in Nigeria. In the case of Southern Nigerian films, or Nollywood, one mode of this melodrama takes the form of what I call an aesthetics of outrage, where the narrative is organized around a series of extravagant shocks designed to outrage the viewer. In the North, Hausa films most often represent insecurity through the unstable and changeable world of love. To do this, Hausa filmmakers have drawn on the equally vivid melodramas of Indian film, from which they borrow heavily and sometimes copy explicitly. Both Southern and Northern films provide a metacommentary on the place of "culture" in contemporary Nigerian society, offering a world that is thoroughly linked up to religious and cultural flows, at the same time as they casually and frequently revel in the difference and uniqueness of Nigerian society. Nigerian culture, here, is figured in the traditional religious culture of the *jujuman*, only exaggerated and distorted to become a stock caricature sold to a Pentecostal audience. With every lip-sync and every dance step, Hausa actors bodily enact Indian film—with all of its complicated hybrid history—within the stories and desires of Hausa society. In a society recently turned to Islamic law, this generates controversy, making these films, like their Southern cousins, objects whereby the meaning and shape of contemporary Nigeria is brought to life and debated.

Cumulatively, Nigerian films represent the aesthetic reaction to the new political, economic, and social architecture of contemporary Africa. When Frederic Jameson (1991) identified postmodernism as the cultural logic of late capitalism, he warned of the danger of periodizing hypotheses that obliterate difference and ambiguity. He responded to this by identifying postmodernism as a "cultural dominant" which while powerfully expressive of shifts in economic and political formations also allowed for a range of competing cultural and political forms. It seems to me that Nigerian films now occupy just such a space in that they express and constitute cultural and political subjectivities in Nigeria. They do this through aesthetic form—the films themselves—but also through their economic mode of production and distribution. Nigerian films represent the waning of state-based visual media (from mobile film units to television dramas) and their ideologies of progress and uplift and represent the shift to privatized media forms, mimicking the larger transformation of Nigerian society. Both form and industrial organization represent a radical reworking of the basis of African cinema and visual culture. Aesthetically, these films dramatize structural transformations brought about by the architecture of insecurity in melodramatic terms, by objectifying and reifying an idea of culture (Nigerian culture, Hausa culture, Yoruba culture) as a sign. In this chapter, I examine the dimensions of the insecurity which mark contemporary Nigeria by examining two cultural forms—Southern English-language Nigerian films and Northern Hausa-language ones. In the case of Southern Nigerian films, I focus on the powerful theme of corruption—financial, sexual, spiritual—that crosses genres, generating the sense of betrayal and insecurity. For Hausa films, I examine the logic of love and romance, intensified by the intertextual presence of Indian cinema, as privileged domains that inscribe social transformation. On a surface level these films appear to adopt very different registers, but ultimately they explore the relation of cultural form to political and social transformations and provide occasions in which the drama of postcolonial Nigeria is both represented and enacted.

The massive success of these films does not obliterate the presence and dynamism of other forms of cultural production in Nigeria, and their popularity should not hide the substantial critique of the films inside Nigeria from both conservative and progressive critics concerned about sexism, gross materialism, the bastardization of culture, and the move away from political and cultural ambitions. And while dominant themes, neither corruption nor love and romance exhaust the diversity of Nigerian film.[3] These do, however, represent two of the themes that most powerfully shape the public perception of these films. Often emphasized by filmmakers as necessary to their films' success, these themes have drawn the most fire from critics fearful of their effects, making them culturally resonant sites for analysis.

NIGERIAN FILMS

Since their introduction in the early 1990s, Nigerian films have transformed the media landscape not just in Nigeria but all over Africa, becoming one of the most dynamic media forms in African history.[4] These films do get to the cinema and on television, and with the rise of the Africa Magic station they are also available by satellite, but the driving force of the market remains the purchase and rental of videocassettes and VCDs.[5] Now more than five hundred films are released in Nigeria each year in three main languages: English, Yoruba, and Hausa. The English-language films dominate other Anglophone nations from Sierra Leone and Ghana to the west, to Kenya and South Africa in the east and south, and they are beginning to cross over into Francophone Africa. Yoruba and Hausa films are dominant in their own linguistic communities, which extend well outside of Nigeria into Niger, Ghana, Benin, and Cameroon. The strength of this industry has turned Nigeria into one of the largest film producers in the world (in terms of sheer numbers). The distributor Charles Igwe points out that six hundred thousand VCDs are pressed each week and that "crates and crates" of VCDs and videocassettes leave Lagos every day by plane for distribution across Africa.[6] This makes Nigeria an emerging force in producing digital media content and in innovating modes of distribution and exhibition.

Because of its reach into every corner of Nigerian society, the film industry has spawned a range of ancillaries that ride the waves of its popularity and are themselves becoming key parts of Nigerian urban cultural life. The fact the film boom coincided with the mass penetration of personal computers and design software into Nigeria, for instance, combined to generate a revolution in African graphic design. The thousands of Nigerian films released each year and the posters that go with them have produced a new visual vernacular—a constant experimentation in photography, coloring, and font design that permeates markets all over Africa, covering the counters of shops and papering the walls of urban areas (see figures 30 and 31). Similarly, the abundant use of song and dance sequences in Northern films means that film music has come to dominate the Hausa music industry (see Adamu forthcoming), just as the popularity of films has spawned a magazine industry geared to reporting on the stories and stars of the industry (figure 32). Cumulatively, the scale of the industry is large. It employs actors, directors, writers, musicians, designers, artists, and choreographers, as well as those employed in sales and distribution. Its ubiquity and international presence means that the Nigerian government

30 and 31. Posters for Hausa video films. Photos by the author.

32. Advertisement for *Albarka* from the back of the Hausa film magazine, *Fim*.

is beginning to recognize films as a major symbol of private initiative and a key force to counter Nigeria's international reputation for corruption and violence, offering a more positive vision of Nigerian culture and industry.

Nigerian films are distinctive in their development of an aesthetic and an infrastructure radically different from the legacy of "African cinema."[7] But in doing so, they have generated considerable controversy. African cinema is not just a body of work but a critical cultural project with roots in the early independence era in Africa and the struggle against cultural imperialism (see Cham and Bakari 1996; Diawara 1992; Pines and Willemen 1989; Ukadike 1994). The early generation of filmmakers sought, first of all, to repudiate the stereotypes of Africans in Hollywood and ethnographic films by revealing the depth of Africa's cultural heritage. From this matured a more complex film practice that was aesthetically and politically avant-garde, and opposed to the universalizing dominance of Hollywood cinema. The aim was to create alternative narrative and visual forms that were distinctly African (such as a "griot" mode of narration). This tied African cinema into the wider effort to combat cultural imperialism and build a "new world information order." As the filmmaker Gaston Kaboré put it: "The ability to picture oneself is a vital need. . . . A society daily subjected to foreign images eventually loses its identity and its capacity to forge its own destiny" (cited in Pfaff 2004: 2). The theorist Mbye Cham summarizes this position well: "These filmmakers deny conventional and received notions of cinema as harmless, innocent entertainment, and insist on the ideological nature of film. They posit film as a crucial site of the battle to decolonize minds, to develop radical consciousness, to reflect and engage critically with African cultures and traditions for the benefit of the majority" (Cham and Bakiri 1996: 2).

Cham's arguments are representative of the intellectual and political effort undergirding the concept of African cinema. This effort draws on a deep legacy of Third Worldist thought that was politically cosmopolitan—in that it made alliances with similar minded film movements in India, Latin America, and elsewhere—but reached that cosmopolitanism by presenting African difference. In parallel with Ngugi Wa Thiong'o's (1986) critique of cultural borrowing as "apemanship and parrotry," African cinema was originally intended to create a space of cultural alterity, made in vernacular languages, where African culture would be bolstered, supported, and protected from foreign cultural domination. Nigerian films, as we will see, share neither the political ambition nor the cultural effort of this earlier generation of film production. The presence of African languages in the films is as much driven by the market advantage of vernacular as by any cultural nationalist ambition. Filmmakers like Kenneth Nnebue quickly dropped Igbo for English when they realized the greater market potential, and since that time English-language films have been the largest and most successful of the genres. Nigerian films effortlessly and unselfconsciously borrow from a wide range of cultural forms and start with an assumption that the audiences and subjects of the film are familiar with and take part in a global mass culture. Culture in these films is as likely to appear as a reified stereotype, part of the backwardness and corruption of a traditional past holding Nigeria back, as it is to be seen as a valued and cherished part of Nigerian society (see Meyer 2003b). Because of this, Nigerian films have been criticized by other filmmakers and in Nigeria itself for concentrating on the underside of Nigerian society—on precisely the sorts of images of witches, ritual abuse, and magic that colonialist documentaries were accused of fixating on. Critics argue that the video films are technically poor, repetitive, and cheaply made. From the point of view of directors trained in film schools, they are a vulgar, populist entertainment with none of the political or aesthetic skill of their celluloid cousin, the lack of technical ability the video filmmakers exhibit making their productions an embarrassment. Jonathan Haynes (1995) has pointed out the lack of an overt political critique in many of the films, contrasting this with the progressivist ambitions of African cinema. To celebrate the films uncritically would be to ignore these issues and silence the voices of more independent and culturally activist filmmakers. But as many other filmmakers recognize, Nigerian films have engaged a popular African audience in a way that African cinema never has. As an art cinema, funded by international and national government grants, African filmmakers never had to win an audience. Their films, while dominant in international film festivals and at the prestigious FESPACO festival in Ouagadougou, Burkina Faso, have rarely been shown in African cinemas or watched by African audiences outside a narrow, elite band. The irony of African cinema is that it refers to the films Africans produce rather than those they watch. Many powerful, artistically excellent films are rarely played for audiences, even in their own nations. Nigerian films, by contrast, receive no outside funding and rely solely on success in an African marketplace, with all the advantages and disadvantages that brings. Charles Igwe, the distributor and producer, commented that, in the beginning of the industry, the first aim of Nigerian filmmakers was not technique or quality but to generate narratives that sold well in the marketplace. Whatever else one can say about Nigerian film, he continued, "we possess the Nigerian audience. There is no question about that."[8]

INSECURITY AND MELODRAMA

African studies has seen a recent burst of work, in many different arenas, that is trying to comprehend the widespread insecurity in contemporary Africa and the emergence of new means of dealing with that insecurity. A great deal of this sense of vulnerability results from the economic and political reordering of African life and is expressed by the forms of social order and imagination of the self that such restructuring generates. Structural adjustment programs, with their forced privatization, hastened the shift of African economy away from state control and salarization and toward what Achille Mbembe (2001) terms "private indirect government." In the early postcolonial period, many African nations were organized around the state and its forms of taxation and employment. Salaried labor, as a civil servant or a parastatal employee, was prestigious, lucrative, and secure. In countries like Nigeria, public-sector employment swelled gigantically during the oil boom. The state's role as employer was supplemented by its continual intervention in the economy through subsidies to key commodities (food, gasoline) in response to pressure form popular political action. As Janet Roitman (2005) and Mbembe (2001) have argued, the economic role of the state, represented in the form of the salary—the monthly wage from which subsistence and development originated—was as much a political technology as it was an economic one. It became the way African subjects were constituted as citizens, drawing them into a political contract with the state. It became less about paying people for completed work and more about rewarding them as clients. Over time, as African economies entered into crisis, the logic of the salary began to mutate. Rapid inflation reduced the purchasing power of salaries enormously, government workers were subject to weeks and months without pay, and the public sector went into decline and lost prestige. Workers who could leave for private companies did so, and those who remained were often compelled to supplement government salaries with private income. As the public sector began to teeter over the abyss, it was given a push by structural adjustment programs that forced African governments all over the continent to reorganize the state sector, privatizing large sections of government and reducing the inflated number of workers. Government's role as provider of employment and salary was overtaken by its role as awarder of contracts, the political technology par excellence whereby economic accumulation, political allegiance, and social hierarchy have been constituted in contemporary Africa.

The consequence of these economic changes has been the shift of large numbers of workers from the public to the private sector. The move away from salary has been one toward ever increasing forms of risk, where one's stability and the routes toward that stability have to be forged outside older networks of education, regular employment, and the salary and within new networks that progressively delink Africa from the official world economy. These networks often rely on what AbdouMaliq Simone (2004) has termed worldliness, the necessity of mobilizing external networks of support, be these religious networks, NGOs, foreign corporations, or wealthy patrons, in an effort to gain some semblance of stability at home. The rise of the informal economy depends on (and generates) an architecture to make this work, which in turn calls into being new forms of community, revalorizes ethnic and kin-based modes of belonging, and constitutes African subjects

NO CONDITION IS PERMANENT

DON'T GIVE UP! YOUR MIRACLE IS ON THE WAY

33 and 34. Stickers found on buses, cars, shops, etc. Collection of the author.

in their relation to the state, the economy, and each other. Where a few decades ago wealth in Nigeria was produced through the production and export of agricultural commodities such as ground nuts, cotton, cocoa, and palm oil, now the creation of wealth has been concentrated largely in the single commodity of oil. As a result of corruption, the awarding of fake contracts, and the siphoning off of funds from government departments, the logics of oil capitalism have created a new symbolic regime of power where wealth is separated from production and seems to appear without effort. It is not won through hard work but seems to derive from an opaque source. The successful in society seem to gain wealth instantaneously, without slow accumulation or even effort, from their connections to mysterious networks (A. Apter 2005; Comaroff and Comaroff 2000). The paths to wealth and security are now unclear, and in that obscurity a range of cultural beliefs has flourished.

One trajectory in recent scholarship has examined how these transformations have fostered belief in the work of the occult operating underneath the surfaces of the observable world.[9] The perceived rise in the presence of witchcraft in everyday life, the widespread beliefs that new elites are part of secret cults, and the urban fear of occult violence demonstrate the intensity of these fears. Religion, whether through the guise of witchcraft or Pentecostal prosperity gospel, has emerged to become the idiom explaining why vast sections of society live in poverty while a tiny elite accumulate fantastic sums of money (see figures 33 and 34). The fear is that behind the operation of this unstable new economy, powerful occult forces are at work. Adam Ashforth (2005) has felicitously coined the term "spiritual insecurity" to refer to the sense of danger and exposure to invisible forces that many contemporary Africans feel. Jean and John Comaroff (1999) have used the overarching term "occult modernity" to characterize how the occult is used as a contemporary idiom through which dislocations in global capital are experienced.

The insecurity that this work identifies needs to be examined as part of a wider register of vulnerability that is at once spiritual, material, physical, political, and social. In Nigeria, for instance, widespread concern in urban areas about the kidnapping of children and their dismemberment in rituals articulates with similar anxieties about the prevalence of armed robbery, ethnic clashes, and religious rioting.[10] The dynamic rise of religious movements such as Pentecostalism and Islamism should be seen in the same vein. Like witchcraft, Pentecostalism and Islamic revitalization movements seek to impose meaning and order on the insecurities of everyday life. Both are part of symbolic economies that represent injustice in the world and promise a means of redress. Certainly, the introduction of shari'a law in the North drew popular support because of the belief that shari'a would finally bring a measure of justice to a profoundly unequal political and economic system. Both Pentecostalism and Islamism are, in their way, radically destabilizing themselves, in that they try to subordinate competing forms of belonging (whether to a family, an ethnic group, a nation) to a transnational spiritual community. Both thrive on vehemently attacking older forms of religious practice, most especially traditional African religions but also alternative forms of Islam and Christianity, from Sufism to Catholicism (see Larkin and Meyer 2005). Pentecostalism and Islamism, while strikingly different in many respects, both provide narratives that moralize political economy, explaining the roots of insecurity and offering a measure of action to combat it (Marshall-Fratani 2002: 85).

AbdouMaliq Simone (2004) argues that contemporary urbanism is marked by an intense provisionality and uncertainty. His interest is in the experiential effects of economic insecurity and Africans' innovative responses to it. As education and industrial labor have been removed as sources of advancement and security in the world, urban Africans are operating with a "more totalizing sense of exteriority" (Simone 2001: 17). To survive, they have to mobilize resources that might exist. Life in poverty becomes a constant state of experimentation, with no clear pattern for success. The anthropologist Conerley Casey (1997, 1998) makes a related argument in more psychological depth in the context of Northern Nigeria.

She explores the psychological consequences of living in a society where a seemingly ordinary quarrel between individuals might at any moment grow into a larger argument between groups, then explode into rioting between ethnic or religious blocs. Casey focuses on the consequences of this sort of provisionality, the everyday, low-level anxiety and preparation for the fact that at any moment, the world might be turned upside down. Simone examines how the growth of Islamic orders from Tijaniyya to Mourides has been fostered by their promise of a measure of economic and social support. Paul Gifford (2004) and others have examined a similar dynamic in the growing power of Pentecostalism. Together, these very different registers of informal economy and Pentecostalism, trading networks and Islamism, witchcraft and capitalism, are trying to represent and in some ways ameliorate the expanding sense of vulnerability and exposure that many Africans feel.

The success of Nigerian films lies in their ability to probe the fault lines of this insecurity in contemporary African urban life and to transform them into cultural productions based on pleasure and play as well as on anxiety. These films are full of stories of the economic dishonesty of elites, of business partners who betray one another, of the sexual corruption of pastors, of the promise of Pentecostal deliverance, or of the malevolence of witches, all of which bear public witness to the ambivalent and unstable nature of urban Nigeria. But in telling these stories, the narratives revel in the costumes and the outrageous transgressions of characters, in the fancy houses and the nouveaux riches who live in them. Comedy is as important a part of this genre as violence, and the inevitable moral at the end of the story cannot quite overcome the sense of play that takes place before. These films wage a political critique through the language of melodrama. Melodrama is excessive, frequently fantastic, and works, as Peter Brooks (1985) has argued, by taking the basic material of reality and charging it with a larger significance, exaggerating it so that the essential moral polarities that underlie everyday life are made clear. Brooks argues that melodrama arose as a genre in postrevolutionary France, when the moral anchors of social stability—church and monarchy—were thrown into abeyance by the rise of a secular republic. By staging moral dramas in excessive terms that reveal the primal ethical forces underlying society, melodrama makes ethics public and dramatically concrete.

Nandy (1998) explores similar issues in an argument compelling for Nigerian films when he asserts that the fantastic and excessive stagings of melodrama have become the dominant political idiom of the popular classes. Nandy argues that Indian masses are marginalized and no longer believe in the false modernism of progressive politics as couched by the state. As politics declines, political action is expressed in a language of fantasy and myth. This language, while vulgar and blatant, is never trivial, he argues. Touching on life's fundamental instabilities, it accounts for people's tremendous emotional identification with films.[11] Nandy develops his argument by exploring how Indian films, for all their blatant exaggeration and seeming simplicity, are anchored in key tensions of contemporary life. Indian films, he argues, represent a slum's view of society in that both slums and the films "show the same impassioned negotiation with everyday survival combined with the same intense effort to forget that negotiation" through fantasy and escapism (2). Under the ideals of Nehruvian rationalist development, popular Indian films were culturally disowned in favor of a politically oriented, realist cinema. Like slum dwellers, Indian films were ever present but socially marginal in the urban landscape. The problem with this, Nandy argues, is that art cinema, in attempting to critique modernity, used the same enlightenment rationality and thus could never find a critical vantage point from which to question modernity's assumptions properly. Popular melodramas, by contrast, because their stories and worldview are rooted in the myths and fantasy of Indian society, offer a critique of modernity from "the point of view of eternal India" rather than from progressive politics (235).

Precisely because it is organized around morality, melodrama offers a means with which to speak about tensions in African society that mimics the idioms of Pentecostalism, Islamism, and witchcraft. It does not ignore questions of the economy, it offers moral justifications for them and explores the changing basis of a society that allows economic insecurity to coexist with fantastic wealth. And it does so in a formal style, never representing life as banal or everyday but always as intense and excessive, mixing formal playfulness with emotional realism. In different ways this is clear in English-language films from Nigeria's Christian South and in Hausa-language films from the Muslim North.

"NOLLYWOOD" AND THE AESTHETICS OF OUTRAGE

Southern Nigerian films, controversially named "Nollywood," exhibit the qualities that Ravi Vasudevan (2000) associates with the cinema of "transitional" societies negotiating the rapid effect of modernity. Here the cinematic address is to an urban class living in a world governed by kinship relations. Plots are often driven by family conflicts, melodrama predominating, with its emphasis on moral polarities, excessive situations, and exaggerated acting. There is a strong element of the grotesque in elites' extreme sexual and financial appetites, their willingness to betray friends and family to gain wealth that they will display in the surface expressions of houses and interior decoration, rich clothing, and beautiful cars. The grotesque, as famously defined by Mikhail Bakhtin (1984) and examined in relation to Africa by Achille Mbembe (2001), is a system of signs whereby the sensory life of power is both depicted and transgressed. It depends on exaggeration, hyperbole, and excess made palpable through rapacious bodily appetites. For Bakhtin, the open mouth, the swollen penis, the defecating anus, and enlarged breasts are all used as a way of ridiculing and parodying the elites of society, commentating on their lust for wealth. Mbembe agrees about the importance of these bodily metaphors but argues that in Africa in the 1980s and 1990s, under the control of dictators, these are the metaphors used by state power itself—this is how elites ritualistically perform their power through a logic of excess. The sheer scale of postcolonial corruption, the outrageous amounts of money stolen from state coffers, the extravagant houses elites build, and the wild rumors that circulate about their sexual proclivities combine not to critique elites but to form the world of meanings whereby power is dramatized. Where Bakhtin and Mbembe come together again is in their sense that the grotesque is not just a system of signs, a collection of images, but a cultural analytic whereby the order of society is made manifest and can be viewed (see also Stallybrass and White 1986).

Southern Nigerian films take the grotesque away from the figure of the postcolonial dictator and place it back inside the family, making it more like melodrama. There the grotesque plays out within and between family members, and the dense political field Mbembe identifies is sublimated into personal relationships. Unlike in Bakhtin's discussion of François Rabelais, there appears to be little irony, with all the distancing and reflexive metacommentary that implies. The films should be seen not as parodies of elite behavior, but as a witnessing to them. They dramatize elites' actions to create a form of ethical evidence that highlights key moral conflicts in society. The grotesque here is harnessed to what I call an aesthetics of outrage, a narrative based on continual shocks that transgress religious and social norms and are designed to provoke and affront the audience. To give one brief example, the character Helen in the film *Glamour Girls* (1994, dir. Kenneth Nnebue) is a prostitute who is picked up from

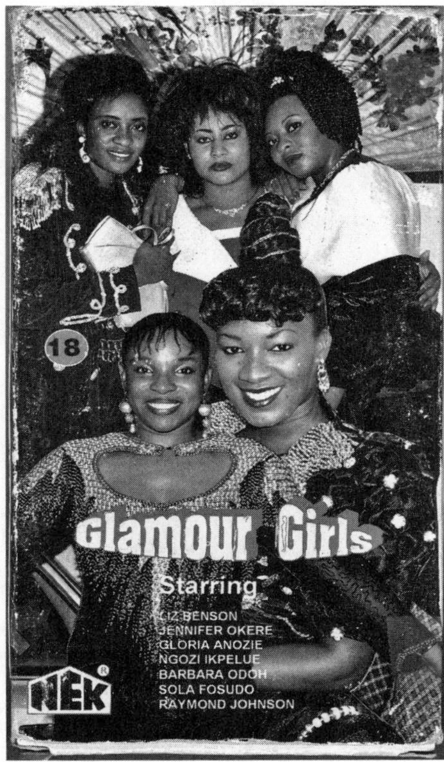

35. Cover of *Glamour Girls*, 1994.

the street and offered as a sexual prize for Martin, an out-of-town guest of a wealthy young Lagosian (see figure 35). When the host goes to fix a price with Helen, he is so overwhelmed by her sexual attractiveness that he strips and makes love with her there and then. Her excessive beauty is brought home because the host is short, and when he appraises her he is eye level with the breasts he is gazing at. When Helen hugs him she seems to overwhelm him. Later, when he goes back to tell Martin it is his "turn," he apologizes for taking so long saying, "I couldn't resist her attraction. She is a mermaid." He also warns that he wants to return once Martin has finished. Martin enters and sees Helen lying semi-naked on the bed, her face turned away from him in semi-sleep. He stoops to kiss her leg and the camera slowly pans up her body as Martin moves up. When she turns to him he shrieks and she jumps up and bolts from the room. A long close-up reveals Martin's stunned reaction. His friend enters to ask what is going on and Martin stutters, "My sister, my only sister," the camera moving into an extreme close-up of him shaking his head.

The aesthetics of outrage is a composite of different elements key to which is the intense transgression of moral and religious norms, often heightened by exaggeration and excess. This scene depicts the casual immorality of the Lagosian elite, who can pay for sex as a simple gift to an out-of-town guest, but swells this dramatically with Martin's (and his friend's) recognition that the sexual turn-taking they were planning was incest. It is a mode of address designed to outrage and provoke the viewer. When I saw this scene with a Nigerian family, it provoked gasps of astonishment, horror, and thrill at the men's open sexism. The negation of morality in the film is designed to stimulate it in the audience, vivifying social norms and making them subject to public comment. The aesthetics of outrage uses spectacular transgression, luridly depicted, to work on the body, generating physical revulsion. Linda Williams (1995) has famously argued that certain genres of film—horror, pornography, tearjerkers, comedies—are designed to stimulate what she calls "spasm," which may take the form of shudders, arousal, tears, or laughter. *Glamour Girls* provokes agitation at the severe moral breaches in which Helen is involved, randomly tricking innocent men and making the viewer both witness to the outrage and helpless to do anything about it. This outrage provides a public witnessing to the sorts of activities people in society are involved in and, through the bodily reaction to them, enacts a moral commentary on society itself. Formally this witnessing is located in the extensive use of the reaction shot. When Martin discovers that the prostitute is his sister, the camera moves into an extreme close-up of his shaking head. After he tells his friend, another close-up reveals the friend's horror at having just had sex with Martin's sister. The reaction shot is used in a number of ways in these films, as we see characters react to the elites' fancy houses and décor, their wonderful clothes, their physical beauty, but it is most common in response to moments of transgression, where it stands in for the audience's judgment, and heightens the sense of the transgression itself. In dramatizing the ways fundamental norms of society have been abrogated, the aesthetics of outrage makes public stark, ethical conflicts at the heart of society[12] at a time when the moral basis of society is in transition. Nigerian films thus represent the instability of modern Nigerian life, but, more than this, they dramatize it, distorting it and transforming it into spectacle, making it something to be bodily experienced and lived.

The experience of the film is what moves these stories from being merely a referent of an external reality. These films are intimately involved in representing the structures of insecurity in Nigerian society, congealing in themselves the ruptures in the social and economic order, but they cannot just be seen as signifiers for events happening elsewhere. The aesthetics of outrage, aimed at bodily stimulation, represents an experience of film integral to the film itself. It is a temporal and corporeal sense of living in and with the film, and it represents the singularity of film over and above political and economic contexts. While films draw their charge from these wider contexts, they cannot simply be reduced to them as if they were neutral referents of a situation outside of the film. The aesthetics of outrage force people to live the film so that external realities are intensified, vivified, and made sensate through the mediation of film narrative itself.

Glamour Girls was one of the earliest "blockbuster" Nigerian films and has had a seminal role in establishing many of the films' key formal features. The narrative of the film revolves around the lives of four "senior girls" who have sex with rich businessmen and politicians to support their extravagant lifestyle. The film opens with one of the girls, Sandra, moving from the East of Nigeria to Lagos to find her friend Doris, to see if she can help her get ahead. Sandra meets Thelma by mistake, and Thelma takes her to Doris's fancy new house. This early scene is key in setting up the formal and thematic conventions of the film. The scene in Doris's house opens with an establishing shot of heavy cream damask curtains, which, after the bell rings, we realize are covering the front door. Sandra enters, looks around, and the camera slowly pans to reveal the furnishings from her point of view. Ruched cream curtains hang over every wall in the room. In front of them are a Louis XIV style sofa and chairs, also in cream damask, with gold leaf legs and arms. A reaction shot of Sandra shows her in awe, taking in the finery and beauty of her friend's house. She sits and tells Doris that life is miserable. She works hard but has no money, has fed and cooked for men, but after a while they leave her for younger women. Framed against the cool cream curtains, Doris and Thelma nod in recognition of men's inconstancy and then change the subject. Doris reveals that she has "joined the payroll" of Chief Obie, a "multimillionaire" who has given her money to redecorate her boutique. They laugh. Thelma observes, "The old, rich men are more generous than the younger ones." She then tells the story of her breakup with a younger man: "When I discovered that the naira was not flowing, I told him bluntly that we don't eat handsome. Handsome men are those with naira power."

Doris and Thelma are representing a world in which relations are not based on love or attraction but on financial gain. Traditional routes to success, such as hard work, are revealed to be a waste of time, and security through love is inherently fragile due to the inconstant nature of men. Doris tells Sandra that the only route to success is through a patron, "You can't achieve the quality of life you want without help," and that "a husband is no longer the prime issue in a woman's life. . . . Once you become rich you can buy yourself a husband." Thelma agrees, saying that even though she has a husband in the United States she still sees wealthy men. "Men who go abroad are all heartbreakers," she observes. "If something goes wrong, I'll have something to fall back on." Sandra cannot believe the outrageous statements her friends are making. When Thelma talks about handsome men being those with money, the camera cuts to a close-up of Sandra looking away, rolling her eyes in disgust at this materialism. But it is a complicated scene. Doris has become wealthy only by relying on the favors of rich patrons. But Sandra herself asks Doris to be her patron, and Doris obliges, making Sandra a "Glamour Girl" and putting her on the payroll of Chief Obie, who makes Sandra rich overnight.

Doris and Thelma trade sexual favors for financial reward and openly flaunt the traditional roles open for Nigerian women. The camera dwells on the surfaces of Nigerian life, the rich décor and beautiful clothing, and emphasizes these through pans, close-ups, and reaction shots that generate a sense of symbolic intensity. What this scene depicts is the admixture of pleasure, even admiration, that often accompanies the portrayal of disgust. The furnishings of Doris's house and the lifestyle she leads are deeply attractive to many besides Sandra, and the independence and authority the glamour girls reveal in the film (where Doris does buy a young husband, shown in one particularly outrageous scene carefully washing and hanging her underwear before serving her dinner) is a powerful inversion of gender relations that offers particular pleasure. This pleasure indicates a level of complicity that accompanies outrage, a complicity frequently justified in the text itself, and which is the reason moral condemnation does not harden into overall political critique.

Glamour Girls depicts a post–oil boom Nigeria where the developmentalist routes to success are bankrupt. Education, even family, are empty of their ability to provide support and protection. The only recourse lies in alternative patrons obtained through sexual favors.[13] This is a world in which people compromise themselves to avoid the suffering of everyday life. It is a world marked primarily by corruption: sexual, political, spiritual, and familial. Indeed, corruption is the single most powerful force underlying the aesthetics of outrage that the films rely on. The film propels viewers through a series of shocks that constantly provoke them with excessive betrayals. Jane finds love only to betray her partner Desmond for Alex, who turns out to be a con man who deceives her and steals her money; Thelma deceives her husband in the United States; Doris treats her much younger husband Daniel like dirt; Sandra betrays her friend Doris and is, in turn, betrayed by Dennis. Helen is a trickster figure. Wholly outside the main narrative about the glamour girls, she is periodically inserted to inject sexual havoc and bursts of sheer outrage. The first time we meet her she is flagging a car to ask for a lift. After the man does her a good turn and stops to drop her off she begins screaming and slapping him, drawing a crowd shouting that the man "booked her" for two thousand naira and now, after sleeping with her, only wants to pay fifteen hundred naira. The innocent man denies this but is confronted by a notoriously unstable Lagos crowd and hands over the money. There is no narrative logic here but shock at her behavior.[14] There is intense moralizing but it is unclear what the alternative is in an unstable and treacherous world. The film presents what the women do as wrong, but ultimately, as Moradewun Adejunmobi (2002) has argued, their actions are justified as necessary responses to the violence of everyday life. They express an implicit recognition of society's failure to provide for its people. Like Sandra, the glamour girls began their activity because of poverty and suffering. Even Helen is revealed to have turned in this direction when, as a high school student, she discovered her father was sleeping with her girlfriends and lavishing his money on them while at the same time refusing to properly support her.

By motivating characters' choices, Southern Nigerian film grounds hyperbolized events in very real, everyday situations of poverty. It often presents characters faced with a difficult situation forced to make a choice. The 2005 film about 419[15] con men, *The Master* (dir. Andy Amenechi),[16] follows the fortunes of a market trader, Dennis, who is defrauded of all his money by a con man and after this comes to join the gang himself and rise as a 419er. Outrage works through a mechanism of distancing: characters are involved in actions so horrible that one cannot identify with them. But at the same time, it depends on similarity: characters come to their actions by choices made to alleviate real hardship. These films present a world of glamour, wealth, and privilege that is wholly foreign to all but a tiny minority of Nigerians, but this is a fantastic response to the adversity that is common to millions. When Helen arranges to stay with a man for a week and bargains up the price by reminding him that she will have to "boycott lectures" and harm her studies, she reminds us that she is making do in a world where the rationalist path to success—education—is now only serviceable as a means of gaining access to powerful male patrons. The scandalous world of Nigerian film is often erected over the much more quotidian struggles of everyday life, and it is the contrast of one with the other that gives these films their charge.

Nigerian films represent a world where modernity is present in the slick material surfaces of Mercedes Benz sedans, large bungalows, stereo equipment, fancy furnishings, and sumptuous dress rather than the world of learning, science, and organization. Society, as it is depicted, is comprised of people who appear to be one thing and are revealed to be something else, where nothing is stable and fortunes can rise or fall in an instant. Nigerian films rely on the generation of excess—sexual, financial, material—that can never be assuaged or fulfilled. It is an excess often born of desperation and a surfeit of desire. This tendency to dwell in life as it is lived at its most heightened is melodramatic, but where Western films often cannot cope with the intensity of melodrama and keep it at arms length through irony and stylized references, Nigerian audiences take melodrama seriously, heeding its moral messages and soaking up its emotional impact. Like horror films, which many films mimic, Nigerian films aim at not just reflection but stimulation. In *Doctor Death* (dir. Fidelis Duker), Morris is egged on by his wife to murder his older brother so he can take over his hospital and then becomes obsessed with seducing his brother's widow, even bewitching her so that she will cast her children out of the house (figure 36). To gain magical powers that will allow him to make his fortune, Amos, one of the main characters in the Nigerian/Ghanaian film *Time* (2000, dir. Ifeanyi Onyeabor) is shown sticking a knife into the stomach of a pregnant woman, then disemboweling her and removing the fetus for a sacrifice (figure 37). These images and narratives are provocations designed to scandalize and disgust. Through that bodily reaction moral reactions are provoked and social ethics publicized. These films work not as realist reflections of society but as inflated, exaggerated imaginings that nonetheless deal with underlying truths. This truth is experienced through the bodily response of revulsion. These are genres designed to generate physical effects. Like the Holy Spirit, they come in to take over your body.

At the heart of many films, crossing genre boundaries of family drama, political thriller, and religious film, is the ever present force of corruption. Corruption is presented as an evil force eating away at the decent ambitions of people trying to get by in life, but also as the prerequisite

36. Cover of *Dr. Death*, 2000.

37. Cover of *Time*, 2000.

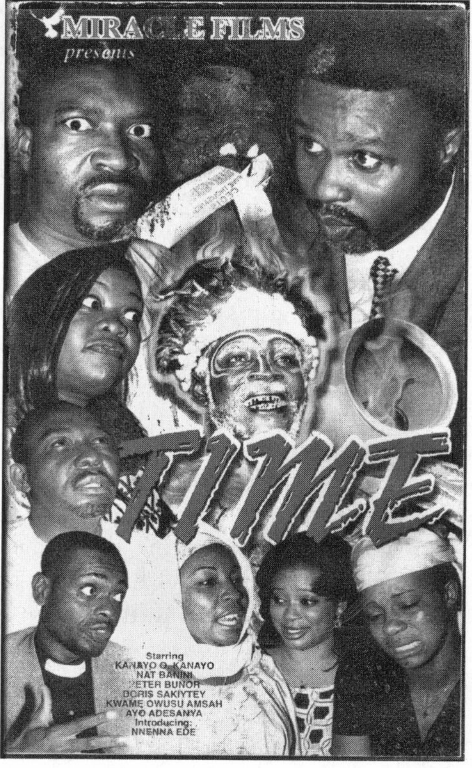

for success. Sandra in *Glamour Girls* has to use her body to gain money, Dennis in *The Master* has to become a 419er and cheat people, Morris in *Dr. Death* murders his brother, and it is only after this turn toward corruption that success comes. Behind this is both a commentary on the failure of modernization in Nigeria and an explicitly Christian logic. In *The Master*, Dennis is robbed by a 419 man who, when he later realizes that Dennis is educated, offers him money to become part of his gang. Dennis at first refuses. His girlfriend argues with him, reminding Dennis, "that man can make you rich." When she leaves, Dennis soliloquizes on his various options. At the end, he becomes a 419er. Similarly, in an even more overt scene in *Time*, the impoverished bank manager Francis makes a pact with a witch. He is offered a pot and told if he drops it and breaks it he will become rich, but as he does so his wife will sicken. Francis is horrified and rejects the offer, running away in fear and desperation. But as he does so, the pot keeps magically appearing in front of him. Spirits materialize and begin to assault him. He panics and keeps running as the maniacal sound of the witch's laughter resounds around him. Finally, he tires. The pot appears at his feet and he picks it up and smashes it on the ground.

In these key scenes, characters are faced with a fundamental choice. Their decision, however motivated and justified, is still a decision they have the moral volition to make, and the audience witnesses them making the wrong one. Like Faust's bargain, these scenes represent an explicit turning away from morality and from God, and we need to see the characters wrestle with that decision to understand the deeply volitional and, in some cases, diabolical, nature of the choice. Corruption here is the force that diverts pilgrims on life's journey, eating away at their resolve, leading them into temptation. In Christian films like *Time*, the forces of darkness can only be controlled by becoming born again and using the Holy Spirit to gain protection (see Meyer 2003b, 2006; Ukah 2003).

Corruption in Southern Nigerian film also addresses the failure of modernization in Nigeria and the atrophying of developmentalist routes to success. Unlike mobile film units or television dramas, Nigerian films are not aimed at producing a rationalist subject—they are about stimulation not cultivation. These films depict a world in which the rationalist figures of the world economy, the bank manager, the politician, and the corporate executive are revealed to be illusions—a system of signs that mask an underlying reality. In *Super Warriors* (2004, dir. Prince Emeka Ani), a businessman, Ugochukwu, runs into difficulties and goes to see his patron, Chief John, to help get them sorted out. Chief John says he can help him,

I AM AFRAID OF MY FRIENDS
EVEN YOU
Let My Enemy Live Long &
See What I Will Be In Future

38 and 39. Nigerian stickers. Collection of the author.

as he has in the past, but that the reason he can is that he belongs to a "family" of "prominent citizens of this country," which he urges Ugochukwu to join. The "family" refers to a secret cult involved in "fetish" worship from which members derive magical powers necessary for success in the business world. Ugochukwu tells the Chief, "I made my money through hard work and not through rituals." Later, he adds that this is against his Christian faith. Chief John reveals to him that all of his success was the result of the cult's powers, not hard work, and that the Chief, too, is a "strong Christian." Hard work, gradual accumulation, success through one's ability, and the recognition of individual merit—the verities of the colonial education system that have palpably failed many Nigerians—are depicted as a veneer that hides underlying forces of spiritual corruption.[17] Value is derived from more obscure means. The corruption characters in Nigerian films are involved in replicates at the level of the family and the individual the wider force of corruption as a dominant system of meaning in society as a whole.

In mixing melodrama with horror and magic and linking spiritual with financial and sexual corruption, Nigerian films have generated a social world where instability is to be found in almost every area of life. Things seem to be one way, and then change utterly for no apparent reason (see figures 38 and 39). As Francis says to a hunter as he is trying to kill himself: "You don't know how it is to be so rich and then to be so poor."[18] In contemporary postcolonial West Africa, where the everyday suffering of the vast majority stands in stark contrast to the gigantic accumulation of the small elite, the tropes of corruption, betrayal, and evil have provided a powerful way to express the inequalities of wealth. They do so through a process of cultural objectification. These films are about making the grotesque public and something to be viewed.

HAUSA FILMS

In the North of Nigeria, both filmmakers and their audiences have been quick to identify the Christian roots of Southern Nigerian Films. Stories about magic, ritual abuse, and witchcraft are less about the actual practices of traditional Nigerian religion and more to do with the global spread of evangelical Pentecostalism, one of the most dynamic forces in contemporary Africa. Pentecostalism objectifies traditional African religious practice, arguing that the traffic with spirits that is such a key part of traditional religion is nothing more than diabolism. These spirits, and the devil, are said to be behind a range of phenomena in contemporary life, from the failure of the state to modernize, to the inability of individuals to prosper and get ahead. Security, in a world of spiritual and material anxiety, can only come from the protection of the Holy Spirit, the acceptance of Jesus Christ as one's personal savior, and the combined efforts, through prayer and charismatic powers, of church affiliation.[19]

Perhaps inevitably because of this, Hausa filmmakers have been wary about making films that deal with issues of ritual abuse and witchcraft. While fear about cult activities or about the negative effects of witchcraft on everyday life are common in Hausa society, and films on this subject are made (see Krings 2006), there is a sense that the un-Islamic nature of these themes should not be objectified and circulated as cultural texts. Both Southern Nigerian and Hausa films remain haunted by the ghost of developmentalism, which hovers over them and provides a critical vantage point from which many of the films are judged. For the South, this is manifest in repeated calls by the Nigerian Film and TV Censors Board for films to stop focusing on "violence, rituals, voodooism and the like"[20] and in demands that they "project Nigeria's image positively" so that "wrong signals [are not] sent to the international community about Nigeria."[21] In the North, the ghost of developmentalism is most intensely felt in the controversy over the influence of Indian film and its role (or not) in corrupting Hausa society. The strength of these critiques indicate how deeply engrained in the Nigerian imagination is the idea that a central function of media is to "represent" culture and the nation in an objectified form. Even while many are critical of the state and its ambitions, the idea that the state should have a role in guiding media, and that media should have a role in upholding cultural values, is widely shared. When I asked the director Tijani Ibraheem why Northern films deemphasized magic as a theme, he said, "as these are negative aspects of our culture," that "we reflect on tradition and the culture" and "pay attention to the type of society we wish to mold."[22] The Hausa response to the perceived Christian roots of Southern films has been to innovate an entirely different genre of filmmaking that does not exist in the South, one that deals with similar issues of insecurity and which adopts a comparable logic of excess. But it does so from a very different tradition, rooted in the songs, dances, and love stories of Indian film.[23]

In Northern Nigeria, the instability of everyday life has been sublimated into the quite different melodramatic arena of romantic love. Love is a profoundly individual emotion but unsettling, potentially excessive, overwhelming people's judgment and sometimes involving them in actions against their will. It is the site of key tensions between individual desire and respect for a social order in which marriages are expected to be arranged, and where individual desire runs up against the ideal of obedience to parents and to the social order. Emmanuel Obiechina (1971), in his exemplary work on the rise of Onitsha market literature, identified the fascination of these writers with themes of love as one of the most powerful indicators of social change and social transformation in Nigeria. Obiechina argued that the idea that people are mutually attracted to each other, that it is legitimate to pursue that attraction and develop intimacy without any interference, and that marriage should develop from this, are ideas wholly without precedent in traditional society. For him, the writers' popularity indicated how transnational cultural flows offer people alternative sets of values (he saw it as Westernization) which they can use to challenge existing social hierarchies. In my own work on Hausa romance fiction (Larkin 1997), I make substantially the same argument: that love has become a key arena in the North where hierarchies between generations are being fought over and revised, a point emphasized by Abdalla Adamu (forthcoming-a, forthcoming-b) in the most sustained analysis of Hausa films so far. Instead of seeing romantic love purely through the prism of an expanding Westernization, though, I look at the mediating influence of Indian film. For decades, Indian film has, for Muslim Hausa, constituted the most sustained cultural form dealing with the tensions around love. If, in Southern Nigeria, films have been marked by melodrama and excess based on an aesthetics of outrage, Hausa filmmakers have drawn heavily on the narrative models and formal styles offered by Indian cinema. To understand the nature of Hausa melodrama, then, it is first necessary to explicate the place of Indian cinema in Hausa society.

INDIAN FILMS AND NIGERIAN LOVERS

Indian films saturate the popular culture of Northern Nigeria, creating a landscape of desire and spectacle and a site for public memory and nostalgia (see figure 40). Ever since the late 1950s, the stars, songs, and stories of Indian film have been the dominant cinematic form in Northern urban areas. These films are popular all over Nigeria, but in the North there has been a special relationship recognized by Southerners and Northerners alike. It has made the imaginative, spectacular world of Indian film an intimate part of Nigerian Hausa popular culture. If one considers African media to be not only what Africans produce, but also the media that they consume, that enter into everyday life and become the public register for desire and anxiety, identification and difference, then Indian films must be considered part of the African cinematic world.[24]

The iconography, sounds, and images of Indian films constitute a vibrant visual and aural part of Hausa urban life. Stickers of Indian stars emblazon trucks, cars, and bikes (figure 41). Famous actors are given Hausa nicknames, such as *Sarkin Rawa* (King of Dancing) for Govinda, or *Dan daba* (Hooligan) for Sanjay Dutt. Many Hausa youth adopt Indian names, and young men try to walk like Sanjay Dutt and talk like Shah Rukh Khan.

The powerful nature of this identification was brought home to me one day in a conversation with Lawan Ahmed, a religious young man who lived in the Muslim neighborhood where I lived. He said the reason he liked Indian films was that unlike American films, they had so much "tradition." By "tradition," Ahmed was referring to an objectified religious and cultural practice that was distinct from Westernization and which, while different from Islam, offered a parallel to Hausa society. Because Ahmed was devout, he commended the fact that in Indian film men and women hardly ever touch and never kiss, consonant with Islam's prohibitions on sexual intermixing. "The devil is always behind us," Ahmed argued, and the sexual demureness of Indian films (at least in comparison to American ones) placed Indian cinema within the Islamic pale.

Ahmed echoed his statement in another conversation I later had with him and a group of his friends. They were vociferously attacking the rising

40. Nigerian poster of Indian film stars. Collection of the author.

41. Indian and Hausa film posters at a motor park, Kaduna. Photo by the author.

popularity of romantic books in Hausa society (Adamu, Y. 2002; Furniss 1996; Larkin 1997). As they saw it, these books "spoiled" women, encouraging them to be sexually active. Indian films, by contrast, "have respect," as one man stated loudly, and several of his friends expressed agreement. He argued that Indian films have *kunya*, an ideal Hausa quality of modesty and a sense of shame. This was especially true for older Indian films, where you could see that "Hausa culture and Indian culture are just the same."

In Northern Nigeria, the common statement that Indian culture is "just like" Hausa culture expressed perceived similarities in custom, fashion, iconography, and formal style. Indian films place kinship at the center of narrative tension. Traditional dress is similar to that of Hausa: men dress in long kaftans similar to the Hausa *dogon riga*, over which they wear long waistcoats much like the Hausa *palmaran*. Women dress in long sarees and scarves that veil their heads in ways that accord with Hausa moral ideas about feminine decorum. Indian films, particularly older films, express strict division between the sexes and between generations. Hausa Muslims are not familiar with the main tropes of Hinduism, but they recognize it as a domain of "tradition" that they see as opposed to "Westernization." This is what Hausa mean when they say that Indian films "have culture." Britain, the United States, and, in a different way, Southern Nigeria are the structuring absences here, the foils against which Hausa can define themselves and their relation to Indian films.

For Hausa viewers, Indian films offer a mode of traditional life similar to their own, and, at the same time offer a vision of modernity different from the West. What is more, they dwell on the tensions involved in moving between the two and, as they do so, create a powerful space with which Hausa viewers can engage. This tension is at the heart of Nandy's analysis, in which he recognizes that in the grandiloquent excesses of melodrama a core critique of contemporary society can be found, one that represents the frustrations and ambitions of a society in transition. Indian films are based on the tension of preserving traditional moral values in a time of profound transition (see also Vasudevan 2000). "The basic principles of commercial cinema," Nandy (1995: 205) writes, "derive from the needs of Indians caught in the hinges of social change who are trying to understand their predicament in terms familiar to them." Commercial cinema tends to "reaffirm the values that are being increasingly marginalized in public life by the language of the modernizing middle classes, values such as community ties, primacy of maternity over conjugality, priority of the mythic over the historical" (202). Characters in Indian films have to negotiate the tension between traditional life and modernity in ways with which Hausa, in a similar postcolonial situation, can sympathize. The choice of wearing Indian or Western-style clothes, the use of English by arrogant upper-class characters or by imperious bureaucrats, even the endemic corruption of the postcolonial state, are all familiar situations with which Hausa viewers can engage.

The circulation of Indian film to Nigeria offers Hausa viewers a way of imaginatively engaging with forms of tradition different from their own at the same time as conceiving of a modernity that comes without the political and ideological significance of that in the West. Indian films offer Hausa viewers a fantastic means of imaginatively engaging with the realities of another culture as a part of their daily lives (see figure 42). It creates a third space, apart from a reified Hausa tradition and an equally objectified "Westernization," from which to imagine other cultural possibilities. When Hausa youth rework Indian films in their own culture by adopting Indian fashions, copying the music styles for religious purposes, or using the filmic world of Indian sexual relations to probe the limitations in their own cultural world, they can do this without engaging with the heavy ideological load of "becoming Western."

42. Nigerian poster of Indian film and cultural icons. Collection of the author.

Nandy's position draws its strength from his recognition that Indian cinema represents and interrogates the tensions of a society in the midst of rapid social and cultural change. This has clear resonances for scholars analyzing Nigerian films as a whole and specific textual overlaps with Hausa cinema in particular. Yet its weakness, at least as far as Hausa films are concerned, is its dichotomizing split between tradition and modernity, indigeneity and Westernization. The rapacious intertextuality of Indian films, which themselves combine elements from Islam and Hinduism, from different regions of India as well as from national and international popular culture, should make one pause before asserting a hard distinction between a Indian subaltern mythos and a singular, rational Western modernity (Kaur and Sinha 2005; Singh 2003). In Hausa films, the heavy intertextual presence of Indian filmic elements exists in a marketplace in which Southern Nigerian films, transnational Islam, and Hollywood films and their perceived Westernization also compete. Here there is no clear opposition between West and non-West but a series of nodes, each with its own cultural influence. Something as seemingly constitutive of Hausa society as Islam on close analysis is revealed to be much more contested. Islam, not surprisingly, is at the heart of the definition of what constitutes Hausa culture and is seen as such not only by Hausa but by other Nigerian ethnic groups. At the same time, however, Islamic reform movements use the term *culture* to refer to the survival of *pre-Islamic* cultural and religious practices.[25] When they do so, Muslim reformers are using *culture* not as the socially valued set of practices that need to be preserved—the best that has been thought and said about Hausa society—but as what is not Islamic and should be driven out in the name of a purer Islam.[26] In this way, Islam in Northern Nigeria rests on its claims to authenticity and to deep roots in Hausa society while at the same time representing an aggressive, transformative modernity (see Kane 2003). For some Nigerians, new Islamic movements are as much a part of new modernities as Western cultural values and are just as vigorously resisted. When Hausa audiences engage with Indian films by copying them in their books and films, in their fashions and forms of talk, in their relations between the sexes and generations, this is only one cultural and religious source they draw on to create a complex field of cultural and social possibilities—a field that is shorn of its richness and complexity when reduced to series of binaries between West and non-West, modernity and tradition, corruption and authenticity. Hausa draw on Indian films to make sense of the changing foundations of the world around them. They translate Indian forms and aesthetics into their own lives as a way of defining the boundaries of Hausa culture and the shape it is to take in the future. In this, they play a role along with influences from the Middle East, the West, Southern Nigeria, and a host of other cultural and religious centers of influence, but this borrowing gives witness to the experimental and shifting ways Hausa fashion cultural forms to interrogate the basis of everyday life.

WASILA

In 2000, the Hausa film *Wasila* (2000, dir. Ishaq Sidi Ishaq) was released onto the Northern Nigerian market, where it sold over two hundred thousand copies and became one of the most influential Hausa films of its time (figure 43). *Wasila* was not the first Hausa film to adopt song and dance sequences from Indian cinema, but its success confirmed the position of its star, Ali Nuhu, as the romantic leader of Hausa film. As Adamu (2005b) argues, after its release the inclusion of song and dance sequences modeled after Indian films became almost obligatory for a film's success.[27] *Wasila* is therefore a good text through which to look at the influence of the Indian film form on Hausa cinema, an issue of considerable controversy in Nigeria, where such borrowing is often attacked for undermining cultural and religious values (Adamu A.U. forthcoming-b; Ado-Kurawa 2004). Most visually and aurally striking in this borrowing are the song and dance sequences, which provide the strongest generic contrast with Southern Nigerian films (where songs are absent) and the clearest mimicry of Indian ones. I also want to emphasize another aspect of borrowing which has been noted by some scholars but is the subject of less public cultural debate: the representation of love, romance, and sexual interaction, perhaps the area where Indian film has had the most sustained cultural influence in Nigeria (Adamu forthcoming-b; Furniss 2005; Larkin 1997). I am particularly interested in the way in Northern Nigeria love is the idiom whereby the issues of betrayal and insecurity, which found expression in Southern Nigerian film through the tropes of corruption and magic, are formed and aired in Hausa society. Love presents the familiar representational terrain whereby people who seem one way turn out to be something else. It offers the same vertiginous rise and fall, where someone who has so much can lose it immediately. Its instabilities are the basis of film form and content, and through it social change and the vulnerability of society is reified and set to music.

Wasila follows the fortunes of a young husband, Jamilu (Ali Nuhu), and

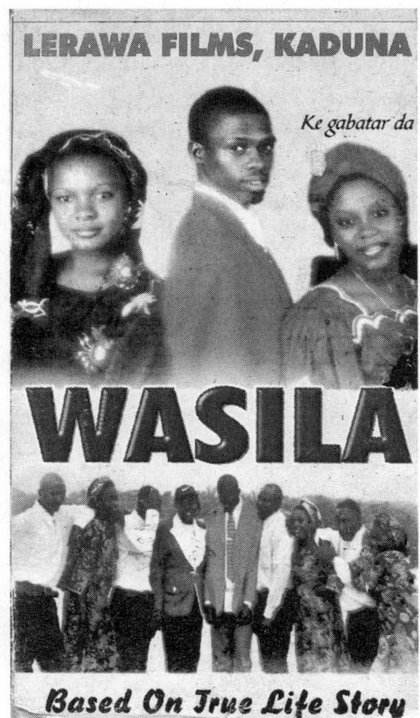

43. Cover of *Wasila*, 2000.

his wife, Wasila (Wasila Ismail), who, as newlyweds, share an intense love for each other. Trouble starts when Wasila awakes in tears from a dream that Jamilu has had a car accident. Her friends realize this is indicative of the depth of her affection, and they question whether it is reciprocated. To find out, they encourage Wasila to pretend she is sick and send for Jamilu, to test his emotional response. Jamilu rushes home from his business and, seeing his lover apparently sick, collapses to the floor with grief and is rushed to hospital. The second half of the film switches gears as Wasila encounters an old flame, Moɗa. Moɗa first approaches her at a shop while Jamilu is inside and she roughly sends him away. But later, Moɗa comes to the house and this time, instead of sending him on his way, she encourages him to come in. When he is reluctant, she teases him and leads him inside the house and then into the bedroom. Jamilu returns unexpectedly to find Moɗa lying on his bed. He is devastated, but remains calm as Moɗa leaves. For a while, he tries to put the incident behind him, but he cannot abide being near his love and withdraws from her to Wasila's great angst. As the film comes to its end, they argue and Jamilu recites the *saki uku*, the public announcement of divorce which, when uttered three times by a man, constitutes legal divorce under Islamic law. Wasila sings a keening lament and the film finishes.

Wasila's fame in Northern Nigeria comes from its being one of the first films to openly use Indian film aesthetics. Early Hausa videos borrowed from Indian film but mainly for plot themes and in the way they depicted relations between the sexes. Films such as *Gimbya Fatima* (parts 1 and 2, 1994, 1995, dirs. Tijani Ibraheem and Aminu Yakasai) and *In da So da Kauna* (1995, dir. Ado Ahmad) depict open, teasing relationships between lovers who share emotional time together, spend leisure time walking with one another, and declare their love openly, all of which, in many ways, were foreign to Hausa gender relations. In traditional Hausa society, a woman was supposed to stay silent in the company of her marriage partner, to keep her eyes averted and not look directly at him (a common practice of respect), and to leave the presence of men as soon as possible. Men and women would spend leisure time with members of their own sex, and courtship was supposed to take place in the presence of chaperones. The political scientist Barbara Callaway (1987: 34) points out that as late as the early 1980s "relationships between unrelated young people of equal status but opposite sex [were] nearly non-existent," and commonly, marriage decisions were the prerogative of parents, not children. Even after marriage, men and women continued to live highly segregated lives in the same house, with men sitting outside or in the *zaure*, a room at the front of the house where men receive visitors, and women controlling the domestic interior of the compound. This was brought home to me in a conversation with a married Hausa friend who grew up watching Indian films in the 1970s. He was complaining about their negative influence on Hausa culture, which startled me, as I knew him to be a big fan of the films. When he was young, he said, he used to like Indian films because of their commitment to the family and the cultural values they showed, but most of all because he liked the way lovers interacted. By this he meant that Indian lovers talk about their problems, they share an emotional life and support each other. The man declares his love for the woman, she declares her love for him, and they embrace. When my friend got married, this was the sort of relationship he was expecting and wanting from his wife, but when he returned home and tried to talk to her, she would turn away, answer as briefly as possible, and then leave. She was acting with the modesty that a good Hausa wife should have, but he wanted the relationships he had seen in Indian films. Because of this he had many problems early in his marriage, and this was why he argued that Indian films were harmful. Indian films, he said, inspired ideas about marriage and relationships that Hausa culture could not support.

In an earlier essay on romance literature (Larkin 1997), I argued that one of the reasons Indian films are so popular is that they provide an imaginative template from which the tensions over arranged marriages and love marriages can be imaginatively explored and critiqued. It is this critical edge that gives Hausa literature and film their emotional charge and sense of social purpose (see also Adamu forthcoming-b; and Furniss 2005). Abdalla Adamu (forthcoming-b) has argued that among the genres that dominate Hausa film—comedies, thrillers, gangster films epics—the two most popular are those about *auren dole* (forced or arranged marriage) and those which plot the tension between wives in a polygynous family. The popularity of issues of love and family reflects the importance of women for the industry, since they are the audience to which most films are aimed. It also helps us understand why so many films are shot in the confines of a house, why domestic interiors dominate, and why shot selection is marked by the dominant use of the two-shot and shot/reverse conventions. This formal style and the settings it depicts pack the wider tensions of Hausa life into the domestic arena and into familial interaction between lovers and among family members. Love is an unruly emotion, representing individual desire, often somewhat out of control, and it is frequently in tension with a wider social order. Love prioritizes individuals over the needs and wishes of family members. Abdalla Adamu (forthcoming-a) argues that underlying Hausa film is the rebelliousness of youths resisting the "tyranny" of the Hausa traditional marriage system, which denies them a choice of partners. This is particularly true for women, for whom marriage is a much larger part of their lives and whose ability to control and shape life within a marriage is more limited. Because of this, fantasies and fears about love and its wayward effects probe the fault lines of social conflict in Hausa society. Struggling for control over love and marriage is one of the few socially legitimate ways that women have agitated for greater independence; when Hausa films dramatize changing sensibilities about relations between the sexes, and about romance, they are pushing at the boundaries of social norms and social order.

Hausa romance literature dramatized the theme of love and the social conflicts around it in powerful ways that partly account for the burst of popularity of Hausa fiction in the 1990s.[28] But the medium of print involved a much greater process of translation and mediation as Indian films came into Hausa novels. What is different about *Wasila* and the films in its tradition is that by including song and dance sequences they make the relation between Hausa and Indian films directly and viscerally present, leading them to seem much more transgressive in a conservative Hausa context.

Like so many other Nigerian films, *Wasila* opens with a scene in the front room of a nice house where Jamilu's parents have come to greet Wasila's. The foursome comment on what a fantastic love the couple share and promise to work together to make sure the couple's marriage succeeds. In a series of shot/reverse shots, the scene sets out an almost ideal scenario. We find out the marriage was a love marriage, driven by the couple themselves, but the parents' obvious delight suggests that this is one of those rare occasions where parental control and individual desire happily coincide. We cut to another interior, this time that of a school, where three of Wasila's friends carry on the previous conversation, remarking on the amazing love that the couple share. As they do so, a camera zooms into close-up on one of the friends, blurs, and we switch from the diegetic world of the narrative and into the fantasy space of a song. Three girls in identical African dress dance in a line as three boys wearing matching black and white Western clothes dance along with them. Jamilu and Wasila appear and all the dancers are on top of a roof, creating a vista and a sense of space falling away behind them, mimicking the hillsides and mountain ranges favored in dance sequences from Indian film. Sometimes the couple dance in synchrony with the backing dancers, but mostly they wind around one another, singing a teasing song to each other, comparing who can love the best. Nearly twenty minutes into the film, this is the first time we see the main characters, as before their presence has been refracted through the tributes to them by friends and family. It is important that their first appearance in the film is a pure declaration of love embodied in song and dance. Songs in musicals are, of course, excessive events that interrupt narrative; they appear in films as proxies for strong emotions that characters cannot speak themselves. As in Indian films, the dancers' costume changes during the sequence, emphasizing its distance from realist narrative and its function as pure spectacle. At the time it was released, this song sequence was electric in Nigeria and captured the (then) still novel sense of transgression at seeing Hausa people performing like Indian film stars. The main star of the film, Ali Nuhu, said that the success of the song, combined with a backlash against it, meant that for a while he could not go out in public to meet his fans.[29]

Wasila made Nuhu into an enormous star, tying his persona to song and dance sequences and to the narratives of Indian film. *Mujadala* (2001, dir. Tijani Ibraheem), released not long after *Wasila*, was another huge hit for Nuhu, with a plot this time wholly lifted from an Indian film, *Dil Lagi* (1999, dir. Sunny Deol). The films tell the story of two brothers brought up after their mother passes away. Both become involved with the same woman. The elder, responsible son (Sunny Deol/Ali Nuhu) falls in love with a college student (Urmila Mantondka/Fati Mohammed) only to find that she is in love with his younger brother (Bobby Deol/Ahmed Nuhu). Complications ensue. Like *Wasila*, *Mujadala* cemented the public link between Nuhu and Indian film adaptations, in which his company, FKD Productions, has come to specialize. These films seem far removed from the spiritual insecurities of *End of the Wicked* or *Time*, or even from the casual immorality of *Glamour Girls*, but they nevertheless are structured around the same sense of vulnerability and impotence in the face of forces beyond one's control. Love is a classic theme of romanticist individualism, and the ability to pursue love is a powerful indicator of individual ambition. But the fact that love can take over one's body and mind erodes that sense of control. It leads lovers to make choices and take actions that go against their judgment, and it leads them into situations of anxious instability. In *Wasila*, love is represented as a form of possession. When we see Jamilu injured in a car crash, we think it is part of the realist narrative of the film, but it turns out to be a dream sequence that ends with Wasila falling to the hospital floor in tears, only to wake and find herself rolling on her sofa, shaking and crying in real life. This dream forces itself into her waking life, clouding the boundaries between real and unreal. It indicates an excessive love, something that is outside of her, controlling her. Similarly, when Jamilu rushes home at the news his wife is sick and sees her apparently ill, he is so overcome by his emotions that he collapses to the floor and is himself taken to hospital. These fits externalize love, taking it outside the body and mind and making it a tactile, physical thing. They present love as something slightly out of control, unpredictable, and dangerous. This instability is driven home by the central betrayal of the film, the seduction of Moɗa. Wasila's errancy comes without motivation: no hint of an ongoing love, no argument to estrange Wasila and Jamilu, no justification of any kind. The fact that the narrative of the film establishes a perfect love and then portrays Wasila cheating with a much less attractive man heightens the sense of instability. Although the film opens with a series of people talking about how powerful the lovers' feelings for each other are, the first time we actually see them is not within the realist narrative but in the alternate fantasy of a song sequence. Abdalla Adamu (forthcoming-b) argues that in Hausa films song sequences are often outside of the narrative, in surrealistic flashback or dreamscape, emphasizing the intimacy between love and forces outside of the everyday world, forces which enter into the body and take it over.

Wasila is primarily about betrayal and the instability of life. If Francis, in *Time*, could be broken by a world in which he is so rich and then suddenly so poor, Jamilu's heart is broken by a similar vertiginous change. The woman he loves most intensely betrays him completely. *Wasila* depicts a world in which people are fundamentally unknowable, in which one is at the mercy of forces beyond one's control. Several scholars of melodrama[30] have emphasized that the emotional force and moral power of the genre rests on putting characters in situations of helplessness so as to heighten the audience's physical experience of "agitation." As Peter Brooks has argued, melodrama represents a world where truth, justice, and ethics have been thrown into question and where political conflicts are shifted onto a personal plane and sublimated into domestic conflicts about love and betrayal.

When Wasila and Jamilu dance on a rooftop in an intertextual evocation of the hills and vistas used in Indian film sequences, or when their story echoes the lives of generations of Indian lovers who preceded them, what is revealed is the power and force of Hausa viewers' imaginative engagement with the world of Indian melodrama. Arjun Appadurai (1996: 53) famously described the importance of this imagination in a deterritorialized world in which "more persons in more parts of the world consider a wider set of possible lives than they ever did before," thanks to the movement of cultural texts brought about by globalization. But in the case of love, at least in contemporary Northern Nigeria, these imaginative investments produce shifts in gender relations and practices of courtship and marriage. At their heart is real social change, manifest most starkly in the movement away from arranged marriages in urban areas and toward a far greater choice for youths in marriage partners, and a greater reluctance of parents to force their choices onto unwilling partners. In an era of change, when the boundaries and force of Hausa values are constantly being negotiated through their interaction with the Islamic and Western worlds, love and marriage are key arenas where Hausa social boundaries are stretched and challenged. It is perhaps because of these real world changes that the debate around the imagined connection of Northern Nigeria to India has become so charged.

CONTROVERSY

The enormous success of Hausa video films and their huge popularity among women and younger men has, perhaps inevitably, led to a strong cultural backlash that accuses the films of degrading and destroying Hausa culture. One man in his early forties told me that the films were ridiculous and the song sequences "very, very controversial."[31] He said the films show lovers walking in the garden holding hands: "You *never* see a Hausa man do that. It is totally against his culture, I can say."[32] This opinion is echoed strongly by many academics, *ulama*, and sometimes, it seems, any male over forty-five. Zulkifi Dakata (2004), in an essay titled "Alienation of Culture: A Menace Posed by Hausa Home Video," makes this argument forcefully. Hausa films at first seemed to promise something new, he argues, but instead the films "unfortunately went on serving us with the same elements that have always threatened to degrade our culture. It is hereby sad to note that instead of using our culture to promote and sustain our indigenous development we take to copying. . . . No right thinking Hausa-Fulani parent would permit their daughter to go to parks and bushes to sing and dance with the boy she loves" (251).

In many respects, arguments like these replay earlier debates about the nature of cultural imperialism and the perils of Westernization. They reveal the powerful hold of the public-service idea of film: that it should "promote" culture and "sustain" development. This language reveals the ghost of state-produced media hanging over the privatized world of Hausa films. It is indicative of the existence of both Northern and Southern Nigerian films in a critical environment formed by an earlier epoch. This environment expects films to be forms of cultural objectification and recognizes that these objects circulate and create cultural and national identity (Ginsburg 1994; McLagan 2002; Myers 2002). They are key arenas where ideas of culture are formed and debated.

The clamorous attack on Hausa film came at the same time as the intensification of religious identification leading to the imposition of Islamic law in Kano state, the center of Hausa film production. Introducing shari'a law inevitably involves a public discussion of the legality of a whole range of cultural practices, but in Nigeria it shifted the direction of the critique in a new way. Sheikh Ameen Al-Deen Abubakar (2004: 256), one of the most prominent of Kano's religious leaders, summarizes this point when he questions whether copying cultural forms constitutes a promotion of a different way of life, citing the hadith "Whoever imitates a given people, he is considered to be with them." Ibrahim Ado-Kurawa (2004) takes this point further, arguing that there is a deeper religious meaning to Indian films that is carried over into Hausa society. This rests on the idea that the dancing and, to some degree, the music in the films, have their roots in religious tradition: "Each step [in the films] has its significance with its own meanings. . . . All dances copied from Indian films are a form of worship for a particular god. . . . By copying the worship of Indian Gods the Muslims are committing *shirk*" (118).

Because of this, he argues, Hausa producers are ignorantly spreading the teachings of Hinduism: "In this respect Hausa home video are serving as agents for the spread of Indian culture of love singing and worship of Hindu gods in contravention of the teachings of the Prophet (SAW) . . . that prohibit such actions" (ibid.: 117).

The fear that Indian films might promote Hinduism in Nigeria is a real concern but, at this point, a minority one, as the vast majority of viewers feel themselves to be deeply Muslim. To make this argument, though, one also has to separate out the "Hinduness" of films from all the other textual and cultural borrowings that make up Indian cinema. While the dancing may have some Hindu roots, song sequences also have very strong Islamic traditions woven into them, as whole sections of the Indian film industry—most famously screenwriting and music—were dominated by Muslims. The influence of Sufi *qawwalis* on Indian film music is perhaps the most famous example of a wide-ranging set of influences that complicates the identification of Indian films as essentially Hindu. This is not to deny the films' intimate involvement with Hinduism, but one must interrogate how that influence works.

The issue of the religious status of Hausa films came to a head after filmmaking was banned following the introduction of Islamic law in Kano state in 2001. In preparation for this action the filmmakers drew up a memorandum to the Shari'a Committee advising it of their plans for the "Islamization of the Film Industry" (Kano Film Industry Operators n.d.). What is fascinating about this document is that it throws the traditional definition of cultural imperialism up into the air. In a commitment to make filmmaking Islamic and stop the degradation of culture, the filmmakers have to carefully parse the idea of "culture" in order to protect it from itself. "Culture is a fabric of interwoven threads," the document argues, "some of which are original and conform with Islamic view while others are alien and inessential." To make Hausa films Islamic, one must not just keep out influences from India which are easily recognizable, but also keep out aspects of Hausa culture that are deemed to be un-Islamic, a process potentially fraught with much greater controversy. The cultural imperialism thesis, based on a dichotomy between indigenous and Western, has no real way to take into account the complexity of Islam, which is both indigenous *and* foreign and which transforms culture into something to be preserved *and* to be protected from. It is only by realizing that Hausa society is made up of Islamic and un-Islamic elements, the filmmakers conclude, that "we shall be able to avoid the erroneous view of sanctity of our cultural heritage. . . . consequently, this will allow us objective examination and distinguishing between cultures with true Islamic roots (which are to be promoted) and those alien that were added at a later date which are to be . . . discourage[d] through the film or movie medium" (ibid.). Culture here takes the figure of the witch or jujuman we saw in *Time* or the secret cult in *Super Warriors*. What was once a constitutive part of cultural identity is now revealed to be beyond the religious pale and reduced to the margins of society. In Northern Nigeria, the slipperiness of the relation between culture and Islam means that filmmakers can be castigated for not "representing the culture," as Ado-Kurawa states, and equally critiqued for the "error" of seeing cultural heritage as sacred.

The extreme self-consciousness about how films "represent the culture" is a survival in Hausa video films of a pedagogical imperative that was central to mobile film units, state-funded television, and the progressivist, nationalist direction of the postcolonial state. It is present in the South and certainly behind the campaign of the Nigerian Film and Video Censors Board to reduce attention to magic and witchcraft in the film industry. In the North, this modernist, nationalist progressive imperative is fueled by the historical conflict between the largely Muslim Hausa-Fulani peoples and the Christian groups of the South. Northern filmmakers, for all their easy adoption of Indian film styles, are very conscious of their role in representing religious and cultural values in their works and of the intense reaction they could face if they overstep established boundaries. When I asked the film star and producer Ali Nuhu why so few Hausa films are devoted to witchcraft and ritual abuse, he responded that this was due to the cultural difference between Southerners and Northerners. "Things go on in their society," he argued, that are not done in the North as "our religion preaches against ritual sacrifice."[33] A film fan told me that Southern films reflected Southerners' deep cultural traditions and their greater reliance on spirits, while Islam "had been in Hausaland for so long" that, while witchcraft existed there, "it was not so much."[34] These comments do not simply indicate the perceived cultural distance between Northern and

Southern Nigeria, they offer an idealized version of Hausa society. Indeed the film fan who argued that witchcraft was not so powerful because of the North's Islamic tradition promptly regaled me with a tale of a *hakimi* (traditional royal leader) whose house had been burned down after he was accused of making ritual sacrifices. A manager of one of the Kano cinemas explained the difference: "The answer is culture. The culture is different. It [witchcraft and ritual abuse] may happen in the North but it is not to be seen by children." Yoruba, by contrast, have no such qualms. "They will play it out—they would like the world to know about it." The manager is here recognizing that these activities go on but that the crucial thing is that they should not be represented on film and should not circulate as objectified representations of Hausa culture. Qasimu Yero, a famous Hausa actor, said the same thing in explaining why Northern filmmakers do not dwell on issues of ritual abuse: "These films go to the U.S. and elsewhere and people say 'this is our culture'"; Hausa filmmakers do not want to be involved in depicting their culture in this way.

Northern filmmakers, audiences, and critics are well aware that Southern films depicting witchcraft and magic have a deeply Christian origin, and while issues of magic and ritual abuse do not necessarily have to have a Christian provenance, the generic ways in which these are formally represented in Southern films bear unmistakable traces of Pentecostalism. Northern filmmakers share a concern for how films objectify and circulate ideas about culture. This concern draws heavily on nationalist ideas of the role of media in fighting cultural imperialism and marries that with an intensified Islamic identity, resulting in a complex and sometimes contradictory film practice. Stars like Ali Nuhu are controversial in Nigeria because of their dependence on Indian film aesthetics. Although they are frequently accused of destroying Hausa culture because of this, they still express clear limits as to what they will borrow and what they will not. For all of his fame as the "Shah Rukh Khan of Nigeria," Nuhu adheres to a belief that films have an important role in upholding, representing, and circulating ideas about culture. Bashir Ɗan Muɗi, one of the leading cameramen in Hausa film and a pioneer of the industry, explains this complexity when he argues that Northern filmmakers realize "there is a lot of Christian missionization" in Southern films. "Indian films are more close to Hausa culture," he notes, adding crucially that "because of language barriers people don't take on all aspects of Indian films. They borrow Indian clothes but do not see it as Hindu. But since we have Christians in our community we see it as a problem."[35] Indian films do not pose the same dangers as Southern films because their distance makes them more of an imagined object and less of an immediate presence. Cultural borrowing relies on the necessary distance that allows one to reject certain elements and adopt others. Hinduness, while controversial, is not the powerful competitor for Islam in Nigeria that Christianity is. When the shari'a ban on filmmaking was lifted and a new censorship body created, one of the panel's first directives was that there should be little use of magic and witchcraft—a clear reference to anxiety about Christianity. As the filmmaker Ado Ahmad put it, "They want you to believe in God in your script."[36]

CONCLUSION

In the Southern Nigerian film *The Master*, Nkem Owoh plays Dennis, a man who, due to poverty, falls into the clutches of a 419 gang and becomes one of them. The film opens with him waking in bed, brusquely ordering his niece to go and buy him some food. When the niece asks for money, he chastises her and sends her on her way. Later, his junior brother, whose house he is staying in, comes into the bedroom and asks why he is not at the market working, and why he blames his situation on other things when really he is just lazy. Dennis replies that he works hard all day but only earns a few naira and that it is not worth it. He then reminds his younger brother that the only reason he is successful now is that Dennis paid for his education earlier on. Dennis then explains that the reason he is so poor, despite his education, is that he borrowed money so he could emigrate and that when he was forced back to Nigeria he lost everything. A few days later, in response to this, the brother returns, saying he has borrowed seventy thousand naira to give to Dennis so he has some capital to conduct business on a bigger scale and will not have to scrabble in the market. It is a peace offering. Dennis embraces him saying he had felt so all alone, but that now, wherever their parents were (in heaven) they would know this is a real family. When Dennis is defrauded of this money by a 419 operation, leaving him broke and his brother in debt, he turns to criminal means to survive.

This brief description sets up a family situation which is complex but recognizable to many Nigerians. The film opens establishing Dennis as a gruff, bullying figure, ordering around his niece and rejecting any idea that he should go out and work for money. At this point Dennis is an unsympathetic figure and a familiar one in Nigerian society. From the junior brother's point of view, he has a senior brother staying in the household, leeching off of him and refusing to work. Family duty prevents the junior brother from telling him to leave. It is a situation pregnant with conflict. The film then gives us a backstory to Dennis, an educated man who has worked very hard but who, through circumstances beyond his control, has lost everything. The junior brother, while angry with Dennis, clearly listens and is moved by the argument that he would be nowhere if it was not for the fact that Dennis "suffered" to put him ahead. That he feels the moral pull of this argument is embodied in the loan he takes out to help Dennis. With the end of the salary as a stabilizing mechanism in Nigerian life, and the reconfiguration of education—which remains crucially important but, as in the case of Dennis, cannot guarantee security and success, Nigerians have been forced into relying on alternative networks in order to find some measure of security in life. Chief among these in a world where hard work and merit count for little is the necessity of finding a patron in order to get ahead. In this world one cannot achieve by one's own efforts—the opposite of the ideal of America—but only through help. Dennis relies on his junior brother just as his junior brother relied on him. His education is recognized and rewarded, but by a criminal who sees that his good English will be helpful in sending 419 letters to unsuspecting foreigners. Packed into this domestic encounter are some of the larger tensions of contemporary Nigeria: the failure of the state to provide employment, the forced reliance on kin, and the rise of new economic networks (in this case, criminal ones). These are situations that stimulate affective responses in the characters: tensions within the family brought about by dependence, a sense of despair and vulnerability, anger and sullen reprimands, the feeling of "being so alone," generosity and happy reunions, love and support. *The Master* emphasizes, like so many Nigerian films, a world where individual advancement and merits are useless unless backed up by a patron. In *Super Warriors*, Ugochukwu only succeeds as a businessman because of the help of Chief Obie who, in turn, derives his success from his participation in a secret cult. The senior women of *Glamour Girls* likewise have foresworn education and marriage as traditional routes to security in favor of cultivating patrons, men with "naira power" on whom they rely to get ahead. These stories dramatize a fundamental shift in the economy and social life of Nigerians. They are a cultural articulation of the transformation of Nigerian political economy. However, these films do not just dramatize the experience of contemporary urban life for many Nigerians, they evoke it in their affective grasp on an audience. Films like these are not just referents to wider realities, representations of conditions that exist elsewhere, they replay these emotions as part of the narrative address of the film. They evoke emotional responses, making people live the experience of characters and react to them with a mixture of empathy and revulsion. There is a physical dwelling in the film, an immediacy and excess, that makes the film not just a representation but a lived experience as well.

Mobile film units and television dramas, by contrast, addressed a developmentalist Nigerian subject through the logic of uplift and progress. Dominated by the state, which set itself up as a protector of cultural values (at the same time as it tried to transform them), mobile film units express the deeply political nature of the relation between media, state, and subject. These values and aesthetics governed the cultural form of Nigerian television and, in certain respects, still do today. There, as the distinguished television actor Qasimo Jero said, you were always "executing government policies."[37] As another former operative of the Nigerian Television Authority put it, television was always involved in "political information dissemination."[38] Nigerian films, by contrast, are loosed from this control. Many filmmakers embody, in their own biographies, the transformation from state to private networks that the films represent. The late Hausa director, Tijani Ibraheem, one of the pioneers of the industry, came to it from a long experience working in television. There, he said, dramas were intended to be pedagogical—to aid state development projects, or to represent the interests of the sponsor. One drama series he directed was sponsored by Allied Bank. While he was free to shape it any way he wished, he had to show characters adopting modern banking methods. In the film industry, by contrast, he remarked that "the idea is usually free" and that "you are not tied up with a public enlightenment sort of thing."[39] Ibraheem's trajectory is mimicked by several filmmakers in both Southern and Northern films, especially by the pioneers of the industry. Filmmakers like these embody the shift in Nigerian society from salaried work to private independent contractors moving from project to project. Nigerian films address a market-driven, liberalized, insecure Nigerian subject. They engage questions of value—moral, financial, sexual—and the intangible and unknowable ways value seems to appear and disappear outside of individual or social control. The state as the arbiter of stability is largely absent. In its wake is the Pentecostal church, the family, the lover, but all of these threaten to betray as much as they promise to help. This is a late capital world of risk, and Nigerian films are inscription machines recording the sense of vulnerability that comes with that risk and rendering it in the register of excessive, fantastic melodrama.

Like Indian cinema, Nigerian films are based on the needs of a people swept up in social change who are trying to understand their predicament in terms that are familiar to them. Whether this is represented in the lurid depiction of corruption and outrage in Southern Nigerian films, or in the tensions between arranged marriage and love marriages in Northern ones, Nigerian film has developed modes of melodrama that represent a society at once rapidly modernizing and still deeply traditional, a society whose religious traditions are as much a part of the globalized world as they are of Nigeria itself. These films constantly attempt to comprehend the economic and social insecurities of everyday life through a moral framework and, by doing so, assert a place for moral and religious belief in the rationalized world of corrupt politicians, 419 con men, and errant lovers. They do this in a postcolonial society where bureaucrats are corrupt, justice is hard to come by, and the family remains the economic, cultural, and emotional center of peoples' lives. In Nigeria, commercial cinema expresses the vulnerabilities, anxieties, pressures, and hopes that affect everyday Nigerians. These stories dramatize the contradictions of a society in rapid change through the central yet constantly uncertain presence of the family—the family in Nigerian films is the force that raises you, that offers you the closest bonds, but could bewitch you, betray your desires, or dominate you. Southern Nigerian films probe this world through an aesthetics of outrage, dramatizing and exaggerating the forces of corruption at work in the world. Northern films do so through complex borrowing from Indian cinema, using the melodrama of one to probe the world of another. They represent the fantasy of playing with other forms as a way of interrogating local norms. In this way, Nigerian films depict and embody the daily "experiments" that constitute the practice of everyday urban life (Mbembe and Nuttall 2004).

7

Degraded Images, Distorted Sounds

NIGERIAN VIDEO AND THE INFRASTRUCTURE OF PIRACY

In Kano, the economic center of Northern Nigeria, media piracy is part of the "organizational architecture" of globalization (Sassen, ed. 2002), providing the infrastructure that allows media goods to circulate. Infrastructures organize the construction of buildings, the training of personnel, the building of railway lines, and the elaboration of juridico-legal frameworks without which movement of goods and people cannot occur. But once in place, infrastructures generate possibilities for their own corruption and parasitism. Media piracy is one example of this. It represents the potential of technologies of reproduction—the supple ability to store, reproduce, and retrieve data—when shorn from the legal frameworks that limit their application. It depends heavily on the flow of media from official, highly regulated forms of media trade but then develops its own structures of reproduction and distribution external and internal to the state economy.

Through this generative quality pirate infrastructure expresses a paradigmatic shift in Nigeria's economy and capital, extending the logic of privatization into everyday life. Piracy's negative character is often commented on: its criminality, its erosion of property rights, and its parasitism on legal media flows that make it a pathology of information processing (Chesterman and Lipman 1988; Coombe 1998; Wang 2003). As important as these matters are, the structural focus on legal issues tends to conceal the mediating nature of infrastructure itself. In the Nigerian case this is seen most strikingly in the phenomenal rise of the video film industry (see chap. 6). This new industry has pioneered new film genres and generated an entirely novel form of reproduction and distribution that uses the capital, equipment, personnel, and distribution networks of pirated media. Nigerian videos are a legitimate media form that could not exist without the infrastructure created by its illegitimate double, pirate media.

In recent years, then, there has been a wholesale shift whereby many entrepreneurs previously involved in the distribution of pirate material have switched to the reproduction and dissemination of legal media. The mass importation of foreign music and film brought about the capital and professional expertise that facilitated the rise of a local film industry. This wandering over the lines that separates legal from nonlegal has been a common feature for urban Africans, who are progressively disembedded from infrastructures linking them to the official world economy and instead have poured energy into developing informal networks—equally global—that facilitate traffic in economic and cultural goods outside the established institutions of world trade (Simone 1998, 2001, 2004; Bayart, Ellis, and Hibou 1999; Mbembe 2001).

In addition to generating new economic networks, piracy, like all infrastructural modes, has distinct material qualities that influence the media traveling under its regime of reproduction. Piracy imposes particular conditions on recording, transmitting, and retrieving data. Constant copying erodes data storage, degrading image and sound, overwhelming the signal of media content with the noise produced by the means of reproduction. Pirate videos are marked by blurred images and distorted sound, creating a material screen that filters audiences' engagement with media technologies and the new senses of time, speed, space, and contemporaneity. In this way, piracy creates an aesthetic, a set of formal qualities that generate a particular sensorial experience of media marked by poor transmission, interference, and noise. Contemporary scholars of technology returning to the Frankfurt school have stressed that technology's operation on the body is a key factor in producing a sense of shock—the complex training of the human sensorium—associated with modern urbanism (Benjamin 1978, 1999; Crary 2000; Doane 2002; M. Hansen 1995, 2000; Kracauer 1995; Schivelbusch 1986). This work is important in understanding the phenomenological and cognitive effects of technology when it is working at its optimum. What is less discussed (but see Schivelbusch 1986; and Virilio 2003) is how technology influences through its failure as much as its success. The inability of technologies to perform the functions they were assigned must be subject to the same critical scrutiny as their achievements. Breakdown and failure are, of course, inherent in all technologies, but in societies such as Nigeria, where collapse is a common state of technological existence, they take on a far greater material and political presence (see Mbembe and Roitman 1995; Verrips and Meyer 2001; and Koolhaas 2001).

Rather than elide pirate infrastructure by using it as a window into legal questions of intellectual property, I wish to foreground it. If infrastructures represent attempts to order, regulate, and rationalize society, then breakdowns in their operation, or the rise of provisional and informal infrastructures, highlight the failure of that ordering and the recoding that takes its place. When we scrutinize the material operation of piracy and its social consequences, it becomes clear that pirate infrastructure is a powerful mediating force that produces new modes of organizing sensory perception, time, space, and economic networks.

INFRASTRUCTURE

Capitalism, as many thinkers from Marx to Henri Lefebvre and David Harvey have reminded us, is not separable from space but produces the spaces through which it operates. All regimes of capital depend on infrastructures—shipping, trains, fiber optic lines, warehouses—whereby space gets produced and networked. Cities, or social space itself in Henri Lefebvre's (1991) terms, take on real existence through their insertion into networks and pathways of commodity exchange, and it is networked infrastructure that provides these channels of communication. Infrastructure is the structural condition of the movement of commodities, whether they are waste, energy, or information. It brings diverse places into interaction, connecting some while divorcing others, constantly ranking, connecting, and segmenting spaces and people (Graham and Marvin 1996, 2001; Sassen 1998; Sassen, ed. 2002).

Infrastructures were key to the first modern corporations, which were organized around the continuous circulation of goods, services, and information on a massive scale (Mattelart 2000). As such they have been enormously influential, organizing territory, standardizing time, and innovating new forms of economic organization. The rise of new electronic communication has intensified these processes, in turn instituting their own effects on people's sense of time and distance and on their conceptions of the present and simultaneity (Kern 1983; Mattelart 1986; Schivelbusch 1986; Virilio 1997).

The difficulty here is that much work on the transformative effects of media takes for granted a media system that is smoothly efficient rather than acknowledging the reality of infrastructural connections that are frequently messy, discontinuous, and poor. Technologies of speed and the infrastructures they create have had a profound impact on societies like Nigeria, but it is painfully obvious to people who live there that they often do not work as they are supposed to. This does not simply reflect national poverty but rather is inherent in the functioning (and the threat of collapse) of all technological systems. What distinguishes poor nations is the systemic nature of these failures so that infrastructure, or the lack of it, becomes a pressing economic and social issue and a locus of political resentment toward the failure of the state and state elites. At the same time, the creation of successful infrastructures sets in motion other types of flows that operate in the space capital provides, and that travel the routes created by these new networks of communication. The organization of one system sets in motion other systems that spin off in different directions.

THE CORRUPTION OF INFRASTRUCTURE

Piracy's success lies in its own infrastructural order that preys on the official distribution of globalized media, thus making it part of the corruption of infrastructure. By "corruption" I mean the pirating of a systems' mode of communication—the viruses that attach to other kinds of official or recognized movement. Technological infrastructure creates material channels that organize the movement of energy, information, and economic and cultural goods between societies, but at the same time creates possibilities for new actions. In Nigeria, this can be seen clearly in the so-called 419 schemes. Sending letters by fax and e-mail, 419 fraudsters claim to be a senior Nigerian official—in a bank or the petroleum ministry—or the relative of a dictator, and state that they urgently need to transfer a large amount of money out of the country (for an overview see Apter 1999; and Hibou 1999). The recipients are told that if they agree to help they will receive a percentage of the money. In this way complete strangers are lured into what the FBI has described as the most successful fraud in the history of the world—and one of Nigeria's main foreign currency earners. The 419ers target foreign businessmen; they make use of international financial arrangements such as bank accounts and international money transfers; and they depend on new communication technologies: first fax machines and now e-mail. It is a form of fraud that depends on a certain cosmopolitanism, on the internationalization of finance, and as a form of action it is inconceivable without the technological and financial infrastructure brought by Nigeria's oil boom. The oil monies of the 1970s and 1980s allowed the deeper penetration of corporate capitalism in Nigeria, creating the professional and technological networks on which 419ers prey. It also inaugurated the spectacular corruption that makes 419 letters believable to their victims. The fraud pirates the discourses and procedures of capitalism but also requires its own infrastructure of communication. In this way, the very success of any infrastructural flows creates possibilities for their own corruption, placing in motion the potential for other sets of relations to occur and creating a ripple effect on movements of people, culture, and religion.

Like 419, piracy similarly operates as a corruption of communications infrastructure that develops its own circuits of distribution using official media. Films made in Hollywood and intended for distribution in an organized domestic circuit are copied by pirates, then sent to Asia or the Middle East where they are subtitled, copied in large numbers as videocassettes, video CDs (VCDs are the dominant technology for media storage in much of Asia) and DVDs, and reshipped, mainly within the developing world. In recent years, as Nigeria has become progressively disembedded from the official global economy (with the single exception of its oil industry), it has become ever more integrated into a parallel, unofficial world economy that reorients Nigeria toward new metropoles such as Dubai, Singapore, and Beirut, what AbdouMaliq Simone (2001) refers to more broadly as the "worlding" of African cities (see also Bayart, Ellis and Hibou 1999; and Mbembe 2001).

Let us take the example of the Kofar Wambai market in Kano. Kofar Wambai is best known for the sale of thread used in the elaborate embroi-

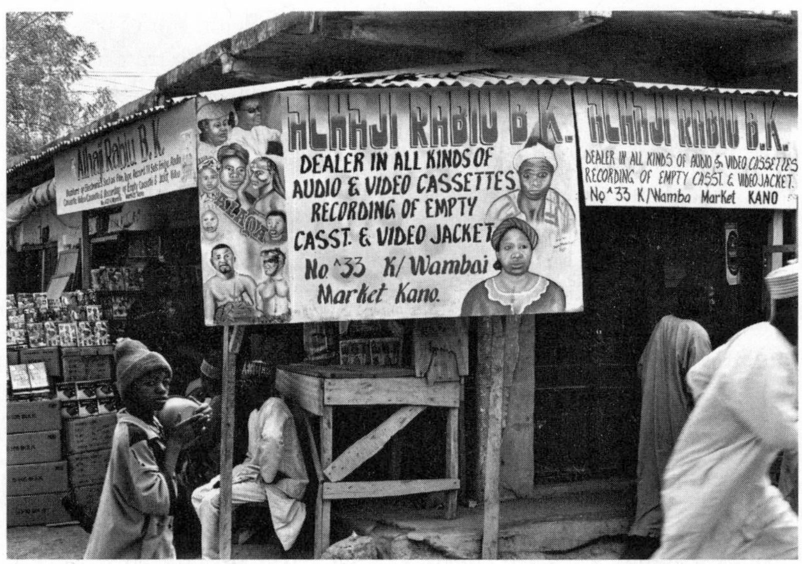

44. Kofar Wambai market, Kano. Photo by the author.

dery of the long Hausa gown, the *babban riga*. Whole tracts of the market are suffused in the bright colors of the thread hanging from the stall doorways, but in one section is lane after lane of small shops specializing in the reproduction and wholesale distribution of audio- and videocassettes: Indian, Sudanese, Western, and Hausa music; Islamic preaching; and Indian, Western, and Hausa videocassettes (see figure 44).

Cassette sellers at Kofar Wambai are represented by the Kano Cassette Sellers Recording and Co-operative Society Ltd. (*Kungiyar Gama Kai Ta Masu Sayar Da Kaset Da Dauka Ta Jihar Kano*), whose headquarters are at Kofar Wambai but whose members spill out far beyond the confines of the market. The success of Kano's cassette reproduction industry is grounded in three developments. First, in 1981, the Motion Picture Association of America (MPAA) suspended the distribution of Hollywood films to Nigeria. This was in response to the seizure of MPAA assets by the Nigerian government, which sought to indigenize the control of Nigerian companies. Second, the oil boom of the late 1970s boosted consumption, allowing for the mass dissemination of cassette-based technologies. Finally, the centuries-old position of Kano at the apex of wide-ranging transnational trading networks facilitated the quick exploitation of these possibilities and the forging of a distribution network that stretches over Northern Nigeria and beyond. The subsequent rise of piracy meant that far from disappearing, Hollywood films have become available at unprecedented speed and volume.

The everyday practice of piracy in Kano was based around the mass distribution of the two most popular drama forms, Indian films and Hollywood films, and the reproduction of televised Hausa dramas and Islamic religious cassettes. Nearly all those who might be described as pirates were at the same time involved in the legitimate duplication and sale of media. The organization that emerged made Kano the regional distribution center for electronic media in Northern Nigeria and the wider Hausaphone area (which covers parts of Chad, Cameroon, Benin, and Ghana and stretches as far as Sudan). The system is this: the main dealers are based at centers in Kano like the Kofar Wambai market. They then sell to distributors in other Northern cities, who in turn supply smaller urban and rural dealers, who supply itinerant peddlers. The system is based on a complex balance of credit and trust; and although it depends, in part, on piracy, it has evolved into a highly organized, extensive distribution system for audio- and videocassettes. The success of the new form of distribution has not been lost on the government, which—though critical of piracy—has used cassette distribution as a way of spreading political messages. As Alhaji Musa Na Sale, president of the cassette sellers association, told me, if something is popular "even the nomads will hear it."[1] The decentralized nature of this distribution system means that neither the government nor the association knows exactly how many people are tied to the industry, especially given its massive expansion with the rise of Hausa video films.

Hausa distributors have had to rely on other ethnic groups for access to foreign videos that were coming from the Persian Gulf. In the 1990s these videos often had the distributor's name superimposed on the tape itself; for example, *Excellence Kano* for Hollywood films and *Al-Mansoor, Dubai* for Indian ones. Hollywood films were imported to Kano directly from the Middle East or transported north from Lagos. Because of the great popularity of Indian films among the Hausa, Kano was and is the main clearinghouse for Indian films. This traffic is controlled by two primary distributors, both based in Kano. For many years the trade was routed through Dubai, and it was common to watch Indian films with advertisements scrolling across the bottom of the screen announcing: "Al-Mansoor's video" followed by a long list of his many shops in Dubai, Abu Dhabi, and other parts of the gulf along with telephone, telex, and fax numbers. These videos often found their way to the Kano television station, CTV, during whose programs announcements for Al-Mansoor's many video shops would scroll by placidly at the bottom of the screen.

With the emergence of VCDs, the routes of the market for Indian film have changed considerably. According to one Indian distributor, the market is now oriented toward Pakistan, where VCD plants make high-quality dubs of Indian films. Master copies are shipped via DHL to Kano, where they are transferred to tape and sold in bulk to Hausa distributors. I was told that the gap between a film's release in India and its appearance in Kano can be as little as seven days.[2] American films are pirated through similar networks. They are copied illegally in the United States and shipped to Dubai or Beirut, often arriving in Nigeria while still on first-run release in the United States. One Jean-Claude Van Damme film I saw had Chinese subtitles superimposed over Arabic ones providing a visible inscription of the routes of media piracy. Frequently U.S. videos contained a message scrolling by at the bottom of the film every few minutes stating: "Demo tape only. Not for rental or sale. If you have rented or purchased this cassette call 1–800 NO COPYS (1–800 662 6787). Federal law provides severe civil and criminal penalties for unauthorized duplication or distribution." However, this message was sometimes obliterated by Arabic subtitles.

Kofar Wambai is the apex of a formal, highly ordered system of reproduction for media goods in Northern Nigeria, and it is one example of how media piracy generates new infrastructures of the parallel economy in Nigeria. It is part of a much larger process whereby the Nigerian economy has split into the traditional official economy, oriented toward legal participation in the international division of labor, and an unofficial economy, each with its own infrastructures and networks, sometimes overlapping, sometimes opposed.

PIRACY

Piracy is an ambivalent phenomenon in countries such as Nigeria. It is widely feared by indigenous film and music makers for siphoning off the small profits they make on their intellectual property. Its effects on indigenous musicians have been disastrous, contributing substantially to the erosion of the industry as a whole. At the same time, many of these same people consume pirate media privately and professionally. Piracy has made available to Nigerians a vast array of world media at a speed they could never imagine, hooking them up to the accelerated circuit of global media flows. Where cinema screens were once filled with outdated films from the United States or India, pirate media allow Nigerian audiences to watch films contemporaneously with audiences in New York or Mumbai. Instead of being marginalized by official distribution networks, Nigerian consumers can now participate in the immediacy of an international consumer culture—but only through the mediating capacity of piracy.

Piracy is part of the so-called shadow ("second," "marginal," "informal," or "black") economy existing in varying degrees beyond the law. It produces profits, but not for corporations, and provides no revenue for the state.[3] The second economy is untaxed and unmonitored and enjoys all the benefits and precariousness of this location. Until Nigerian video, media infrastructures in Nigeria have been predominantly state controlled, organized around providing publicity for state projects. Piracy, by contrast, is based in unofficial, decentralized networks, and Nigerian video represents the migration of these networks into the mainstream.

The rise of a privatized media phenomenon represents not so much an erosion of state power but a larger movement in which the shadow economy has reconfigured the state itself. According to U.S. State Department figures, Nigeria is the largest market for pirate goods in Africa, and one estimate suggests that up to 70 percent of the current Nigerian gross domestic product is derived from the shadow economy, making it, in percentage terms, one of the largest such economies in the world, matched only by that of Thailand (Schneider 2000). Figures such as these are always provisional and, like many statistics about Nigeria, often simulacral, being not so much a numerical representation of an existing state of affairs but rather a mimicking of rationalist representations of economic life. But in Nigeria the second economy has grown to such a scale that no one really knows how to represent it. No one is sure how large the GDP is; no one can calculate the balance of payments or even the size of Nigeria's population (Bayart, Ellis, and Hibou 1999; Hecht and Simone 1994). Strong forces are at work to make sure that revenue streams from major industries, like oil, are obligingly opaque. Jean-François Bayart, Stephen Ellis, and Beatrice Hibou (1999) have argued that illegal activities in Nigeria—such as fraud, corruption, and the import and export of illegal oil, drugs, and videos—have grown to such a degree that they now form part of the routine operation of the state rather than a pathology outside it. Nigerians have become famous in Africa and beyond for migrating as workers, importers, exporters, smugglers, drug carriers, and fraudsters. While the federal state continues to take part in the formalized ritual of the official economy, many

Nigerians see a widening gap between that representation and the everyday reality of how Nigeria functions. Piracy is part of this larger reconfiguration of the Nigerian state and economy.

Ravi Sundaram (1999) argues that informal processes in the Indian media ecology should be seen as a pirate modernity—a mode of incorporation into the economy that is disorganized, nonideological, and marked by mobility and innovation. This formulation nicely captures the ambivalence of piracy, refusing the simple equation that piracy is an alternative or oppositional modernity (though there are elements of this in people's justifications that pirate goods redress economic inequalities between developed and undeveloped countries). Piracy is nonideological in that it does not represent a self-conscious political project in opposition to capitalism—it is not tactical media in that sense (Garcia and Lovink 2001). But it is also worth stressing the high degree of formality that marks this "informal" world. A focus on the mobility, innovation, and provisionality of piracy elides the fact that pirate networks are highly organized, and determinative of other sets of relations.

HAUSA VIDEO

In the 1990s media distributors in the North who had been involved with the reproduction and distribution of religious, Hollywood, and Indian cassettes began to turn their attention to Nigerian and especially Hausa-language videos which were coming to dominate audio- and videocassette production. Figures 45 and 46 show the office of Alhaji Rabi'u B. K., former vice president of the Kano Cassette Sellers Recording and Co-operative Society Ltd. In 1995, Alhaji specialized in recording religious cassettes that he dubbed in his studio/shop in Kofar Wambai. Figure 45 shows the hardware and equipment involved in cassette distribution. The explosive market for Hausa video films transformed his business, so that by 2002 it was almost wholly devoted to the reproduction and distribution of Hausa films. Figure 46 shows his shop in 2002: the dubbing facilities have been moved off site, the audiocassette machines are gone, and the walls are lined with video jackets. His shop now primarily functions as a place to meet clients traveling to Kano. This transformation is common among most, if not all distributors. Many still sell Indian and American films, of course; their sales do not seem to have suffered even though their proportion of the market has dropped with the unprecedented popularity of Hausa and Nigerian videos. The shift in businesses like this indicates that, in the

North, Hausa video films have fed off of the networks of piracy much in the way piracy fed off networks of official media.

As Hausa film exploded in popularity, the style and shape of the video market changed considerably. Hausa videos have come to dominate the market, creating a huge demand that was not there previously.[4] Hausa video film production has become highly organized and regulated, with producers, distributors, and camera operators organized into their own professional associations. An established system of production, postproduction, and distribution has been put in place: a producer puts up the initial money, finds a writer, director, and actors and produces the film. Once the film is made, editing complete, and the covers for the tapes printed, the film enters into a waiting list for release, which ensures that no more than six films come out a month. On the release date, the producer takes the film to one of the distributors in Kano and sells a master copy of the tape and several hundred copies of the jacket for about fifty naira each (about 50 cents). The film then sells for two hundred naira each. Intellectual property is vested not so much in the tape, which belongs to the distributor, but in the jacket, which is created and controlled by the filmmakers themselves (see figures 47, 48, and 49). The jackets for Hausa films—wraparound sleeves in which cassettes are inserted—are the only way to distinguish pirate from legal media (see figures 50 and 51).

The distributor covers the cost of dubbing machines, the capital outlay, and provides important access to the network of distributors. No money is paid to the producer until the tapes have been sold. Unsurprisingly, this system has been the source of considerable tension between producers and distributors as it leaves producers carrying all the risks of failure. On at least one occasion producers in the Kano State Filmmakers Association threatened to boycott distributors in order to increase the price of jackets. Some filmmakers do exhibit films at the cinema and others try and sell to television stations, but the economic heart of the industry is the exploitation of domestic video technology.

Video filmmaking, like many aspects of the informal economy, is a precarious and highly volatile business. The tension between distributors and filmmakers is a struggle for control of the industry, but both remain vulnerable to the leveling out of the market. In recent years, the early boom period of Hausa video and Nigerian video—when it seemed that anyone who made a film could make money—has passed. Now filmmakers say they have to work harder for less profit. The precariousness of the industry in the North also comes from increasing moral criticism of the films

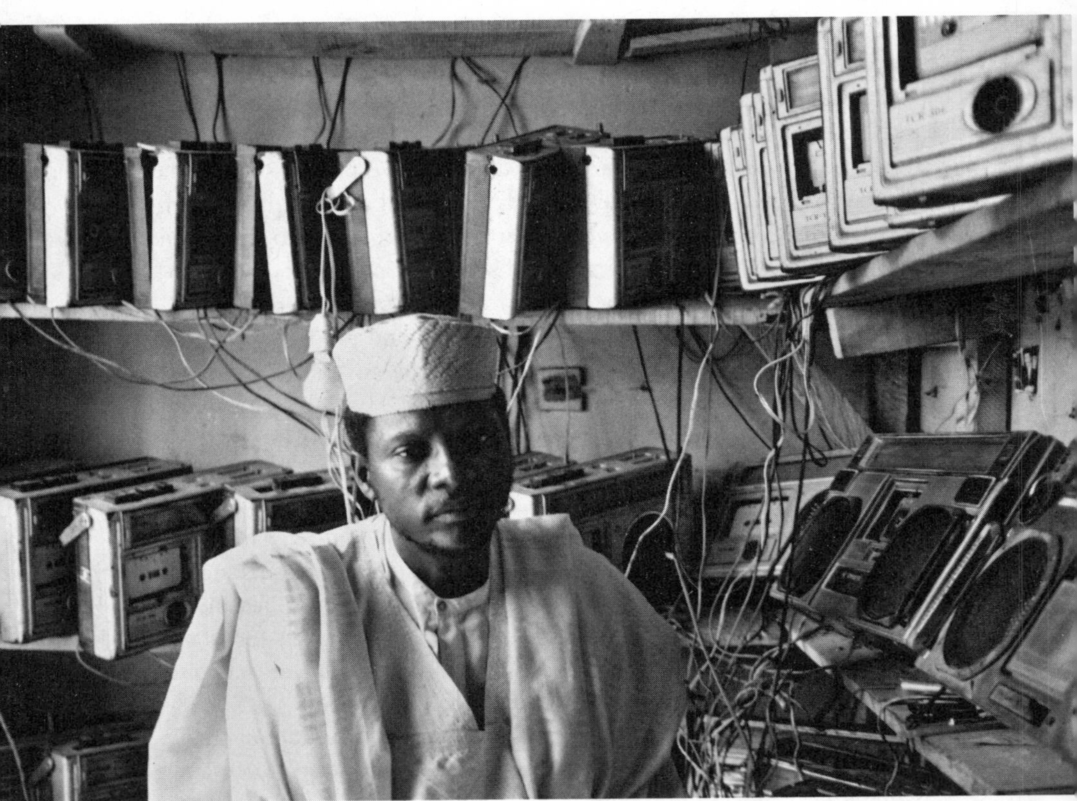

themselves. This threat was heightened in 2001 when, following the introduction of shari'a law in Kano state all Hausa filmmaking was banned. Filmmakers responded to the government's ban by organizing themselves under the Kano State Filmmakers Association, a formal interest group that could negotiate with the government. Because filmmaking was such a new phenomenon, most filmmakers were young (many in their thirties) and lacked connections to senior patrons in older forms of trade. Still, the association found several ways to pressure the government. First, magazines such as *Fim* argued that film was not inherently un-Islamic, since many Islamic states such as Iran and Egypt had film industries. Periodicals such as *Bidiyo*, in more tabloid fashion, noted that shari'a law was being applied "only" to filmmakers—there was no question of banning Indian, Hollywood, or Southern Nigerian films—and threatened to run popular actors and actresses as candidates against incumbent politicians. In a meeting with the Kano State Ministry of Information, the association pointed out

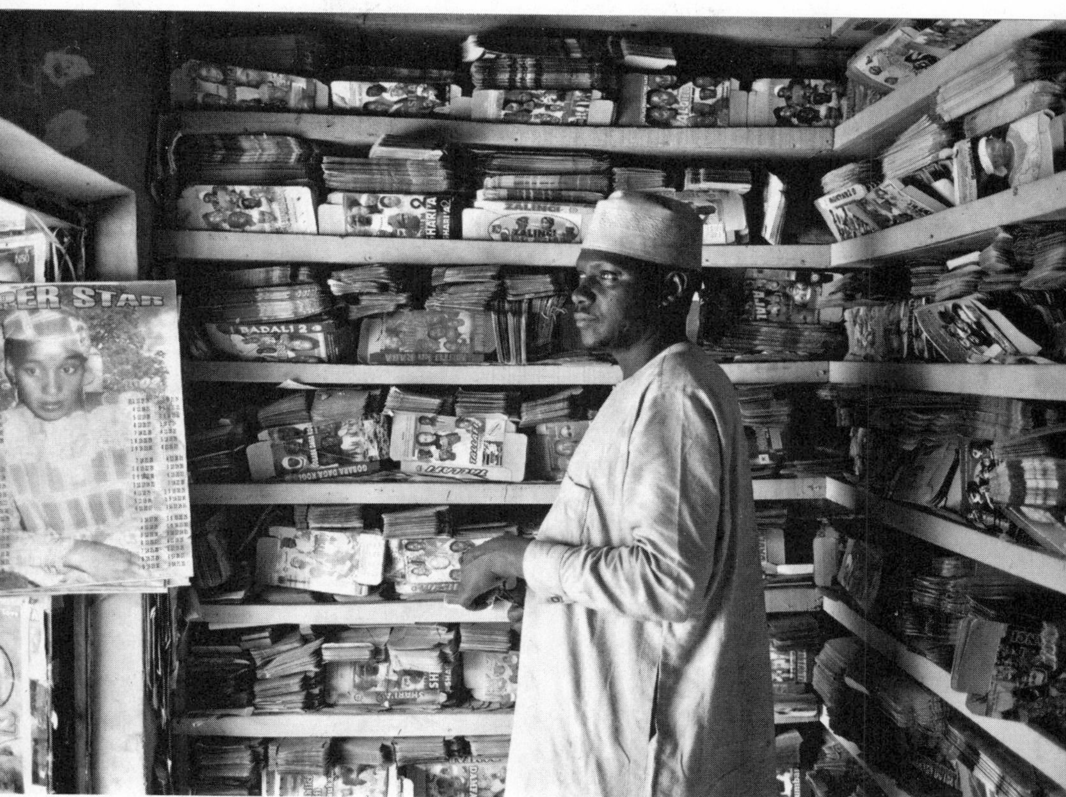

(opposite) 45. Alh. Rabi'u B. K. in his shop, Kofar Wambai market, Kano. 1995. (above) 46. Alh. Rabi'u B. K. in his shop, Kofar Wambai market, Kano. 2001. Both photos by the author.

that when Zamfara state (the first in Northern Nigeria to adopt shari'a law) banned prostitution, it supplied prostitutes with alternative forms of employment, and when it closed down cinema halls, it compensated the owners.[5]

Given this precedent, the filmmakers argued, the Kano state government should now be responsible for the welfare of the producers, directors, actors, musicians, composers, writers, editors, and graphic designers employed in this industry. Since the industry was so large and established there was no way such compensation would be possible. As a compromise, the filmmakers proposed establishing a censorship board that would certify the Islamic and cultural acceptability of films but allow filmmaking to

47, 48, and 49. Pirate videocassettes of a Hollywood and Indian film. Note how the cover of the (legal) early Hausa film *Gimbya Fatima* (Dir. Tijani Ibraheem) follows the form of the pirate videos.

continue. When the proposal was accepted in March 2001 and the censorship board put in place, one of its first moves was to ban mixed-sex song sequences in films.

The market for Hausa films has solidified, so that five main distributors dominate the industry. Cassettes are dubbed in bulk and sold on a wholesale basis through wide-ranging networks forged when Hausa films did not exist. Kano, long important as a media center for Indian films and religious cassettes, is now the dominant site for the much larger market for Hausa film. Small distributors travel there from Northern Nigeria, Chad, Cameroon, and Ghana. Hausa distributors have their own distribution networks that are restricted almost wholly to the Hausa-speaking diaspora (see figures 52 and 53).

The roots of all Nigerian film (whether in English, Hausa, or Yoruba) in piracy means that the physical quality and look of Nigerian video film has been determined by the formal properties of pirate infrastructure. Piracy standardized a particular quality of reproduction; both filmmakers and distributors alike believe that while people like Nigerian videos, they will

50. Hausa videos on sale. Note the wraparound covers. Photo by the author.

51. Jackets in a distributor's warehouse, waiting for tapes to be dubbed. Photo by the author.

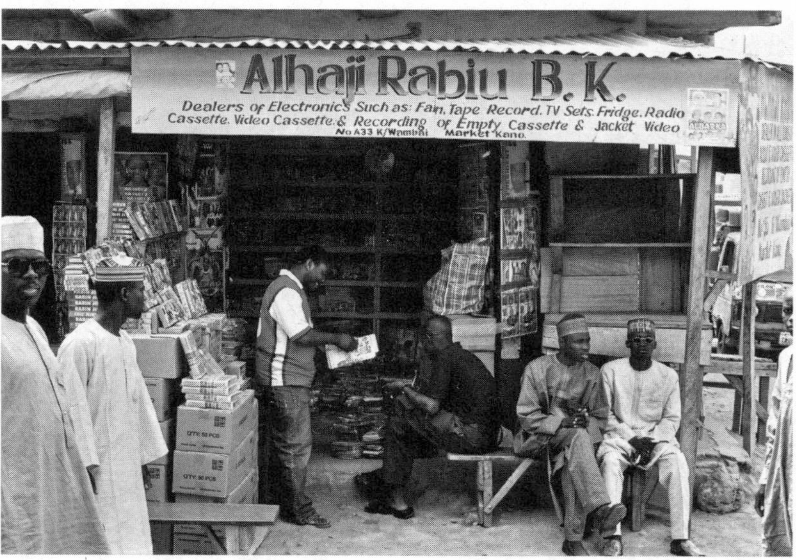

52 and 53. Video shops in Kano, Nigeria. Both photos by the author.

not pay higher prices for better image or sound quality. Because the new Hausa videos are dubbed using the same machines as pirate films, because they rely on the same blank cassettes and are distributed through the same channels, piracy has created the aesthetic and technical horizons for non-pirate media. It is this question of aesthetic to which I now turn.

THE MATERIALITY OF PIRACY

In the film *Kumar Talkies*, the director Pankaj Kumar evokes the role of cinema in small-town Indian life. In one scene a group of men talk about going to watch films in a nearby city. The newness of the films there, the high quality of their reproduction, and the experience of moviegoing come to stand for a temporal and cultural difference between the town and the city. One man says that he does not watch films in his town because he never gets to see the entire film. Kumar then cuts to the local cinema owner who explains that indeed that is the case: in order to save electricity and costs he takes out a few reels from each film, imposing enormous jump-cuts on the formal integration of the text, slicing whole chunks of narrative from the audience's view. The big city, not surprisingly, becomes the place where this fracture can be repaired, where films are shown in their entirety and audiences do not have to confront their physical and cultural marginality every time they attend the cinema.

I have argued elsewhere (Larkin 1998–99) that media technologies do not just store time, they represent it. As Stephen Kern (1983) has written, different societies can feel cut off from history or excessively attached to the past—without a future or rushing toward one. Technology, especially media, often provide the conduit for our experience of being "inside" or "outside" of history. The materiality of media creates the physical details and the quotidian sensory uses through which these experiences are formed. In *Kumar Talkies*, the everyday operation of cinema provides a symbol for marginality and provincialism. In postcolonial societies such as India or Nigeria this is intensified because of the powerful link between technology and colonial rule and the offering of modern technology as part of the civilizing mission of colonial power.

BREAKDOWN

In Nigeria, the ubiquity of technological breakdown and repair imposes a particular experience of technology and its cultural effects. Contemporary urban theory has, perhaps understandably, been slower to explore these cultural articulations, focusing instead on the reconfiguration of urban space brought about by new media. Paul Virilio, in typically contradictory fashion, lobbies fiercely for both sides of the argument. On the one hand, he proclaims with dystopian excess that the immediacy of real-time technologies has fundamentally transformed our ability to understand time and space. Instead of being marked by duration, or the unfolding of events in succession, time, he argues, is now exposed instantaneously (Virilio 1997, 2000). Events that take place at a distance are experienced immediately, thanks to the telepresence brought about by real-time technologies. Speed, here, is the crucial dimension (see also Kern 1983). Speed conditions our experience of time, producing temporal compression and allowing us to act at a distance. Cities, which used to be organized around entrances and exits—nodes that regulate the exchange of people and goods—have given way to the immaterial interface of information exchange. This is certainly the case in Nigeria, where a series of technological changes over the last ten years, including the rise of satellite TV, the growing penetration of Internet culture, and the belated arrival of mobile phone networks have all created new technological portals through which Nigerians engage with each other and the world beyond.

The difficulty with this side of Virilio is that the experiential transformations he identifies presume a stable, smoothly operating infrastructure. The transition he identifies is totalizing, penetrating homogenously, organizing universally. It partakes of a world of fast-operating computers, clear-picture televisions, and constant telecommunication signals. But Virilio (2003) also notes that with the invention of the first train came the derailment, and few thinkers have been as insistent as he that the development of technology is tied to the development of catastrophe. My interest in technological collapse is somewhat different, not in extravagant spectacles like collapsing bridges or exploding space shuttles but in the small, ubiquitous experience of breakdown as a condition of technological existence. For Nigerians, cars, televisions, VCRs, buses, and motorbikes are often out of service. Even when they work electricity supplies are unreliable and prone to surges that damage consumer equipment. NEPA, the Nigerian Electric Power Authority, is famously known as "Never Expect Power Always,"[6] and phone lines are expensive and difficult to obtain. Poverty and the organization of the Nigerian economy means that consumer technologies such as scooters and cars arrive already used and worn out. After their useful life in Belgium or Holland, cars are exported to Nigeria as "new" secondhand vehicles.[7] After these vehicles arrive in Nigeria, worn parts are repaired, dents banged out, and paint resprayed, to remake and "tropicalize" them (for an excellent account of this, see Verrips and Meyer 2001). This renewal is, of course, temporary. Other parts expire, secondhand parts break down, and local "innovations" and adjustments designed to make cars, televisions, and VCRs work, fail. A cycle of breakdown, repair, and breakdown again is the condition of existence for many technologies in Nigeria. As a consequence, Nigeria employs a vast army of people who specialize in repairing and reconditioning broken technological goods, since the need for repair is frequent and the cost of it cheap (Sundaram 1999; Verrips and Myers 2001).

Critical work on urbanism has argued that utopian theories of technology and urban transformation deemphasize the fact that entire societies are excluded from the new information infrastructures (what Manuel Castells [1998] terms "technological apartheid"; see also Castells 1996; Graham and Marvin 1996, 2001; Sassen 1998; Sassen, ed. 2002). Some of these arguments recur in the debate over the so-called digital divide and the division of the world into technological haves and have-nots. My difficulty with this move is the dichotomizing logic it promotes and its assumption that the economic and cultural effects of new technologies are absent from "disconnected" societies. The danger is that this polemic looks through rather than at the object at hand and fails to examine the structuring effects of technologies and their failures in everyday life. Virilio's account of the experience of speed in contemporary urbanization is highly relevant to societies such as Nigeria but perhaps not in the ways he imagines. There is no question, for instance, that new technologies have indeed resulted in profound temporal acceleration for Nigerians. But the poor material infrastructure of Nigeria ensures that as the speed of Nigerian life increases, so too does the gap between *actual* and *potential* acceleration, between what technologies *can* do and what they *do* do. Thus, even as life speeds up, the experience of technological marginalization intensifies, and the gap between how fast society is moving and how fast it could move becomes a site of considerable political tension.

The poor condition of infrastructure and the ubiquity of breakdown bring about their corollary: repair as a cultural mode of existence for technology. This is a consequence of both poverty and innovation. Breakdown and repair structure the ability of subjects to use and be used by technologies. The culture of repair rests on the experience of duration in the everyday use of technology. Breakdown creates a temporal experience that

54. Recording machines wired together to dub cassettes. Photo by the author.

has less to do with dizzying, real-time global integration than with waiting for e-mail messages to open, machines to be repaired, or electricity to be restored. In Nigeria, all technologies are variously subject to the constant cycle of breakdown and repair; the promise of technological prosthesis is thwarted by the common experience of technological collapse. Each repair enforces another waiting period, an often frustrating experience of duration brought about by the technology of speed itself. The experience of slowness comes as a consequence of speed-producing technologies, so that speed and acceleration, deceleration and stasis are relative, continually shifting states.

In figure 54 we see the stringing together of cassette recorders used to dub audiocassettes in Kano. The covers—intended to protect the cassette while recording—have been ripped off for ease of ejection. Wires hang loosely, sometimes tangled in bunches; many machines have their casings broken; and all are exposed to the harmattan winds that deposit layers of dust on every surface in the city. Piracy depends on infrastructural forms like these that create material effects on the storage and retrieval of data. In Nigeria, the infrastructure for media, especially pirate media, is often marked by disrepair and noise.

Nigerian dealers in the legal and illegal reproduction of media record data on cheap tapes with low-quality machines. This information is retrieved for the most part through old VCRS, televisions, and cassette players marked by distortion and interference. Watching, say, Hollywood or Indian films on VCRS in Nigeria, where there is no official distribution of nonpirate media, means necessarily watching the dub of a dub of a dub. As the same dealers, using the same equipment and same blank cassettes, dub Hausa video films, the result is that the visual standard for pirate media remains in place. Pirated images have a hallucinogenic quality. Detail is destroyed as realist representation fades into pulsating light. Facial features are smoothed away, colors are broken down into constituent tones, and bodies fade into one another. Reproduction takes its toll, degrading the image by injecting dropouts and bursts of fuzzy noise, breaking down dialogue into muddy, often inaudible sound. This distortion is often heard in the vibrating shrillness of the tape players used by the *masu saida kaset*, itinerant cassette hawkers who travel around the city, selling eclectic collections of music and Islamic preaching (see figures 55 and 56).

The quality of the tape recorder used by these cassette sellers is standard in Nigeria. As the seller travels, the cassette player blares out Indian film songs, Islamic preaching, or Hausa music at such high volume that the signal degenerates into the pure vibration of the machine. In this the machine actually mimics the sound of live musical performances in Kano, which often rely on the distorted amplification of microphones, loudspeakers, and portable generators. Christopher Waterman (1990) points out that in the South of Nigeria distortion by amplifiers became such an accepted part of live performance that juju musicians would intentionally destroy new loudspeakers to achieve the standard "buzzing" sound.[8] This distortion affects many media in Nigeria. Film prints, for instance, arrive at the end of long, picaresque journeys, beginning in the metropolitan cinematic centers of India or Europe and crossing the cinema halls of many countries before winding up their lives on the Nigerian circuit. There they are often shown until they literally fall apart. All are scratched and heavily damaged, full of surprising and lengthy jump-cuts where film has stuck in the projector and burned. Although the sound and image of video are poor, Ghanaian video filmmaker Willy Akuffo has warned video makers against nostalgia for the "quality" of film, which forgets how terrible film prints actually were. As a former projectionist he had to deal with repairing burned film and fixing the previous repairs that the prints had accumulated on their journey to Africa.[9] Likewise, the quality of video projection, with its low-resolution

55 and 56. Cassette Seller, Kano Nigeria. Both photos by the author.

ghostly images, can be highly variable depending on the age and quality of the equipment. In the poorer cinemas that converted to video in the mid-1990s there were terrible problems with tracking and with inaudible sound. The projected image often filled only a portion of the cinema screen or would be distorted into an hourglass shape. At other times the corner of the images was pinched and vibrating as if it were a photograph peeling off.

The infrastructure of reproduction, like most contemporary infrastructure in Nigeria, is marked by cheapness, faulty operation, and constant repair. "All data flows," the media theorist Friedrich Kittler (1999: 14) reminds us, "must pass through the bottleneck of the signifier," and in doing so they are vulnerable to being "engulfed by the noise of the real." The "real" here is precisely the fuzziness of cinematic images or the hissing of tape recorders—the noise produced by the medium of transmission itself as it encodes and disseminates data. Yuri Tsivian (1994) has termed this effect the "semiotics of interference" and has analyzed the operation of early Russian cinema, arguing that the physical conditions of media exhibition—scratches on the film and noise and vibrations from projectors—became part of the "message" of films themselves.[10] For Nigerians, the costs of consuming and producing world media require operating on the margins of technology. Distortion on an audio tape, dropouts on a video, and a slow connection to the Internet are the material conditions of existence for media. While media infrastructure creates the reality of being ever more connected to a globalized world, it does so by emphasizing Nigerians' marginalization at the same time. Electricity blackouts, snowy television images, difficulty getting international phone lines, and distorted loudspeakers on cassette players all create a technological veil of semiotic distortion for Nigerians.

Some of this distortion is taken for granted, rendered invisible to people by its ubiquity. It is clear, for instance, that many of the most popular transnational media forms, such as sports (especially wrestling), action films, and Indian films, are highly visual and thus capable of overcoming both linguistic differences and the audio degradation that makes words hard to hear even when languages are well understood. But this degradation is rarely commented on. Instead, what these films evoke is the fantasy of other countries where deficiencies in infrastructure are believed not to exist. For many Northern Nigerians, Saudi Arabia is a place where electricity always flows, where roads have no potholes, and where hospitals are of the highest quality—just as everyone in Europe and America is thought to own televisions and mobile phones.[11] These fantasies represent implicit and sometimes explicit critiques of the failures of the Nigerian state to provide basic infrastructures for everyday life. The breakdown of infrastructure provides a conduit for critiques of the state and of the corruption and ethnic favoritism of political elites (Verrips and Meyer 2001).

CONCLUSION

In his exhaustive study of the rise of print, the historian Adrian Johns (1998) argues that piracy, rather than being an aberration of an "original" mode of text production, is central to the way print operates and spreads over time and space. The qualities we now associate with print—its fixity, guarantee of authorship, and commodity form—were not inherent in the technology but the result of a social compact, the institution of a technological order of reality. Johns is instructive in reminding us that, in many parts of the world, media piracy is not a pathology of the circulation of media forms but its prerequisite. In many places piracy is the only means by which certain media—usually foreign—are available. And in countries like Nigeria the technological constraints that fuel pirated media provide the industrial template through which other, nonpirated, media are reproduced, disseminated, and consumed.

Piracy and the wider infrastructure of reproduction it has generated reveals to us the organization of contemporary Nigerian society. They show how the parallel economy has migrated onto center stage, overlapping and interpenetrating with the official economy, mixing legal and illegal regimes, uniting social actors, and organizing common networks. This full flowering media, and the infrastructure it relies on, presents a stark contrast to the state sponsorship of media in the colonial and early postcolonial era. Now political control exercised through the governmental, pastoral care of developmental media has been replaced by an economy shorn of its political objectives. The infrastructure piracy creates generates its own mode of spatiality, linking Nigeria into new economic and social networks. Piracy means that Nigerian media production and circulation no longer depend on the intervention of the state (colonial or postcolonial) but are captured by the logic of privatization and gradually extend over differing areas of social experience. Sundaram (1999: 61), writing about everyday electronic culture in India—self-trained programmers who build computers and servers by cobbling together secondhand computer parts—refers to this as "recycled modernity," one that is "everyday in its imaginary, pirate in its practice, and mobile in its innovation." Rem Koolhaas has explored a similar phenomenon in the collapse of traffic systems in Lagos, a city overwhelmed by cars and the lack of roads (Koolhaas et al. 2001). There traffic jams and bottlenecks force detours through "nonflow" areas, spreading traffic off the planned grids and expanding the motorable space of the city. As cars back up for longer periods of time they create markets for hawkers. Over time the markets get formalized, roadside mosques are marked out to service the workers, and new infrastructures emerge to paper over the inefficiencies of the old (see also Mbembe and Roitman 1995; Simone 2001; and Verrips and Meyer 2001).

The infrastructure of reproduction created by piracy generates material and sensorial effects on both media and their consumers. Cheap tape recorders, old televisions, videos that are the copy of a copy of a copy, so that the image is permanently blurred, the sound resolutely opaque—these are the material distortions endemic to the reproduction of media goods in situations of poverty and illegality, and they shape the ways these media take on cultural value and act on individuals and groups. The dialectic of technological breakdown and repair imposes its own cultural experience of modernity, an alternate speeding up and stasis, and a world where gaps in space and time are continually being annihilated and reinforced.

Conclusion

In 2003 a blackout in New York City halted everyday order and turned life upside down. People who were working stopped, those from the suburbs stayed in the city, and strangers talked together. Relieved that it was not terrorism, proud there was little rioting (unlike during the 1970s), New Yorkers celebrated a moment of communitas. When society came to a shuddering halt for a few days, people took this total transformation of everyday life as a moment to bond, a reminder of the coming together that followed September 11. It was, in this sense, an event and thus marked by its singularity, its excess and exceptional difference from everyday life. After the event, everyday life was expected to continue as before, albeit haunted by a sense of the vulnerability of Western infrastructural networks to terrorism. The intensity of this fear was generated, of course, by the unexpectedness and exceptional nature of the blackout.

In Nigeria, when electricity disappears things similarly come to a standstill. For about two minutes. There is mild surprise, irritation but no shock. Then people walk around to the back of the house and turn on small generators. Businesses fire larger ones. People fill their lamps with oil, light candles, and in a few minutes everything is going on as before, with people trading, dancing, praying, and eating: the warp and woof of everyday life.

While in New York blackouts brought a sense of vulnerability and revealed the dependence of Western societies on a constant flow of power, in Nigeria, no building is constructed without the knowledge that state infrastructures fail. In older buildings, the corners of garages are reserved for generators. In new ones, special annexes are built to house generators, like the small mosques in wealthy family compounds. The necessity of electrical autonomy is a basic factor in the architectonics of built space, the structures of planning, and the form and experience of Nigerian urban life.

Wolfgang Schivelbusch (1995) argues that one of the most important transformations of networked urban life came with the rise of the gas lamp. Gas represented the industrialization of light and an end to the autonomy of oil lamps and candles. It was gas that made individual households nodes of a centralized power source, tying them into a collective system, linking the domestic and intimate to larger structures of capital and the state, and these linkages of networked infrastructures were fundamentally modern. The rise of the electric gird furthered this process. Electricity represents the intrusion of capital and then government into everyday life, tying citizens into a new sort of collectivity. In Nigeria, the beginning of this effort is tied to colonial rule but its vast extension in the postcolonial period was driven by the modernizing ambitions of the nationalist, independent state. As the urbanists Stephen Graham and Simon Marvin (2001) have written, the provision of networked infrastructures such as the electricity grid were seen as mechanisms that controlled the relation between the individual and the state, instigating waves of societal progress: "Across the urban world, fragmented islands of infrastructure were joined up, integrated and consolidated toward standardized, regulated networks" (40), networks that became the embodiment of what it meant to be modern.

In Nigeria, the grand modernist project of infrastructure, manifest in the robust presence of a state whose involvement in everyday life was to be present in the turning of a switch or the flushing of a toilet, has broken down. Infrastructures once embodied the promise of a new, progressive world: Okwui Enwezor (2001: 52) writes evocatively about the modernist buildings of Lagos erected in a burst of energy after independence, when "the newly minted political class demanded monumental architecture to appease the Gods of independence." This high moment of national and cultural self-confidence was followed by what Achille Mbembe (2001) calls the "reappropriation of the state" by postcolonial dictatorships, after which government began a slow slide to simulacra. Previously, infrastructures drew on their technical achievements to express a symbolic power—

a form of technopolitics, where political rule was mediated through the workings of a railway, roads, or power plants. In the age of what Mbembe terms *private indirect government*, infrastructures are important not for their technical properties but because they are a political mechanism whereby actors can make claims on the state and governmental elites can award contracts and so purchase political allegiance. Under this logic, infrastructures are still haunted by the developmentalist ambitions of the nationalist period, but these ambitions are evacuated of any real meaning and infrastructures themselves became repetitions, devoid of substance. Large-scale infrastructures were important as translation mechanisms to turn oil revenues into patron-client networks, which is why during the oil boom Nigeria became peppered with enormously expensive infrastructural development projects that were technically inefficient and often not completed (A. Apter 2005; Watts 1992). Now instead of citizens' being linked to the state through the smooth network of the electric grid, the generator dominates Nigerian life. Loud, smelly, coughing smoke into the air from the backs of houses all through urban neighborhoods, the generator provides the ambient sounds and smells of the city. Its presence bears witness to the collapse of the integrated infrastructural idea and the reconfiguration of the state's ambition to provide developmental progress. Even the gasoline the generator feeds on is sold on the black market by *'yan daba* from individual drums throughout the city. All over Nigeria, when electricity supply disappears and people walk around to the back of the house to bring the generator coughing to life, this simple sensual experience of contemporary urban living highlights the link between technologies and political order. In the disaggregation from networked electricity to autonomous generators lies the shift in Nigerian society from the developmental state to new forms of individual, competitive, liberalism.

INFRASTRUCTURES ARE NOT JUST TECHNICAL BUT CONCEPTUAL OBJECTS

My interest in the conceptual mechanisms that lie behind infrastructures comes out of a questioning of what is at stake in the encounter between Hausa subjects and new media technologies. Before the radio program was listened to, the film watched, the cinema entered, there is a confrontation between subject and technology staged by the enormous efforts of colonial administrators, Islamic leaders, technical advisors, and nationalists, whose efforts combined in various ways to give technology its meaning in colonial (and postcolonial) Nigeria. Michel Foucault referred to this as the condition of exteriority. In *The Archaeology of Knowledge* (1972), he was interested less in the semantic content of archives and more in the systemic conditions of possibility that allowed certain statements to emerge, be sustained, and, over time, transform. My aim has been to highlight the political exteriority from which infrastructures emerge. This is what I mean when I argue that infrastructures are not just technical but conceptual objects. In urban theory, infrastructures are often noted for their invisibility, their taken-for-grantedness, until they break down or something goes awry; but in the colonial and postcolonial context, infrastructures command a powerful presence, and their breakdown only makes them more visible, calling into being governments' failed promises to their people as specters that haunt contemporary collapse. They are a mode of regulating society by publicly performing and thus constituting relations between the state and its citizenry. The building of the Baro-Kano railroad and the Kano Water and Electric Light Works was intended to move trains and to provide electricity, but it was also a mode of address whereby the colonial state offered development and technological progress in return for political subjection. Progress was the knowledge of how to use and live in a world ordered by such technologies, and it figured one as a citizen, a member of a society made up of equivalent individuals offered equal access to the benefits of technology. For most of the twentieth century, infrastructures were based on an idea that the provision of railways, or electricity, or radio networks should be available to all citizens at a standard price with little regard to regional differences: Hausa were not charged more for electricity than Yoruba, Christians were not offered a different telephone rate than Muslims, commoners traveled the same free roads as the aristocracy. Infrastructures embodied a relation between the state and its citizenry, expressing shared ideas about the state's role in society. Infrastructures were intended to be a universal public good in which every member of society was presumed to be equal to everyone else. It is easy to critique the ideological basis of this offer: to note that infrastructures were organized for the economic exploitation of the colony, that European countries received infrastructural benefits far in excess of their African colonies, that rural areas received less attention than urban ones. But while this is true, to dismiss the egalitarian command of infrastructure would be a mistake: not only a key ideology of colonial rule, it passed easily into the postcolonial period and was a major part of nationalist African agendas.

In an era of privatization, with the collapse of the idea of infrastructure as a universal public good owned by the state, has come the move instead toward "enclave" infrastructures. Access to private roads, satellite television, the Internet, and electricity is regulated not by the state but by how much individual consumers (as opposed to citizens) can pay for generators, bribes for preferential service, black market gasoline, and a range of goods that once were expected to be freely (or cheaply) available in the public domain. This free access was always an expectation, of course, a status rarely achieved but a useful one from which Nigerians could critique the waste, inefficiency, and corruption of the Nigerian state. For most of its history, Nigeria has persevered with poor infrastructural conditions which have tended toward collapse. This collapse structures the rhythms, practices, and shape of everyday urban life. In Nigeria, most people use their bath not for bathing but for storing water, knowing that service will be discontinued for hours and sometimes days at a time. Large plastic barrels in kitchens and bathrooms are crucial water reservoirs for cooking, drinking, and washing. Everyone owns a variety of candles, oil lamps, battery powered torches, and, if one is lucky enough, gasoline-powered generators of varying sizes. Mobile phones are for communication but are also flipped open to give light when a blackout occurs and one is waiting for a generator to start. Despite, or more likely because of, the cheap, subsidized price of gasoline, it is often unavailable from official gas stations, where lines of cars snake back from the pumps and up the road for hundreds of yards. Owners leave them there waiting until gasoline has been delivered to the station. In turn, every urban area is covered with black market gasoline stalls where one or two youths stand with a barrel and a funnel offering higher price gas to those who can pay. Waste slowly moves through sewers, rubbish is not picked up, electricity and water supply is intermittent, and Nigerian urban life takes place in interaction with this lack of infrastructure. Ayodeji Olukoju (2004) brilliantly charts the cat-and-mouse games that take place between citizens, who sometimes steal energy supplies because the Nigerian Electric Power Authority (NEPA) is inefficient and corrupt, and NEPA authorities, who cut off whole blocks and areas in response. Cumulatively, these breakdowns, the innovations they demand in compensation, and the informal social practices that grow up around them mean that, for very different reasons than the colonial and postcolonial state intended, the presence, functioning, and repair of infrastructure in Nigeria is not invisible or taken for granted but an inescapable feature of everyday life. Olukoju writes that in Lagos, when power is restored after a blackout, all the children in the area shout, "UP NEPA!" (ibid.). Infrastructures have become the means to critique the state and lament the failed promises of elites. They become the justification for throwing one's hands up at the promises of nationalist elites and turning instead to religious and other networks that might prove more reliable.

In the early chapters of this book, I laid out how colonial governments attempted to tie infrastructures to a mode of rule. The complex symbolic work that surrounded these imposing edifices, the thousands who turned out to see the ceremonial opening of the Baro-Kano railway bridge, or the newspaper reports about the newly electrified city of Ilorin, were attempts by British colonialists to stabilize the symbolic logic of infrastructures. Debra Spitulnik (1998–99) similarly describes how radios were incorporated into colonial patronage systems, handed out by administrators to chiefs as evidence of the benevolence and progressiveness of colonial rule. There was a dual aspect of this work, reflecting the heterogeneous and internally contradictory nature of colonial rule itself. On the one hand, infrastructures were part of the colonial sublime, an attempt by rulers to use technology as a mode of difference to show the superiority and power of colonial rule and the world of science and technological expertise it represented. Immanuel Kant (1952: 92) argued that the feeling of the sublime overwhelms us, inciting us to "abandon sensibility," resulting in a feeling of submission and prostration. The British sought to use this experience of awe and power as part of the aesthetics of infrastructure, where the idea of the sublime rested on the sharp difference between the world of the colonialists and the world of their subjects. At the same time, and against this, was the logic of similarity, the governmental promise that colonial rule proffered: Nigerians who accepted this rule could be made to be more like Europeans; they could be taught to master these technologies, be educated in their uses, so that the sense of awe could be tamed, the sublime reduced, and development brought about. Both these tendencies, toward difference *and* similarity, were inherent to the practice of indirect rule in Nigeria.

To comprehend how this logic worked is to understand how infrastructural technologies can only conceptually exist because of what Bruno Latour (1993) refers to as the "networks of production," the institutional, discursive contexts that accompany objects and which establish them as facts in the world. This is similar to Foucault's interest in the archive not as a collection of documents or things but as the form of political exteriority that makes objects appear to have certain meanings (and not other ones). To show that infrastructures represented the governing principles of Empire is not to say that they always succeeded, or that they were smoothly efficient, but it does foreground the institutional efforts to make infrastructures mean in a particular way. The British ran into tension with other forms of discursive tradition mobilized by nationalist and religious elites, each of these groups itself fragmented into different interests, and all working to create the conceptual frames whereby technologies were brought into comprehension. This indicates what was at stake in the encounter between European technology and colonial subject and perhaps why both colonialists and Nigerians reacted to infrastructures in the way they did. In the postcolonial period, the tie to European rule was lost, but it is remarkable how much of the modernist ideology of infrastructure remained. Nationalist governments, whether civilian or military, embraced the contract that development would be facilitated by the provision of infrastructure, that this was a key, perhaps *the* key way that the state's ambition was to be manifest to its people and their relation to it configured. Radio talks on the workings of the water supply system might have been replaced by newsreels of nationalist leaders opening factories, inaugurating power plants, or welcoming dignitaries to the commemoration of bridges and dams, but the intense effort to stabilize and fix the symbolic logic of these technologies was sustained.

INFRASTRUCTURES ARE NOT JUST CONCEPTUAL BUT TECHNICAL OBJECTS

The link between infrastructures and modes of rule was a fragile, vulnerable thing. While these public works could seem massive and terrifying, involving thousands of workers, leveling hills, fording rivers, and reorganizing territories, at other times the ability of objects to maintain the aura invested in their construction was brittle. In the case of the sublime, especially when tied to technology, objects cannot maintain their sublime status. In order for the idea of the sublime to be redeployed, it has to be continually renewed. Steamships render sailing ships slow, airplanes destroy steamboats' apparent speed, and jets make propeller planes anachronistic, nostalgic emblems of a previous era. Each of these technologies, in its moment of innovation, is deeply transformative, unmooring peoples' sense of space and time and the speed of everyday life. None can maintain that power. When that idea of the sublime is tied to the representation of colonial power it builds in a fragility that forever haunts its efforts. The electric lights that awed the citizens of Ilorin and Kano became familiar and unexceptional. The fear of magic that once attended radio broadcasts largely dissipated. With the passage of time the work of technology becomes familiar and quotidian, and the ability to use the sublime for political purposes is made vulnerable by the need for constant technological renewal.

The sublime was also threatened by the technical and material qualities of infrastructures, which created possibilities for action in excess of the colonial ability to fix order. The building of the railroad, for instance, spurred the massive theft of railroad keys (bolts) by Hausa blacksmiths, who saw the rail network as an enormous source of raw material. Preventing this theft was a main preoccupation expressed in railway police and secret service reports in the 1920s.[1] The television system launched in 1961, designed to represent Hausa traditional culture and to promote development with Western programming, was immediately besieged by demands (by the Hausa members of the Broadcast Corporation Advisory Committee, opposed by its British members) that it show Hindi films.[2] Material objects are funded and initiated with specific intentions in mind, but, as the anthropologist Webb Keane (2001: 74, 71) has argued, the physical life of objects can "expose semantics to objective circumstances" making them vulnerable to "all that can happen to things." For Keane, signs should not be reduced to their communicative function, the materiality of the signifier made transparent to the communicative event or to its relation to other signs in a system. Borrowing from C. S. Peirce, Keane (2005: 186) argues that signs should be treated as material things, "vulnerable to causation and contingency." Embodying a value in material form necessitates bundling that value with other material qualities an object possesses, shaping its capacity to create meaning and social action. The redness of an apple, Keane suggests, comes along with its spherical shape, light weight, sweetness, and a tendency to rot. In a larger cultural formation it is tied to ideas about health and doctors, sin and culpability, poison and innocence. If one chose another object to connote redness, say, a fire engine, that object would tie into qualities of speed, hardness, and machinery, ideas about masculinity, danger, and public service. Keane calls this process bundling, the material quality of embodiment inescapably binding qualities to other qualities. It gives rise to the processual form in which "signs give rise to new signs in an unending process of signification" (ibid.). This is a point also made by Fred Myers (2001) when he writes that the physical embodiment of objects is crucial to their ability to be resignified and recontextualized over time.[3]

It is this materiality of media as objects, their sensual qualities and the contingencies those qualities exert, that generates the excess (or lack), which creates a semantic fragility. Objects break down, power plants fail, water supply dries up, radio broadcasts are sometimes too weak to be heard, bad phone lines render voices unintelligible, and connections fail. The British made totems out of technology and placed them center stage in society, where they were expected to carry out the work of progress, enlightenment, and development. Technologies became the material objects through which relations between ruler and ruled were embodied, but it was while they were center stage that their failures became manifest. Once built, they exposed their ability to objectify social relations to the physical contingencies of rain, harmattan winds, poor repair, theft, and so on. These technical qualities proved to be unruly and difficult to control, and their failure to carry out their technical and symbolic function is as important in shaping urban Nigeria as their success.

PRODUCING URBAN SPACE IN AFRICA

The material properties of infrastructures are also important in creating the physical ambience of the city, the sounds, smells, visual backdrop, and built space that make up its sensual life. In treating media technologies as parts of a much wider logic and form of infrastructure I have sought to open up new ways of thinking about the production of Nigerian urban space over time. Moving between the imaginative texts produced and consumed by Nigerians, the spaces of association in which these texts take on phenomenal lives, and the social practices that cluster around them, my aim has been to bring out the variety of urban Africa, to tie the creation of built form to the rich sociality that forms creates, to keep in mind the disrepair of everyday life but insist on the imaginative force that overruns that breakdown. Since Ulf Hannerz (1987) made his famous call for an anthropology of African urbanism that examined the structures of meaning that make up urban life, there has been a shift in the way that scholars in anthropology and African studies have conceived of urbanism in Africa. Hannerz argued that African urbanism was too focused on issues of poverty, economic and political exploitation, and unequal relations between developed and developing societies. As Achille Mbembe and Sarah Nuttall (2004) have recently noted, this had led to a tendency to depict African societies as in continual crisis. Hannerz, in urging attention to the richness of popular urban life, was promoting the idea that, as David Hecht and Maliqalim Simone (1994: 13) put it, "the need to survive does not . . .

swallow up the need to imagine." In recent years, a slew of work in history, anthropology, ethnomusicology, and art history has followed Hannerz's lead in examining urban Africa through the leisure practices and cultural forms of its inhabitants, rather than through production and their forms of labor.[4] This work starts from the premise that urban sites are spaces made up of a "creativity of practice," as Mbembe and Nuttall (2004: 349) have it, where urban life is better read as "a place of manifold rhythms, a world of sounds, private freedom, pleasures, and sensations" (360) than as a "theater for capitalist accumulation and exploitation" (356).[5]

I have less interest in theoretically opposing the urbanism of infrastructures, extraction, and inequality to the urbanism of fantasy and imagination. The creativity in the Nigerian film industry lies as much in its forms of economic organization and distribution as in the brightly imagined images of the films themselves. Bridges, factories, radio networks, and railways are as much objects of fantasy and imagination as are forms of fashion, literature, and film. The building of something like the Abeokuta steel mill, one of the most expensive infrastructural projects in Nigeria, is nothing if not an aesthetic form that tells us as much about the melodrama of Nigerian politics as it does about production and economics. All over the world, highway projects, corporate headquarters, and the laying of fiber optic cable networks occupy that messy conceptual boundary where the economic and rational meet the symbolic and fantastic.

As well as being objects of desire, infrastructures are conduits shaping the networks that constitute urban life. If the city is an event, as Georg Simmel has argued, and urban experience the outcome of a ceaseless series of encounters, then those encounters in Kano are constituted within the limits of the networks that bump up against each other there. Sufi religious brotherhoods, Lebanese businessmen, Ibo traders, and Hausa politicians are based in Kano but embedded in their own discrete networks that extend in different directions over the world. Space, as Henri Lefebvre (1991) argues, is the outcome of relations of exchange, relations that create the peculiar sets of networks that exist in any particular urban place. For there to be movement of cultural goods—be they Indian films, hip-hop from the United States, or high fashion from Europe and Japan—a formal and informal infrastructure has to be established creating the material channels that allow transnational cultural flows to occur. "Flows," for all their seemingly disembodied nature, require material conduits. They appear because a place—in my case urban Kano—is embedded in precise networks of social relations built over time.

Successive regimes of capital destroy and rebuild infrastructures, reconfiguring space in their own image (Harvey 2000). When shipping lines, warehouses, roads, railways, workers' quarters, telephone lines, and fiber optic cable networks are built not only do these infrastructures organize the flow of exchange and the sets of cultural, religious, and economic networks with which the city will be involved, but they give rise to the city's physical shape. Lefebvre argues that as space is continually reformed by the necessities of capital, newly developed networks do not eradicate earlier ones but are superimposed on top of them, creating a historical layering over time. As he memorably put it, this makes space seem flakey like a *mille-feuille* pastry rather than homogenous and discrete (Lefebvre 1991: 86). At any one point, then, urban space is made up of the historical layering of networks connected by infrastructures. These are the conduits that dictate which flow of religious and cultural ideas move and therefore which social relations get mobilized in their wake. Their historical layering helps explain why dormant cultural, religious, and economic forms can suddenly gain purchase again, reawakening and becoming reenergized in a new situation.[6]

Out of this historical layering come the modes of affect and excitement that give experiential meaning to the lives of the city's people. The building of the cinema theaters, their marginality in Hausa society and the aura of excitement and illicitness that surrounds them, the imaginative engagement of generations of Hausa youth with Hindi cinema, and the rise of Nigerian films are all consequences, often unintended, of infrastructural orders established under the British that have been progressively distorted and reshaped into something quite different. When we refer to the "urban experience" partly what we are referring to is the particular assemblage of sets that forms the unique configuration of a city. These are layered over time and new layers interact with preexisting ones, reenergizing some and closing off others. This evolution orients a city like Kano internally toward Southern Nigeria but also across the Sahara to North Africa and the Middle East, over the Atlantic, and increasingly across the Indian Ocean to Asia. Northerners chase modernity through Muslim connections to Saudi Arabia, Dubai, and other Islamic centers, as well as through connections to the West. All this makes Kano integrated with yet distinct from cities in the South, and infrastructures provide the material conduits that bind these loose connections into sustained networks.

AFRICAN CINEMA

One of the starting points of my research and this book was to pose the question of what a theory of media would look like if it began from Nigeria rather than Europe or the United States. Would it look the same? Would the conditions of existence for media—the political exterior of colonial and postcolonial rule, the religious and cultural discursive traditions in contest with that rule, the physical being of technology, the modes of sociability and imaginative life that media provoke—make media theory look different? Is this just a case of exceptionalism, a vivification of anthropological difference inscribed in media theory? Or do these differential conditions interrupt assumptions about media, highlighting processes played down in analyses that ground media in the social and political configurations of the United States or Europe? How then, do we identify processes common to technology as technology—the determinism that is always a part of media's ability to shape and produce the subjects that consume them? My intent has been to use a sustained analysis of media in Nigeria not to emphasize difference for its own sake but to give greater analytic prominence to problematics common to media but often underexamined. These involve the link between media and infrastructure, the role of breakdown and repair in the working of media systems, the heterogeneous nature of cultural flows, the competition between discursive systems (religious, colonial, nationalist) that attempt to stabilize the logic of media, the ontological instability of technologies themselves, their locus as sites for political contest, and thus their open-ended contingency. None of these processes are unique to Nigeria, and indeed one could well argue that they only exist due to Nigeria's interaction with other social worlds, but there they have a prominence which makes them key parts of the contested world of the country's media. At the same time, my research has tried to use media theory and film theory to broaden the frame of anthropology, to take seriously the cultural forms through which social life is objectified, and to force the consideration of media as central to the experiential sense of what it is to become and be urban.

While my main theoretical effort in this book has been to push the analysis of media to conceive of them within a larger conception of infrastructure, I have at the same time been conscious of writing a history of African cinema that, because it starts from the point of view of the films Africans watch, and the way cinema enters into African lives, takes a trajectory radically different from the historical narrative and theoretical questions of African cinema. I have ended up with a study of cinema in Africa rather than one of African cinema. As I argue in chapters 5 and 6, "African cinema" refers to an avant-garde, art-film aesthetic practice usually based on the works of great directors such as Ousmane Sembene, Djibril Diop Mambety, and Souleymane Cisse (Cham and Bakari 1996; Diawara 1992; Givanni 2001; Okome and Haynes 1995; Thwackway 2003; Ukadike 1994). Emerging from the crucible of the fight against cultural imperialism, these films were often based on the politics of affirming African cultural values and forms through cinema. They did this through self-conscious resistance to foreign cinematic forms, particularly those of Hollywood. Even as many of the filmmakers have taken a less overtly political stance, this commitment to alterity and resistance has continued to mark the scholarship on African cinema (as can be seen in titles stressing that "Africa Shoots Back" [Thwackway 2003] and calling for "Decolonizing the Gaze" [Barlet 2000]). Both the artistic texts and the critical discourse that surrounds them have been of huge importance to African intellectual life, but there are several conceptual tendencies inherent in this work. Perhaps, with a changing intellectual climate, what seems the starkest is the emphasis on African alterity and prioritizing those modes of cultural production least "contaminated" by influences from elsewhere. The danger of this is, of course, that we draw a portrait of African societies that reifies what Mbembe and Nuttall (2004) refer to as a metanarrative of difference, and construct Africa as being apart from the world, eliding its long historical connections to places elsewhere. Emphasizing difference also made it difficult to see the popularity of film traditions and cultural styles emanating from elsewhere in anything other than negative terms. It is hard to integrate work on the identification of South African blacks with American gangsters and jazz stars (Nixon 1994), the rise of cowboy youth culture in the Congo (De Boeck 2006; Gondola forthcoming.), or the fascination of East African and Nigerian audiences with Hindi film stars within the rubric of African cinema (Behrend 1998; Fugelsang 1994; Larkin 1997, 2004). This difficulty results partly from the focus on *production* by Africans as the legitimate signifier of what constitutes African cinema—despite the fact that most of these films circulated outside of the continent—leaving undeveloped the analysis of film cultures in Africa itself. My aim has been to pay greater attention to forms often seen as marginal to the idea of African cinema. In the portrait of cinema in Africa that emerges here, colonial films—usually seen as the grainy, didactic forms against which African cinema defined itself—are central rather than marginal, Indian films are a constitutive part of African cinematic heritage, and Nigerian video films represent its burgeoning future. By analyzing how cinema has existed in Nigeria over the last five decades, I trace how it has fed into Nigerian social lives, creating new modes of sociality, new aesthetic forms, and new templates for desire and imagination. Media are tied to the forms of political order and objectify these forms, helping to constitute subjects within that order. But media are also more than this. They have their own material agency, their built spaces, flickering images, evanescent sounds that meander through urban spaces creating the moods and affects that are part of the stuff of urban life. These affective experiences of media and urban living are tied to these physical forms, and their vulnerability to the contingencies of everyday life. Media are also productive, their sounds and images being constantly reinvented, constantly recycled in Nigerian songs, films, television shows, fashions, nicknames, modes of lovemaking, forms of address, comportment, desire, and fantasy. They offer up in vivid color the emotions and creativity of contemporary Africa. This book tries to give a different sense of African urbanism and a new way of thinking media into anthropology and anthropology into media. It aims to trace out a genealogy of media's past and the path for the future.

Notes

INTRODUCTION

1. This theme is repeated in Joyce Cary's (1939) description of the manic road builder Rudbeck in *Mr. Johnson*; see chapter 1.

2. For interesting discussions of the first contact narrative, see Burke 2002; Ginsburg 2002; Moore 2000; and Taussig 1993.

3. Interview with author, 23 January 1995, Kano, Nigeria.

1 COLONIAL SUBLIME

1. The Native Administration (NA) was the Nigerian-administered government that worked in tandem with the colonial administration.

2. In this he was correct: many did say it was a waste of time. Col. Walter Crocker (1937: 138), a colonial official, saw the project as a perfect example of the British tendency to concentrate on wasteful, splashy projects while "old Audu out in the Bush" got nothing. Crocker here is referring to a wider problem of British support for urban aristocracy over the needs of the rural poor. He argues that the money should have gone for digging wells and water troughs in rural areas. But for British administrators the importance of the project was symbolic as well as technical. For them, the plant was evidence of their ability to train a progressive,

modernizing class of Hausa civil servants who saw modernization as an important aspect of government.

3. On the writing of Hausa language, see Brenner and Last 1985.

4. Perhaps an even more important target were colonialists in Southern Nigeria, who argued that support for the Northern aristocracy would maintain a feudal elite and never bring about development and modernization. The Water and Electric Light Works were thus visible proof of the success of the Northern policies of indirect rule. See below.

5. Rhodes House (RH), Papers of Robert Heussler, Mss. Brit. Emp., S4802 7, "The Problems of Northern Nigeria as the Natives See It: Account of an Interview with Lord Lugard."

6. It is hard to read colonial records without coming across the intense and sustained antipathy Northern colonialists felt toward Southern Nigerians. "When I came here," wrote Crocker (1937: 55) of his time among the Idoma, "all the contractors were Ibos or Yorubas, Southern Nigerian literates, typical products of a system that teaches men to read a little and to write less, and to speak pidgin English and to wear European clothes. . . . If Southern Nigeria produces them it can keep them is the policy I follow so far as it touches me." This attitude dramatizes Chatterjee's argument about the rule of colonial difference: it is no accident that the more Southerners became like the British, the more intense the reaction toward them became. One district officer recounted that over time, "most Europeans were automatically rude to Southerners, so institutionalized had matters become" (Smith 1968: 17). The British antipathy toward Southerners came from many quarters, inspired not least by the Southern tendency to condescend and "humiliate" Northerners for their lack of education (a fact that Crocker mentions frequently), but there is no doubt that a large measure of this feeling came from British resentment and fear of Southern nationalist tendencies—a resentment that was rendered in cultural terms. Crocker (1937) writes of being approached by a Southerner "dressed in the height of African clerk dandyism" (97), which he later describes as "dressed in topees, woolen golf hose and the like" (144). Compare this to his description of the emir of Misau: "He is young, thirty to thirty-five. . . . He represents the Fulani aristocrat at its best and most ideal; very good looking, beautifully dressed, and with a dignity and courtesy so fine and yet to easy that one felt as a Westerner feels in a Japanese home, a shade gauche. What a world of difference there is between his sort and the Negro" (149).

7. RH, Papers of J. H. Carrow, Mss. Afr. s.1489.

8. RH, Papers of J. E. A. Baker, Mss. Afr. s.312, Letter by C. T. Money to J. E. A. Baker, 6 April 1945.

9. RH, Papers of J. H. Carrow, Mss. Afr. s.1489.

10. Ahamdu Bello, the Sardauna of Sokoto, was the leader of Northern Nigeria at independence.

11. RH, Papers of J. H. Carrow, Mss. Afr. s.1489.

12. Northern Nigeria is home to many different ethnic groups of which the largest by far is the Hausa. The 1803 jihad of Usman Ɗan Fodio that established the Sokoto caliphate resulted in the imposition of Fulani royal elites on largely Hausa subjects. Over time intermarriage has meant that many refer to the ethnic mix of the North as "Hausa-Fulani" and often refer to Fulani leaders as Hausa.

13. RH, Papers of J. H. Carrow, Mss. Afr. s.1489.

14. See Nye 1994. The political scientist Toby Dodge (2003) provides a striking example of this in his chapter on "the despotic power of aeroplanes," which examines how the British used aerial bombing as a means of striking terror and subjugating Iraqi civilians in the 1920s.

15. The Baro-Kano railway was authorized by Winston Churchill, then undersecretary at the Colonial Office. In a written response, he found it justified by the "enormous administrative and military difficulty in holding so vast a territory as Northern Nigeria without line of rapid communication," and by the "importance of British enterprise reaching extensive cotton growing areas in Northern Nigeria" (cited in Jaekel 1993: 93).

16. Adeline Masquelier (2002: 829) incisively captures the dislocation involved in forced labor in a Hausaphone area in the neighboring country of Niger: "When I asked old men what they remembered of the colonial period they would invariably recall being conscripted for roadwork. They would evoke poignant memories of having to leave behind entire fields ready for sowing or harvest, knowing that their absence would mean starvation, illness and despair the following year."

17. Poems—songs—were a standard form of literary expression for Hausa Muslim intellectuals.

18. *Bid'a*, innovation, is a key Islamic term that refers to the Qur'anic prohibition on innovation in matters of religious practice. Because Islam does not make the same distinction between religious and nonreligious realms that Christianity does, innovation is a key concept through which changes in social, cultural, and religious arenas are debated.

19. See the file Abubakar Sokoto, Hiskett Archives, Herskovits Library, Northwestern University.

20. Dikko is unusual in that he was the most important example in Northern Nigeria of the sort of future-oriented, progressive emir the British were attempting to fashion. The Resident of Katsina, in reporting on progress in the province, rhapsodized about the emir, "Muhammadu Dikko needs no testimonial: for he is one of the most widely known and respected of the Moslem chiefs in Nigeria. . . . From the start his qualities were recognized," foregrounded by "his interest and belief in modern inventions," from "installing electric light in his house last year" to "the purchase of a motor-car as early as 1913" (*NPN*, 1 November 1935, 15; for a sustained discussion of Dikko, see Umar 1997).

2 MAKING OF RADIO

1. J. F. Wilkinson, Program Office for the Northern RDS, NAK/MIA/A.201, Officer of the Broadcasting Services, Movements of.

2. Interviews: Alh. Adamu Salihu, Kano, August 1995; Alh. Maitama Sule, Ɗan Masanin, Kano, August 1995; Hassan Suleiman,July 1995 Kano.

3. Later to be renamed the Radio Diffusion Service; see Ladele, Adefela, and Lasekan 1979.

4. I thank Anderson Blanton (pers. comm.) for bringing this to my attention through his research on missionary radio.

5. Take, for example, *Zaria Calling*, the broadcast of the RDS in Zaria city, for the week beginning Sunday, 25 July 1948. Programming opened at 6:30 am with *Hindustani Records* or *English Records*. From 7:00 am to 6:30 pm was the *General Overseas Programme* of the BBC. Local programming resumed at 6:30 pm with *Arabic Broadcast* (servicing the large Lebanese community). Between 7:15 and 8:30 was *Local Broadcast*, followed by *Hausa Artist* between 8:00 and 9:00. *Vernacular Records* concluded programming, ending at 10:00 pm. NAK/INF 5, Zaria Local Broadcasting Charts, Weekly Programmes.

6. Interviews of Maitama Sule, August 1995, Kano; Alh. Adamu Abdallah, December 1994, Kano; and Hassan Suleiman, August 1995, Kano.

7. RH, Papers of J. H. Carrow, Mss. Afr.s 1489; interview with Maitama Sule, August 1995, Kano. On the rise of a 'yan boko as a new "counterelite," see Yakubu 1996.

8. RH, Papers of J. H. Carrow, Mss.Afr.s 1489.

9. See also Ferguson 1999, chapter 6.

10. Adamu Salihu, interview with author, 2 August 1995, Kano.

11. Nasir Kabara, interview with author, 23 January 1995, Kano. Elsewhere in Africa the British often vacillated between emphasizing the scientific and the magical aspects of technologies such as radio. Heike Behrend (2003, 2005) has written on how colonialists in Uganda explicitly copied missionary arguments that technology usurped the magical forces once associated with local spirits and that the force inside them had a magical origin. Terence Ranger (1993) describes the broadcast of the British king's coronation in Uganda, a key event for radio, as all over the Empire radio sets were erected to carry the king's broadcast to his colonial subjects. Ranger describes the ceremony that accompanied the broadcast, which included a tattoo, bonfire, a fireworks show, forty spotlights, and a parade of African warriors in leopard skins, who disappeared to reemerge as modern soldiers. "The sensation of the evening," though, was the broadcast of the king's message, which issued from loudspeakers that Twining, the colonial officer in charge, had concealed so that the sound seemed to issue forth as if from nowhere. Ranger's description is a great example of the profound tensions at work in colonialism between the representation of technology as science—and

a means for training, mutability, and progress (leopard-skin warriors into soldiers)—and as wonder, magic, and the sublime.

12. RH Papers of J. H. Carrow, Mss. Afr. 1489; see also Heussler 1968.

13. NAK/Kano Prof. 4364 RDS.

14. RH Papers of J. H. Carrow, Mss. Afr.s 1489, "Some Rough Thoughts on the Administration and Progress Made during 1919 to 1939," handwritten ms.

15. NAK/Kano Prof. 4364 RDS.

16. Letter, J. H. Carrow to the Secretary, Northern Province, 24 November 1944, NAK/MIA Kaduna, 2nd collection, vol. 1, no. 765, Radio Diffusion Service, Northern Region.

17. NAK/Kano Prof. 4364/s.13, Circular, D. B. Wright for Ag. Civil Secretary, Kaduna, to Resident Kano, 28 September 1952.

18. NAK/MIA Kaduna, 2nd collection, vol. 1, no. 765, Radio Diffusion Service, Northern Region.

19. NAK/Kano Prof. 4364/s.13, Radio Distribution Service Programme Subcommittee and Advisory Committee.

20. NAK/Kano Prof. 4364/s.13, Radio Distribution Service Programme Subcommittee and Advisory Committee, 25 May 1951.

21. NAK/MIA Kaduna, 2nd collection, vol. 1, no. 765, Radio Diffusion Service, Northern Region, List of Five-Minute Talks Given on the Zaria RDS.

22. NAK/Kano Prof. 4364/s.13, Radio Distribution Service Programme Subcommittee and Advisory Cttee, 25 May 1951.

23. NAK/Kano Prof. 4364/s.13, Radio Distribution Service Programme Subcommittee and Advisory Committee, 10 December 1950.

24. *Nigerian Citizen*, 3 September 1953, included in NAK/MIA/R.2231.

25. Ibid.

26. NAK/MIA Kaduna, 2nd collection, vol. 1, no. 765, Radio Diffusion Service, Northern Region; Kano State History and Culture Bureau (hereafter HCB)/INF/8 Radio Distribution Service Minutes of Meetings.

27. NAK/MIA/R.2231.

28. Letter to the Secretary Northern Province from the Acting Divisional Engineer, 7 June 1950, NAK/MIA Kaduna, 2nd collection, vol. 1, no. 765, Radio Diffusion Service, Northern Region.

29. NAK/MIA, 2nd collection, vol. 1, A201, Officers of the Broadcasting Services, Movements of.

30. Letter by R. E. G. Wilkins, Ag. Director Posts and Telegraphs, Lagos, to L. H. Goble, 4 July 1950, NAK/MIA Kaduna, 2nd collection, vol. 1, no. 765, Radio Diffusion Service, Northern Region.

31. In 1949, L. W. Turner, a BBC engineer, and F. A. W. Byron, an engineer for the Crown Agents Telecommunications Department, were commissioned by the Colonial Office to survey radio in Nigeria, the Gold Coast, Sierra Leone, and the Gambia. The Nigerian service was seen as inadequate. In their 1949 report they

condemned the poor facilities and advised a switch to a wireless service (Ladele, Adefela, and Lasekan 1979).

32. NAK/MIA/R.1756, Radio Diffusion.

33. Minute appended to a letter sent from NBS Lagos to Resident Adamawa, 1951, NAK/MIA Kaduna, 2nd collection, vol. 1, no. 765, Radio Diffusion Service, Northern Region.

34. NAK/Kano Prof. 4364/s.13, Circular, D. B. Wright for Ag. Civil Secretary, Kaduna to Resident Kano, 28 August 1952.

35. Notes on interview with Mr. Bunting of the NBS, NAK/MIA/R.1756, Radio Diffusion.

36. Cable Resident Ilorin to Civil Secretary, Kaduna, 26 July 1954, NAK/MIA/A170 Nigeria Broadcasting Services, Programmes.

37. Letter, Controller, Northern Region to the Director of Broadcasting, Lagos, 9 April 1954, NAK/MIA, 2nd collection, vol. 1, A201, Officers of the Broadcasting Services, Movements of.

38. J. F. Wilkinson, 1st Tour Report: Nigeri, Ilorin, Kabba, March–April 1954, NAK/MIA, 2nd collection, vol. 1, A201, Officers of the Broadcasting Services, Movements of.

39. Tour of Gusau, Sokoto, Birnin Kebbi, Kontagora, Minna, Abuja, Lapai, Ilorin, Lokoja, Jos, April–May 1955, J. F. Wilkinson, Programme Officer, Northern Region, NAK/MIA, 2nd collection, vol. 1, A201, Officers of the Broadcasting Services, Movements of, 1952–58.

Gusau, it should be noted, was part of the same region that 10 years previously J. H. Carrow demanded should have RDS because of its inhabitants' tendency "to be parochial and wholly disinterested in matters outside their own area"; RH Papers of J. H. Carrow, Mss. Afr.s 1489. Less than a decade later the problem was reversed: they wished to connect with areas outside their own—just not necessarily the areas the British wanted them to.

40. Letter to Director of Broadcasting, Lagos from Controller, Northern Region, 9 May 1954, NAK/MIA, 2nd collection, vol. 1, A201, Officers of the Broadcasting Services, Movements of, 1952–58.

3 COLONIAL FILM AND POLITICAL FORM

1. NAK/AR/REP/1/13, Annual Report 1932, Idoma Division. See also *Northern Provinces News*, "Opening of the Benue Bridge," 23 July 1932, 23. I thank Moses Ochonu for bringing this cinema exhibition to my attention.

2. It is, of course, one of the great ironies of the film that the story hinges on the idea of British technical excellence contrasted to the inept and technically inferior Japanese.

3. Friedrich Kittler (1994) continues Virilio's attention to the genealogy of state military power and media systems. He argues that crucial aspects of the tech-

nology for television were perfected to monitor missile launches in the Second World War. More than that, World War II initiated the shift from the world of free-floating tubes, electrical coils, and condensers and introduced the circuit board. The war's significance for Kittler is not so much in any particular invention but in innovating systems whereby individual opinion and decision making becomes subordinated to the logic of the system itself which is now autonomous and self-regulating: "The self-guided weapons of World War II eliminated the two modern concepts of causality and subjectivity and introduced the present as the age of technical systems" (332).

4. NAK/Kano Prof. 2393, Health Propaganda Unit.

5. Recall that the precolonial state that made up much of Northern Nigeria was a sultanate divided into different emirates. At the apex stood the sultan of Sokoto. Each emirate was headed by an emir, advised by an emirate council made up of other aristocrats—the *galadima, waziri, ciroma,* and so on—and divided into districts, each with its own district head (*hakimi*). This formed a tightly organized hierarchical society based on the power and prestige of traditional royal elites: the emir and his council in urban areas and the district heads in rural ones.

6. NAK/Kano Prof., Annual Report 1939.

7. Kano Province, Annual Report 1937.

8. "Reports from Overseas: Nigeria," *Colonial Cinema* 4.3 (1946): 63. For a historical overview of the CFU, especially in regard to East Africa and to the context of British cinema at the time, see the work of Smyth (1979, 1983, 1988, 1992) and Burns (2002). See also Vaughan 1991.

9. In Northern Rhodesia cinema operators would attract great crowds by playing gramophone records; "Reports from Overseas: Northern Rhodesia," *Colonial Cinema* 4.3 (1946): 64.

10. Abdulkarim Umar Ɗan Asabe, interview with author, 5 December 1994, Kano.

11. NAK/MOI Kaduna, 3rd collection, vo1.2 CIN/5, Cinema Show Report, Zaria Province, 1957–60.

12. Abdulkarim Umar Ɗan Asabe, interview with author, 5 December 1994, Kano.

13. Touring Return of No. 1 Mobile Cinema Unit, September 1957, NAK/Kano Prof., 2nd collection, INF/54 Mobile Cinema—Kano N.A. Touring Returns.

14. NAK/MOI Kaduna, 3rd collection, vol. 2, CIN/5, Cinema Show Report, Zaria Province, 1957–60, Zaria city, 7 December 1958.

15. Abdulkarim Umar Ɗan Asabe, interview with author, 5 December 1994, Kano.

16. Qasimu Jero, interview with author, 20 January 2001, Kaduna.

17. Alh. Maitama Sule, interview with author, Ɗan Masanin, Kano, 1 August 1995.

18. "Reports from Overseas. Northern Rhodesia," *Colonial Cinema* 4.3 (1946): 65.

19. "The Cinema and You: By, an African Commentator," *Colonial Cinema* 5.1 (1947): 2–3.

20. "The Mobile Cinema Van in the Villages: By, an African," *Colonial Cinema* 3.1 (1945): 11–14.

21. Peter Morton-Williams, interview with author, London, 20 March 1996.

22. Ibid.

23. The *West African Pilot* was the newspaper edited by the leading nationalist figure in Nigeria, Nnamdi Azikwe (later president of Nigeria).

24. Letter to Secretary, Northern Provinces, from D. F. McBride, NAK/MOI/50 Cinema and Films.

25. NAK/INF/54, Mobile Cinema, Kano NA Touring Returns, Letter to Information Officer from Special Duties Officer, Kano, 24 December 1956.

26. This was acknowledged as much by a director of information in England writing to the Nigerian government in response to their critique of the film *Challenge in Nigeria*: "We are painfully aware of the delicate issue of making films about the Colonies which displease the local intelligentsia and especially Colonial students in this country who are (quite understandably) very sensitive to any display of the more backward, even though typical, features of Colonial life and who think in consequence that we are engaged in a deliberate attempt to ridicule and belittle Colonial people as primitive folk"; NAK/MOI/50, Cinema and Films/Letter to Colonial Office from K. W. Blackburne, Dir. of Information Services, 2 October 1948. This was an issue of intense concern in Nigeria. After the independence of India, Nigerians were successful in having Hollywood films such as *Sanders of the River* censored there as part of India's solidarity with other colonized peoples. And after Nigerian independence, Nigerians studying in England wrote back frequently to the Sardauna to complain about primitivist images of Africans in British documentaries. This is the prehistory of the rejection of ethnographic films by the first generations of African filmmakers—as these films were seen within a long European tradition of ethnic and national stereotyping.

27. It was mainly shown in a shortened version called *Giant in the Sun* (1959).

28. Bello is one of the most important political figures of independent Nigeria. A member of a prominent noble family (*sardauna* is a royal title), he emerged as one of Northern Nigeria's most important political figures at independence.

29. This is most powerfully seen in ubiquitous representations of the *jahi* charge, where the emir's retainers dressed in their finery charge down at the emir as if to attack him before pulling up at the last moment in salute. Jahi charges remain an important part of the symbolic performance of loyalty and authority (for a critique, see Apter 2005).

30. NAK/MIA, 2nd collection, vol. 2, INF: 2, Filmmaking.

31. NAK/MOI Kad, 3rd collection, vol. 1, Cin. 12, vol. 2, Show Reports Kano, 1962–64.

32. Kano Prof., 2nd collection, INF/54 Mobile Cinema, Kano N.A. Touring Reports.

33. NAK/MOI Kaduna, 3rd collection, vol. 2, CIN/5, Cinema Show Report, Zaria Province, 1957–60, 23 July 1959, Soba.

34. NAK/MOI Kaduna, 3rd collection, vol. 2/CIN/5/Cinema Show Report, Zaria Province, 1957–60, Kagoro, 3 November 1961.

35. NAK/MOI Kaduna, 3rd collection, vol. 2/CIN/5/Cinema Show Report, Zaria Province, 1957–60, Kubacca, 2 May 1957.

36. See also Sellers 1953; Burke 2002; Smyth 1979; and Vaughan 1991. Burns 2000 devotes a chapter to Sellers's theories of visual literacy. These ideas have, of course, been thoroughly critiqued by African film scholars both at the time and in more recent critical work. For contemporary critiques, see Baeta 1948; and Odunton 1950. More recently see Diawara 1992; Okome and Haynes 1995.

37. See esp. Baeta 1948 and Odunton 1950. As early as 1936 the zoologist Julian Huxley, who brought with him on a trip to East Africa three Empire Marketing Board films to test African reaction, found no difficulties in comprehension (Huxley 1936).

38. Columbia University Rare Books and Manuscripts Library (hereafter CU)/BASR/Box 23, Minutes of the International Radio Project Meetings.

39. CU/BASR/Box 23/B0370, The Comparative Sociology of Communication Systems, Memo prepared for the VOA for discussion at the meeting of 28 April 1950.

40. This statement (quoted in Powdermaker 1953: 55) was made at an experimental seminar held at the Wenner-Gren Foundation for Anthropological Research and organized by the anthropologist Hortense Powdermaker. Attending were senior BASR figures such as Lazarsfeld and the director, Charles Glock, along with Daniel Lerner (then a member of the BASR), Leo Löwenthal (then chief of the Program Evaluation Branch, International Broadcasting Division, Department of State), Harold Lasswell, Robert Merton, and others.

41. Kracauer was probably chosen by his good friend Löwenthal. In a reminiscence, Löwenthal (1991) writes of Kracauer's financial vulnerability as he tried to make a life in the United States and of his own frequent efforts to send work Kracauer's way. Löwenthal cites a letter where Kracauer refers to "the necessity of my securing an existence here [in the United States]" (13); it seems highly likely that the choice of Kracauer for the State Department was driven in part by a desire to provide him with employment. Kracauer's famous study of German cinema, *From Caligari to Hitler* (1947), was written first of all as a study of the fascist mentality for the Department of State, and many academics were involved in similar government projects during the war years (see, e.g., Mead and Metraux 1953). His later book cowritten with Paul Berkman, *Satellite Mentality* (1956), in which they analyze the political and propaganda susceptibilities of Soviet-bloc nations, was also a qualitative summary, sponsored by Löwenthal, of quantitative country reports carried out by the BASR. Kracauer, however, was an uneasy

fit at the BASR and, like Adorno before him, found the quantitative bias of the emerging discipline of mass communication uncongenial to critical thinking. In an essay, "The Challenge of Qualitative Analysis" (1952b), published in *Public Opinion Quarterly*, almost the house journal of the BASR, he critiqued the intellectual bias and supposed claims to "objective" hard data underlying quantitative research as a whole and the work of the BASR in particular. It was also during this period of working for the BASR that Kracauer researched and wrote what came to be his *Theory of Film* (1997).

42. See the report "The Influence of Islam on Communication Behavior in the Middle East" (CU/BASR/Box 22, author unknown, listed for staff circulation only, June 1951) which outlines many standard ideas about the inertia and fatalism of the Arab mind and the barrier Islam presents to modernization. This was written after the first country reports on Greece and Turkey were completed and may represent an early summary of the BASR's conclusions. In his report, Kracauer writes that the lower strata of Middle East society do not use media because "cultural and religious prejudices . . . seem to hamper any changes in this situation." He continues, arguing that Oriental notions center "around the belief that man is not primarily called upon to change his social environment," that "spiritual preoccupations may overshadow his concerns with poverty and injustice," and that "this belief. . . . breeds fatalism" (Kracauer 1952a).

43. In *Theory of Film* Kracauer cites an interview with Sellers published in French as part of a wider piece on the work of the CFU (Maddison 1948).

44. Burns draws on Burke's (2002) insightful essay on African reactions to mosquito films.

45. For a comparative analysis of the developmentalist logic of state television, see Abu-Lughod 2004; and Mankekar 1999.

4 BUILT SPACE OF CINEMA

1. The Nigerian government has used cinema politically to show films as a way of reaching a broader population for political purposes. For instance, after the Maitatsine riots of 1991, all Northern cinemas showed a government-made film depicting the devastation caused by the millenarian Muslim leader Muhammad Marwa and, crucially, showing his dead body to confirm his mortality. But these occurrences are rare.

2. In the 1930s, 1940s, and 1950s, mainstream Nigerian cinemas were dominated by British and American movies. In the 1950s cinemas began screening the odd Egyptian and Indian film. By the mid-1960s Egyptian films had disappeared and Indian films had begun to vie with Hollywood for popularity. Hong Kong cinema rose in popularity during the 1970s. Until the rise of Nigerian videos, African films have rarely been shown regularly at mainstream cinemas in Northern Nigeria, the notable exception being the traveling Yoruba films which emerged

from the Yoruba traveling theater tradition. For the most part these films were screened not in mainstream theaters but in rented halls formerly used for theatrical performances.

3. The Russian film historian Yuri Tsivian (1994) provides an elegant account of cinema-going as a sensory activity, paying attention to the temperature of the auditorium, the placing of the projector, the quality of light, and the nature of aural and visual interference.

4. For an interesting discussion of the symbolic distinctions between European and "traditional" quarters, see Mitchell 1991.

5. T. S. Rice, Memorandum on Segregation and Town Planning, 1921, KNA (Kano Native Authority) Kanolocauth 5/2 142/1923; cited in Frishman 1977.

6. This phrase, which may well sum up the entire symbolic value of Sabon Gari in the eyes of Kano Hausa, was coined by Resident Alexander of Kano in a speech to the Conference of Residents in 1926; *Record of the Proceedings of Conference of Residents, Northern Provinces, 1926* (Lagos: Government Printer, 1927); cited in Allyn 1976: 138.

7. This mode of exhibition mimics the history of film in the United States and Britain, where the first films were often shown as part of a wider program of burlesque (see M. Hansen 1991), or vaudeville (see Chanan 1996 [1982]), sandwiched between singers, comedians, and dancers so that they were only one element of the evening's entertainment.

8. Nigerian National Archives, Kaduna (NAK), Kano Prof. 1391, Kano Township Annual Report 1934.

9. NAK, Kano Prof., 2600, The West Africa Picture Co., (1) Application for C. of O., (2) General Correspondence.

10. NAK, Kano Prof., 4430, Mr. J. Green Mbadiwe, application for permission to erect a hotel and cinema at Kano.

11. Ibid.

12. NAK, Kano Prof. 2600, The West Africa Picture Co., (1) Application for C. of O., (2) General Correspondence.

13. After a few months the loophole was closed and the sale of alcohol banned; ibid.

14. NAK/MIA Kaduna, 2nd collection, vol. 2, R.1493, Cinematograph Audience, 1932–1952, Letter No. 16497.10A, Secretary, Northern Provinces, to Chief Secretary Lagos, 6 February 1932.

15. While Masquelier is right that markets have these larger cultural resonances, they also contain more earthly dangers. Thieves and hooligans (*'yan daba*) also frequent the market, and since 1953 the Sabon Gari market has been perhaps the greatest flashpoint for interreligious and interethnic rioting in Kano.

16. Several informants spoke to me about these fatwas but in a very general way; I was unable to find any written fatwas.

17. Sheikh Nasiru Kabara, interview with author, 23 January 1995, Kano.

18. Later, of course, this name began to be applied mainly to mobile film units.

19. Both terms were later replaced by the more neutral *sinima* or *silima*.

20. Sheikh Nasiru Kabara, interview with author, 23 January 1995, Kano.

21. This word is used to refer specifically to Islamic teachers but more generally to any adult male.

22. Minute by M. H. (?), 20 October 1954, in response by a letter from the director of education, Northern Region, 15 September 1954, requesting an assessment of censorship, HCB, Simple list of files removed from cabinet, R918, Films and Film Censorship.

23. Letter, E. K. Featherstone, resident, Kano, to secretary, Northern provinces, 9 January 1948, HCB, Simple list of files removed from cabinet, R918, Films and Film Censorship.

24. Ibid.

25. *Boko* refers to Hausa language written in roman script as opposed to precolonial Hausa which was written in Arabic script (*ajami*). *'Yan boko* derives from Western education but came to refer largely to the elites working in the new bureaucracy. Initially it was a term of abuse, directed at those whom many Hausa Muslims regarded with deep suspicion. For a discussion of this, see Tahir 1975.

26. *'Yan daba* do indeed have relations with traditional hunting groups in rural areas, though in contemporary Northern Nigeria they are largely seen as urban hooligans. Then as now, the fact that they travel with hunting dogs (in Islam dogs are seen as unclean animals) heightens both their relative autonomy from traditional religious norms as well as the basic intimidation factor that surrounds them; see Ɗan Asabe 1991; and Casey 2002.

27. In using "moral" I refer to two things: cinema in Kano is defined as an immoral, sexualized space, one that (unlike in the United States) never achieved social legitimation; on another, underlying level, I follow T. O. Beidelman's (1993) concept of morality as the set of images and practices through which people both comprehend their world and act within it in ways that conform and subvert their moral understanding. Space, for Beidelman, is a "moral metaphor," a social product that encodes the imagined order of society and personhood and reveals basic ideas about, and conflicts between, the individual and society. Beidelman's assertion of the active presence of the imagination in moral space has the advantage of foregrounding the concept of space as formed by human action, as something produced.

28. Interview with Alh. Maitama Sule, Ɗan Masanin Kano, 1 August 1995, Kano.

29. Lawan Abdullahi, interview with author 2 April 1995, Kano.

30. See *Report of the Commissioner Appointed by His Excellency the Governor to Enquire into the Circumstances in Which a Fire Caused Loss of Life at, and Destroyed, the El-Dunia Cinema, Kano, on the 13th Day of May 1951*, Justice Percy E.

Hubard, NAK, Zaria Prof., vol. 2, EDU, 5 Cinema Cinematographs, Cinema Office, (2) Mobile Cinema Routine Correspondence. See also NAK, Kano Prof., 7564, El Dunia Disaster. Colonial Office, 583/317/8, Cinema Disaster at Kano, 1951.

31. The power to curse (*tsine*) is a powerful magical attribute in Hausa society as elsewhere in Africa. Certain people are believed to have the power to make their curses come true, though if they are not evil people they may have this ability and not realize it. One person explained the rumor to me by saying that so many people were cursing the construction of the El Duniya that the combined weight of all these curses brought the theater down.

32. NAK, MOI (Ministry of Information), 55, Broadcasting, Radio Diffusion Service and BBC.

33. NAK, Kano Prof., 4364/s.13, Radio Distribution Service Programme Subcommittee and Advisory Committee.

34. Alhaji Abdullahi Adamu, interview with author, 2 April 1995, Kano.

35. NAK, Kano Prof., 6945, Jakara Palace Cinema, Letter to S. D. O. K. from Senior Superintendent of Police, Kano, N.A. P.G.F, Sewall, 6 September 1952.

36. Alh. Maitama Sule, Ɗan Masanin Kano, interview with author, 1 August 1995, Kano. Jakara and Maɗataye are both quarters in Kano birni. The song clearly refers to Hausa fears of encroaching Westernization and immorality in Muslim areas.

5 IMMATERIAL URBANISM

1. It is a truism that popular culture is, in part, "escapist." But in many parts of Africa popular culture is also expected to be instructive or "educative," as Nigerian English has it. Audiences expect and desire didactic moral instruction in popular narrative forms. For an excellent account of this, see Karin Barber's (2003) magisterial study of Yoruba traveling theater. Barber's book details the social life of a popular cultural form (theater), but it is also one of the best accounts of the emergence of a public, secular culture in colonial and postcolonial Africa.

2. Cinto Usman, interview with author, Kano city, 7 April 1995.

3. Previously I translated this term as "prostitute." The usual Nigerian English translation is "harlot," but *karuwai* refers as much to a state of life and a set of practices as it does to an economic mode of selling one's body for sex. Therefore Hausa commonly refer to "unattended women" or "women who have left home" when discussing women who are outside the supervision of their family and especially of a senior male—a father, brother, or husband. This situation in itself can constitute immorality and lead to being defined as a karuwa, whether one is involved in sexual activity or not. For an explication of *karuwanci*, see Pittin 1979. For a brilliant insight into the life of a woman who "leaves home" in a Muslim West African society, see Chernoff 2003.

4. Jibrin Magashi, interview with author, Kano city, 1 August 1995.

5. Yakubu Ahmed, interview with author, Kano city, 28 April 1995.

6. Ado Ahmad Gidan Dabino, interview with author, Kano city, 28 June 1995.

7. Lawan Ahmed, interview with author, Kano city, 12 October 1994.

8. Bashir Ɗan Ladi, interview with author, Kano city, 18 May 1995.

9. On the event as a temporal phenomenon, see Doane 2002. On the event, or the moment, as an assemblage of series of singularities, see the discussion of Deleuze in Singh n.d.

10. 'Yan daba are famously accused of *daukar amarya* (literally, "taking the bride") kidnapping women and sometimes raping them.

11. The popularity of Westerns was widespread all over Africa, called "Billism" in Belgium, and "Copperbelt cowboys" in Zambia; Ambler 2001; De Boeck 2006; Gondola forthcoming.

12. Ishaq Adefemi Agboola, interview with author, Kano city, 23 January 2002.

13. For an extended description of one form of bariki culture, see Werthmann 2002.

14. For a description of bikis and an analysis of 'yan daudu, see Gaudio 1997, 2005.

15. Literally "son of the wind." *Iska* is also the word used for supernatural spirits who possess humans.

16. Casey (2002) argues that their desire for shari'a was motivated less by an attachment to a globalized Islamist renaissance and more by a sense that shari'a would bring justice and an end to oppression by elites.

17. Sani Habib, interview with author, Kano city, 29 April 1995.

18. Michell Issa, manager, Cinema Distribution Circuit, interview with author, 15 May 1995, Kano.

19. Ibid.

20. In this I follow the intellectual move pioneered in the study of early cinema. See, e.g., Charney and Schwartz 1996; Gunning 1986, 1994; and M. Hansen 1991.

21. A fact very clear to anyone caught in a rainstorm inside the theater.

22. Ado Ahmad, interview with author, 28 June 1995, Kano. Since this interview, Hausa video films, including Ahmad's own, have adopted song and dance sequences.

23. Sani Bashir, interview with author, Kaduna, 28 December 1994.

24. In the past, Hausa women were often expected to marry at the onset of menses, around the age of 13.

25. Sani Bashir, interview with author, Kaduna, 28 December 1994.

26. Ado Ahmad, interview with author, 28 June 1995, Kano.

6 EXTRAVAGANT AESTHETICS OF NIGERIAN FILM

1. For several reasons, the name of this film practice is varied. Since their inception, these films have gone by the name home video in popular usage and

Nigerian video film in academic usage—the latter emphasizing the use of video (and later digital technology) in production. This was cemented by the landmark early collection edited by Jonathan Haynes (2000). More recently, since their popularity has come to global attention, these films have been referred to as "Nollywood," a term academics have been wary of because it places Hollywood as a dominant center from which other film histories (Bollywood, Nollywood) are derivative. However, "Nollywood" has become a dominant term used in Nigeria, and, as Haynes (2005) has argued, it does encode filmmakers' genuine aspiration of how they would like their media to be viewed (this stands in striking contrast to earlier generations of African filmmakers, whose ambition was to create a film practice in opposition to Hollywood). Over time, the use of *video* has been replaced by that of *film* in recognition that *film* is the default term for feature-length dramatic narratives—which Nigerian films clearly are. In this book, I will use the term *Nigerian film* notwithstanding the fact that no film is used anywhere in the process. This raises, however, a second issue.

I use *Nigerian film* to refer to all filmmaking in Nigeria, encompassing English-, Hausa-, and Yoruba-language motion pictures (though I do not discuss the latter in this chapter) especially because I want to identify thematic and formal conventions that cut across different film genres. I use *Southern Nigerian film* to refer to English-language films.

2. On fast capitalism, see Watts 1992. On informal markets, see Bayart, Ellis, and Hibou 1999; MacGaffey and Bazenguissa-Ganga 2000; Mbembe 2001; and Simone 1998, 2001, 2004. On Pentecostalism, see Corten and Marshall-Fratani 2002; Gifford 2004; Meyer 2004a, 2004b; and Marshall-Fratani 2001. On Islamism, see Kane 2003; Launay and Soares 1999; Loimeier 1997; Umar 1993; and Westerlund and Rosander 1997. On witchcraft, see Ashforth 2005; Comaroff and Comaroff 1999; Fisiy and Geschiere 1990; Geschiere 1997; and Moore and Sanders 2001.

3. Graham Furniss (2005) has noted the roots of many Hausa films in oral literature; see also Ahmad 2004. Yusuf Adamu (2002) has examined the influences of Hausa market literature on the same films, and many have noted the basis of Yoruba films in Yoruba traveling theater (e.g., Haynes, ed. 2000; and Ogundele 2000).

4. For an introduction, see Haynes, ed. 2000; Ukadike 2000.

5. VCD stands for "video CD," a cheaper version of a DVD that is the dominant storage form for media in many parts of the non-West. For an illuminating account of the origin of VCD technology, see Wang 2003.

6. Charles Igwe, conversation at the conference, Nollywood Rising: Global Perspectives on the Nigerian Film Industry, Los Angeles, 15 June 2005.

7. For a discussion of this, see Haynes, ed. 2000.

8. Charles Igwe, conversation at the conference, Nollywood Rising: Global Perspectives on the Nigerian Film Industry, Los Angeles, 15 June 2005.

9. The work in this tradition is now voluminous, but see Ashforth 2005; Comaroff and Comaroff 1999; Geschiere 1997; Meyer and Pels 2003; and Moore and Sanders 2001.

10. Since the return to civilian rule, Nigeria has been beset by an extraordinary amount of ethnic, economic, and religious violence, which has produced some of the worst atrocities since the Nigerian civil war—most especially in Kaduna city in 2000 and 2002.

11. Lila Abu-Lughod's (2004) analysis of Egyptian soap operas provides one of the more in-depth studies of how melodrama works in a postcolonial situation. Her work both overlaps with the argument I am making here and substantially differs. In Egypt, melodramatic television serials represent an "education in sentiment" in that they both translate wider political issues into interpersonal relations and, because they are on state television, publicize state initiatives. In the Nigerian and Indian cases, however, melodrama represents a space of extravagant action outside of and in contradistinction to state cultural forms.

12. This is an argument Peter Brooks (1985) makes for melodrama as a whole.

13. It is worth noting that many of the men in the film also trade sexual favors for patronage.

14. The next time we see her she is accompanying a wealthy man into a hotel. Outside the man's wife is waiting to confront them. When she does so and refers to Helen as a "harlot," Helen begins to abuse her loudly, hitting her until the wife is dragged off. On top of the husband's sexual betrayal, Helen's actions represent a full-blown public degradation of the wife's status and position.

15. The term *419* is legal code in Nigeria for fraud; con men involved in fraud are known as "419ers" (see chapter 7).

16. I thank Philip Cartelli, a student in my class on African popular culture, for bringing this film to my attention.

17. Bereft of religious overtones, the same ideas are at work in *The Master*, where Dennis dresses up in a series of different costumes to try on identities for his frauds. In one classic scene, he is caught practicing in front of the mirror, saying "No, no, no. What you want me to do, Mr. Robinson, is against banking policy" over and over again, emphasizing different words and gestures, practicing various alternatives to make his fraud seem plausible. Clearly this fraud involves pretending to be a corrupt bank manager. For his first job, his boss gives him money to buy a smart business suit and a black leather suitcase for him to look like a rich importer. When they later embark on a new, more audacious fraud, the boss tells Dennis that "we have to take your profile up a bit so when the man sees you he will believe you have the money." Thereafter, Dennis is only seen wearing traditional Nigerian clothes, a beautiful pink *babban riga*. "It is all about perception and misdirection," the song on the soundtrack tells us. "This is the modern way of making money," the boss confides. When Dennis sells a trader fake battery acid, he tells him, "I thought I could do something good for my country." Here

the logic of tradition, development, and nationalism is useful only as a ploy to authenticate a con.

18. Later, after making the pact with the witch, Francis comes across a village friend while driving his new SUV. "Tell me, Francis," the friend asks. "How did you make it so big in so short a time?"

19. What Birgit Meyer (2004a) has argued for Ghana is equally true for Nigeria: the system of meaning and the tropes Pentecostalism uses have migrated from a specifically religious sphere to public culture more broadly. Franklin Ukah (2003) has similarly argued that in their stories about cults and ritual abuse, Nigerian films give concrete form to activities widely rumored to go on in the real world, and the appearance of the pastor at the end of the film driving out the forces of darkness reveals the explicit religious logic that animates them. In video stores, many of these films are shelved under the genre category, "Christian film," but many more, using very similar themes, fall under the general category of "drama." The negative portrayal of witchcraft, secret cults, and ritual abuse are elements that can appear in any genre, from comedies to thrillers. This bears out Meyer's assertion that even when seemingly divorced from any explicit Pentecostal base, the style of representation of magic and traditional religion has its roots in Pentecostal theology.

20. "Censors Board Wields the Big Stick," *This Day*, 16 November 2004; www.thisdayonline.com/archive/2001/11/28/20011128art02.html.

21. Alaba Ojomo, chairman of parliamentary committee on information and national orientation; Afrol News, www.afrol.com/articles/13938.

22. Tijani Ibraheem, interview with author, Kano city, 9 January 2001.

23. See A. Adamu 2005a, 2005b; Larkin 1997, 2004; and Adamu, Adamu, and Jibril 2004.

24. See Larkin 1997, 2004. There is a growing literature on the influence of Indian films in Africa. Emmanuel Obiechina (1971) makes some short but insightful comments on their influence on Onitsha market literature. Minou Fugelsang (1994) and Heike Behrend (1998) separately explore the influence of Indian film on gender in East Africa. More recently Isolde Brielmaier's (2003) study of popular photography in Kenya examines in detail how modes of lighting, posing, and narrative emotion derived from Indian film were incorporated into Kenyan studio photography. Paralleling this chapter, Abdalla Uba Adamu (forthcoming-a, forthcoming-b) has written on the influence of Indian film on Hausa home video. Gwenda Vander Steene's emerging research explores a similar situation in Senegal, where "Indophilia" has long been a part of public culture.

25. Bori spirit possession is one example. While undoubtedly a part of "Hausa culture," it is rejected and marginalized by Muslim reformers for being un-Islamic.

26. Hausa history, in fact, is marked by the emergence of revivalist religious movements that have come to prominence by attacking pagan or backsliding-

Muslim practices in the name of a more authentic Islam. The most famous example is the 1803 jihad that established the precolonial Hausa-Fulani state, the Sokoto Caliphate. The jihad was justified by the need to correct the religiously corrupt and syncretic practices of Hausa kings. These kings and many of their allies thought of themselves as Muslims but the reformist rhetoric of the caliphate leader, Usman ɗan Fodio, redefined them as pagans, and the power of his armies ensured that his definition prevailed. See Last 1967.

27. A. Adamu forthcoming-b is the most sustained look at the influence of Indian film on Hausa video. Basing his conclusions on a statistical study, Adamu argues that after *Wasila* the percentage of Hausa films that were musicals increased markedly even as the overall number of videos released continued to climb yearly.

28. There is now a broad literature on the breadth and variety of Hausa fiction (of which love is only one genre). See Y. Adamu 2002; Furniss 1996, 2005; Furniss, Buba, and Burgess 2004; and Whitsitt 2002.

29. Ali Nuhu, interview with author, Kano city, 25 January 2002.

30. See Elsaesser 1995; Gledhill 1987; Singer 2001; and Williams 1995.

31. Bawa Ishaq, interview with author, Kaduna city, 19 January 2002.

32. Ibid.

33. Ali Nuhu, interview with author, Kano city, 25 January 2002.

34. Garba Ibrahim, interview with author, Kaduna city, 19 January 2001.

35. Bashir Ɗan Muɗi, interview with author, Kano city, 26 January 2001.

36. Ado Ahmad, interview with author, Kano city, 28 June 1995.

37. Qasimo Jero, interview with author, Kaduna city, 20 January 2001.

38. Ado Abdullahi, interview with author, Kano city, 24 January 2001.

39. Tijani Ibraheem, interview with author, Kano city, 9 January 2001. And the training Ibraheem went through in television betrays the long shadow of colonial film units over postcolonial television production.

7 INFRASTRUCTURE OF PIRACY

1. Musa Na Sale, interview with author, Kano city, 17 August 1995.

2. This could be true, but there is likely an element of showmanship, too. In 1993, when distribution was still by video, I was told that films could arrive in Kano as little as seven days after their release in India. In 2002, I was told by the same distributor (but a different person) that the reason for the shift to VCDs was to increase speed and quality, and that the problem with videos was that they could take up to a month or more to be received from Dubai; interviews, June 1993, March 1995, January 2002.

3. Except, as Jonathan Haynes pointed out to me, through the taxing of blank cassettes.

4. This trend is confirmed by Indian film distributors, who told me their sales remained constant during the rise of Hausa film and that sales currently remain

strong. Certainly Indian films are still hugely popular among Hausa filmmakers and continue to be a source of inspiration, technical ideas, and narrative themes for Hausa film.

5. Ironically, when filmmakers from Kano traveled to Zamfara to shoot a film they were invited to the governor's mansion to meet Zamfara's first lady, a huge fan of Hausa film.

6. When it became a PLC they added "Please Light Candles."

7. For an interesting comparative example, see the trade in secondhand clothing analyzed in K. Hansen 2000. Also, Gerald Lombardi's (1999) study of computer use in Brazil includes a fascinating example of the practice of obtaining telephone lines, the prerequisite for an on-line culture, and the huge informal (and illegal) market in brokering phone lines that feeds off of this infrastructural inadequacy.

8. Thanks to Andrew Apter for reminding me of this. This practice is common among musicians in many parts of Africa. The so-called Congotronics music of Konono No. 1, a Congolese band that plays traditional Bazombé spirit music, is a good example. The members of Konono No. 1 are migrants to Kinshasa who have electrified traditional music using homemade amplification fashioned from old car batteries. The result thrusts continual buzzing and distortion into the performance of the music itself.

9. Birgit Meyer reminded me that Willy Akuffo described this during a workshop organized by the International Study Commission of Media, Religion, and Culture, in Accra, Ghana, 19–27 May 2000.

10. James Ferguson (1999) makes an interesting but different argument on the role of "noise" in globalization. He focuses on the traffic in cultural meanings, arguing that cities are culturally "noisy" in that all sorts of forms of cultural flows clash and are available to urban dwellers. Ferguson's central question is "Which of the bits floating in the swirl of events does any given social actor 'get' in this semiotically noisy environment?" (208), rather than how noise might be a function of mediation itself.

11. Writing about the sexual relations between Hausa *'yan daudu* (men who act like women) and men in Saudi Arabia, Rudolf Gaudio (1997: 113) argues that when these 'yan daudu return from Saudi Arabia they parade their sophistication and cultural savoir-faire—part of which involves raving "about the creature comforts that Saudi Arabia [has] to offer: telephones, air conditioning, a constant supply of electricity and running water. *'Ba abin da babu'* they would say, 'there's nothing that isn't there.'" See also O'Brien 2000.

CONCLUSION

1. NAK/SNP/11/325M/1921; see Rogers 1994.
2. NAK/MOI/100 BCNN, Programme Material and Advisory Panel.
3. For other examples of attention to this sort of materiality, see Spitulnik 2002.

4. The body of work on this is now huge. For a limited introduction, see Akyeampong and Ambler 2002; Askew 2002; Barber 1997; Barber 2003; Buckley 2000–2001; Diawara 2002; Enwezor 2001; Enwezor et al. 2003; Fair 2001; Ferguson 1999; Gondola 1996, 1999; Martin 1995; Mustafa 2002; Nixon 1994; Oguibe 2004; Wendl 2001; and B. White 2002, 2004.

5. For a materialist riposte to this, see Watts 2004.

6. This approach can be applied to the history of Kano. For example, in precolonial times Kano was an important node of the trans-Sudanic and trans-Saharan trade routes. This trade involved the maintenance of elaborate trading networks, the institution of Hausa as a trading lingua franca, the cultivation of Islam as a common bond connecting diverse ethnic groups, and so on. Colonial conquest and amalgamation into Nigeria reoriented the Kano economy away from the trans-Saharan trade to the mass production of crops for export to the world market. The building of the Lagos-Kano railway in 1911 decisively oriented Kano south to Lagos, and as crops went south, traveling north on the same railways were Southern Christian migrants coming to staff the new European companies and colonial bureaucracies. With them came new modes of education, new forms of popular culture, commitments to transnational communities wholly independent of Islam, and a world of cultural and religious differences, whose tensions mark Nigeria's political economy to this day.

Bibliography

Abubakar, Ameen Al-Deen

2004 Hausa Society and Entertainment. In *Hausa Home Videos: Technology, Economy and Society*, ed. Abdalla Uba Adamu, Yusuf M. Adamu, and Umar Faruk Jibril. Pp. 255–59. Kano, Nigeria: Centre for Hausa Cultural Studies.

Abu-Lughod, Lila

2004 *Dramas of Nationhood: The Politics of Television in India*. Chicago: University of Chicago Press.

Adamu, Abdalla Uba

Forthcoming-a "The Song Remains the Same": The Hindi Cinema Factor in Hausa Video Film Soundtracks. In *Global Soundtracks: The Culture of World Film Music*, ed. Mark Slobin. Middletown, Conn.: Wesleyan University Press.

Forthcoming-b Media Parenting and Construction of Media Identities in Northern Nigerian Muslim Hausa Home Videos. In *The Media and the Construction of African Identities*, ed. John Middleton and Njogu Kimani. London: International African Institute/Twanzega Communications.

Adamu, Abdalla Uba, Yusuf M. Adamu, and Umar Faruk Jibril, eds.

2004 *Hausa Home Videos: Technology, Economy and Society*. Kano, Nigeria: Centre for Hausa Cultural Studies.

Bibliography

Adamu, Yusuf M.

2002 Between the Word and the Screen: A Historical Perspective on the Hausa Literary Movement and the Home Video Invasion. *Journal of African Cultural Studies* 15(2): 203–13.

Adas, Michael

1989 *Machines as the Measure of Men: Science, Technology and Ideologies of Western Dominance*. Ithaca, N.Y.: Cornell University Press.

Adejunmobi, Moradewun

2002 English and the Audience of an African Popular Culture: The Case of Nigerian Video Film. *Cultural Critique* 50: 74–103.

Ado-Kurawa, Ibrahim

2004 Hausa Films: Negotiating Social Practice. In *Hausa Home Videos: Technology, Economy and Society*, ed. Abdalla Uba Adamu, Yusuf M. Adamu, and Umar Faruk Jibril. Pp. 111–18. Kano, Nigeria: Centre for Hausa Cultural Studies.

Ahmad, S. B.

2004 From Oral to Visual: The Adaptation of Daskin-Da-Ridi to Home Video. In *Hausa Home Videos: Technology, Economy and Society*, ed. Abdalla Uba Adamu, Yusuf M. Adamu, and Umar Faruk Jibril. Pp. 154–61. Kano, Nigeria: Centre for Hausa Cultural Studies.

Akyeampong, Emmanuel, and Charles Ambler, eds.

2002 Leisure in African History, an Introduction. *International Journal of African Historical Studies* 35(1): 1–16.

Allyn, David Edley

1976 The Sabon Gari System in Northern Nigeria. PhD diss., University of California, Los Angeles.

Ambler, Charles

2001 Popular Films and Colonial Audiences: The Movies in Northern Nigeria. *American Historical Review* 106(1): 81–105.

Amladi, Parag

1997 New Apprehensions: The Ambivalence of Modernity in Early Indian Cinema, 1913–1939. PhD diss., New York University.

Andriopoulos, Stefan

2005 Psychic Television. *Critical Inquiry* 31: 618–37.

2006 The Terror of Reproduction: Early Cinema's Ghostly Doubles and the Rights to One's Own Image. *New German Critique* 99: 151–70.

Appadurai, Arjun

1996 *Modernity at Large: Cultural Dimensions of Globalization*. Minneapolis: University of Minnesota Press.

Apter, Andrew

1999 IBB = 419: Nigerian Democracy and the Politics of Illusion. In *Civil Society and the Political Imagination in Africa: Critical Perspectives*, ed. John L.

Comaroff and Jean Comaroff. Pp. 267–307. Chicago: University of Chicago Press.
2002 On Imperial Spectacle: The Dialectics of Seeing in Colonial Nigeria. *Comparative Studies in Society and History* 44(3): 564–96.
2005 *The Pan-African Nation: Oil and the Spectacle of Culture in Nigeria*. Chicago: University of Chicago Press.

Apter, David E.
1965 *The Politics of Modernization*. Chicago: University of Chicago Press.

Asad, Talal
1993 *Genealogies of Religion: Discipline and Reasons of Power in Christianity and Islam*. Baltimore: Johns Hopkins University Press.

Ashforth, Adam
2005 *Witchcraft, Violence and Democracy in South Africa*. Chicago: University of Chicago Press.

Askew, Kelly
2002 *Performing the Nation: Swahili Music and Cultural Politics in Tanzania*. Chicago: University of Chicago Press.

Baeta, A. R.
1948 General Discussion: Gold Coast. In *The Film in Colonial Development: A Report of a Conference*. Pp. 38–39 London: British Film Institute.

Bakhtin, Mikhail
1984 *Rabelais and His World*. Bloomington: Indiana University Press.

Barber, Karin
1997 Preliminary Notes on the Audience in Africa. *Africa* 67(3): 349–62.
2003 *The Generation of Plays: Yoruba Popular Life in Theater*. Bloomington: Indiana University Press.

Barkindo, Bawuro M.
1993 Growing Islamism in Kano City since 1970: Causes, Forms and Implications. In *Muslim Identity and Social Change in Sub-Saharan Africa*, ed. Louis Brenner. Pp. 91–105. Bloomington: Indiana University Press.

Barlet, Olivier
2000 *African Cinemas: Decolonising the Gaze*. London: Zed.

Barnouw, Eric, and S. Krishnaswamy
1980 *Indian Film*. Oxford: Oxford University Press.

Barthes, Roland
1980 Upon Leaving the Movie Theater. In *Apparatus, Cinematographic Apparatus: Selected Writings*, ed. Theresa Hak Kyung Cha. Pp. 1–6. New York: Tanam.

Bayart, Jean-François, Stephen Ellis, and Beatrice Hibou, eds.
1999 *The Criminalization of the State in Africa*. Oxford: James Currey.

Behrend, Heike
1998 Love à la Hollywood and Bombay in Kenyan Studio Photography. *Paideuma* 44: 139–53.

2003 "Call and Kill": Zur Verzauberung und Entzauberung westlicher technischer Medin in Afrika. In *Signale der Störung*, ed. Erhard Schüttpelz and Albert Kümmel. Pp. 287–300. Cologne: Fink.
2005 Zur Medialisierung okkulter Mächte: Geistmedien und Medien der Geister. In *Gespenster: Erscheinungen—Medien—Theorien*, ed. Moritz Bassler, Bettina Gruber, and Martina Wagner-Egelhaaf. Pp. 201–11. Würzburg, Germany: Königshausen und Neumann.

Beidelman, T. O.
1993 *Moral Imagination in Kaguru Modes of Thought*. Washington, D.C.: Smithsonian Institution Press.

Bell, H. Hesketh
1911 Recent Progress in Northern Nigeria. *Journal of the African Society* 10(40): 377–91.

Beller, Jonathan L.
1994 Cinema, Capital of the Twentieth Century. *Postmodern Culture* 4(3). postmodern_culture/v004/4.3/beller.html.

Benjamin, Walter
1978 The Work of Art in the Age of Mechanical Reproduction. In *Illuminations*. Pp. 217–51. New York: Schocken.
1999 *The Arcades Project*. Cambridge, Mass.: Harvard University Press.

Brenner, Louis, and Murray Last
1985 The Role of Language in West African Islam. *Africa* 55(4): 432–46.

Brielmaier, Isolde
2003 Picture Taking and the Production of Urban Identities on the Kenyan Coast. PhD diss., Columbia University.

Brooks, Peter
1985 *The Melodramatic Imagination: Balzac, Henry James, Melodrama and the Mode of Excess*. New York: Columbia University Press.

Buckley, Liam
2000–2001 Gambian Studio Photography. *Visual Anthropology Review* 16(2): 71–91.

Buck-Morss, Susan
1989 *The Dialectics of Seeing: Walter Benjamin and the Arcades Project*. Cambridge, Mass.: MIT Press.

Burke, Timothy
1996 *Lifebuoy Men, Lux Women: Commodification, Consumption and Cleanliness in Modern Zimbabwe*. Durham: Duke University Press.
2002 Our Mosquitoes Are Not So Big: Images and Modernity in Zimbabwe. In *Images and Empires: Visuality in Colonial and Postcolonial Africa*, ed. Paul S. Landau and Deborah Kaspin. Pp. 41–55. Berkeley: University of California Press.

Burns, James
2000 Watching Africans Watch Films: Theories of Spectatorship in British

Colonial Africa. *Historical Journal of Film, Radio and Television* 20(2): 197–211.
2002 *Flickering Shadows: Cinema and Identity in Colonial Zimbabwe*. Athens: Ohio University Press.
Callaway, Barbara.
1987 *Muslim Women in Nigeria: Tradition and Change*. Syracuse: Syracuse University Press.
Carbine, Mary
1990 "The Finest outside the Loop": Motion Picture Exhibition in Chicago's Black Metropolis, 1905–1928. *Camera Obscura* 23: 9–41.
Cartwright, Lisa
1995 *Screening the Body: Tracing Medicine's Visual Culture*. Minneapolis: University of Minnesota Press.
Cary, Joyce
1939 *Mr. Johnson*. New York: New Directions.
Casey, Conerley
1997 Medicines for Madness: Suffering, Disability and the Identification of Enemies in Northern Nigeria. PhD diss., University of California, Los Angeles.
1998 Suffering and the Identification of Enemies. *Political and Legal Anthropological Review* 21(1): 1–25.
2002 "States of Emergency": Islam, Youth Gangs and the Politically Unseeable. Paper presented to the Sawyer Seminar, Emory University, 26 September.
Castells, Manuel
1996 *The Rise of the Network Society*. Oxford: Blackwell.
1998 *The Information Age: Economy, Society and Culture*. Vol. 3, *End of the Millennium*. Oxford: Blackwell.
Cham, Mbye, and Imruh Bakari, eds.
1996 *African Experiences of Cinema*. London: BFI.
Chanan, Michael
1996 [1982]. *The Dream That Kicks: The Prehistory and Early Years of Cinema Entertainment in Britain*. London: Routledge.
Charney, Leo, and Vanessa Schwartz, eds.
1996 *Cinema and the Invention of Modern Life*. Berkeley: University of California Press.
Chatterjee, Partha
1993 *The Nation and Its Fragments: Colonial and Postcolonial Histories*. New York: Oxford University Press.
Chernoff, John
2003 *Hustling Is Not Stealing: Stories of an African Bar Girl*. Chicago: University of Chicago Press.
Chesterman, John, and Andy Lipman
1988 *The Electronic Pirates: DIY Crimes of the Century*. London: Routledge.

Cohn, Bernard

1983 Representing Authority in Victorian India. In *The Invention of Tradition*, ed. Eric Hobsbawm and Terence Ranger. Pp. 165–209. Cambridge: Cambridge University Press.

Comaroff, Jean, and John Comaroff

1999 Occult Economies and the Violence of Abstraction: Notes from the South African Postcolony. *American Ethnologist* 26(2): 279–303.

2000 Millennial Capitalism: First Thoughts on a Second Coming. *Public Culture* 12(2): 291–343.

Coombe, Rosemary J.

1998 *The Cultural Life of Intellectual Properties: Authorship, Appropriation and the Law*. Durham: Duke University Press.

Corten, André, and Ruth Marshall-Fratani, eds.

2002 *Between Babel and Pentecost: Transnational Pentecostalism in Latin America and Africa*. Bloomington: Indiana University Press.

Cosander, Roland, André Gaudreault, and Tom Gunning

1992 *Une invention du diable? Cinéma des premiers temps et religion* [An Invention of the Devil? Religion and Early Cinema]. Québec City: University of Laval Press.

Crary, Jonathan

2000 *Suspensions of Perception: Attention, Spectacle and Modern Culture*. Cambridge, Mass.: MIT Press.

Crocker, W. R.

1937 *Nigeria: A Critique of British Colonial Administration*. London: Allen and Unwin.

1949 *Self-Government for the Colonies*. London: Allen and Unwin.

Crowder, Michael

1964 Indirect Rule French and British Style. *Africa* 34 (3): 191–205.

Cubitt, Sean

2005 *The Cinema Effect*. Cambridge, Mass.: MIT Press.

Curtin, Philip D.

1992 Medical Knowledge and Urban Planning in Colonial Tropical Africa. In *The Social Basis of Health and Healing in Africa*, ed. Steven Feierman and John M. Janzen. Pp. 235–55. Berkeley: University of California Press.

Dakata, Zulkifi A. G.

2004 Alienation of Culture: A Menace Posed by Hausa Home Video. In *Hausa Home Videos: Technology, Economy and Society*, ed. Abdalla Uba Adamu, Yusuf M. Adamu, and Umar Faruk Jibril. Pp. 250–54. Kano, Nigeria: Centre for Hausa Cultural Studies.

Ɗan Asabe, Abdulkarim Umar

1991 Yandaba: The "Terrorists" of Kano Metropolitan? *Kano Studies* Special Issue: Youth and Health in Kano Today 85–112.

De Boeck, Filip, with Marie Francoise-Plissart
2006 *Kinshasa: Tales of the Invisible City*. Antwerp, Belgium: Ludion.
de Certeau, Michel
1986 *The Practice of Everyday Life*. Berkeley: University of California Press.
Diawara, Manthia
1992 *African Cinema: Politics and Culture*. Bloomington: Indiana University Press.
2002 1960s in Bamako: Malick Sidibe and James Brown. *Black Renaissance/ Renaissance Noire* 4: 59–63.
Doane, Mary Ann
2002 *The Emergence of Cinematic Time: Modernity, Contingency and the Archive*. Cambridge, Mass.: Harvard University Press.
Dodge, Toby
2003 *Inventing Iraq: The Failure of Nation Building and a History Denied*. New York: Columbia University Press.
Elsaesser, Thomas
1995 Tales of Sound and Fury: Observations on the Family Melodrama. In *Film Genre Reader* 2, ed. Barry Keith Grant. Pp. 350–80. Austin: University of Texas Press.
Elsaesser, Thomas, with Adam Barker, eds.
1990 *Early Cinema: Space, Frame, Narrative*. London: BFI.
Enwezor, Okwui
2001 Lagos in the Culture of Twentieth-Century Modernity. In *Century City: Art and Culture in the Modern Metropolis*, ed. Iwona Blazwick. Pp. 44–57. London: Tate Gallery.
Enwezor, Okwui, Carlos Basualdo, Uta Meta Bauer, Susanne Ghez, Sarat Maharaj, Mark Nash, and Octavio Zaya, eds.
2003 *Under Siege: Four African Cities—Freetown, Johannesburg, Kinshasa, Lagos*. Ostfildern, Germany: Hatje Cantz.
Fair, Laura
2001 *Pastimes and Politics: Culture, Community and Identity in Post-abolition Urban Zanzibar, 1890–1945*. Athens: Ohio University Press.
Ferguson, James
1999 *Expectations of Modernity: Myths and Meanings of Urban Life on the Zambian Copperbelt*. Berkeley: University of California Press.
Fika, Adamu Mohammed
1978 *Kano Civil War and British Over-rule, 1882–1940*. Oxford: Oxford University Press.
Fisiy, Cyprian F., and Peter Geschiere
1990 Judges and Witches, or How Is the State to Deal with Witchcraft? Examples from Southeast Cameroon. *Cahiers d'études africaines* 30(2): 135–56.

Flood, Finbarr Barry
2002 Between Cult and Culture: Bamiyan, Islamic Iconoclasm and the Museum—Afghanistan. *Art Bulletin* 84(4): 641–59.
Foot, Sir Hugh
1964 *A Start in Freedom*. New York: Harper and Row.
Foucault, Michel
1972 *The Archaeology of Knowledge*. New York: Pantheon.
1991 Governmentality. In *The Foucault Effect: Studies in Governmentality*, ed. Graham Burchell, Colin Gordon, and Peter Miller. Pp. 87–104. Chicago: University of Chicago Press.
Friedberg, Anne
1993 *Window Shopping: Cinema and the Postmodern*. Berkeley: University of California Press.
Frishman, Alan
1977 The Spatial Growth and Residential Patterns of Kano, Nigeria. PhD diss., Northwestern University.
Fugelsang, Minou
1994 *Veils and Videos: Female Youth Culture on the Kenyan Coast*. Stockholm: Stockholm Studies in Social Anthropology.
Furniss, Graham
1996 *Poetry, Prose and Popular Culture in Hausa*. Edinburgh: Edinburgh University Press.
2005 Video and the Hausa Novella in Nigeria. *Social Identities* 11(2): 89–112.
Furniss, Graham, Malami Buba, and William Burgess
2004 *Bibliography of Hausa Popular Fiction, 1987–2002*. Cologne: Rüdiger Köppe.
Gailey, Harry A.
1974 *Sir Donald Cameron, Colonial Governor*. Stanford, Calif.: Stanford University Press.
Garcia, David, and Geert Lovink
2001 The ABC of Tactical Media. In *The Public Domain: Sarai Reader 01*, ed. Sarai, the New Media Collective, and the Society for Old and New Media. Pp. 90–93. Delhi: Sarai, the New Media Initiative.
Gaudio, Rudolf P.
1997 Men Who Talk Like Women: Language, Gender and Sexuality in Hausa Muslim Society. PhD diss., Stanford University.
2005 Male Lesbians and Other Queer Notions in Hausa. In *Readings in African Gender*. Andrea Cornwall, ed. Pp. 47–59. Oxford: James Currey.
Geschiere, Peter
1997 *The Modernity of Witchcraft: Politics and the Occult in Postcolonial Africa*. Charlottesville: University of Virginia Press.
Gifford, Paul
2004 *Ghana's New Christianity: Pentecostalism in a Globalizing Economy*. London: Hurst.

Gilsenan, Michael
1992 *Recognizing Islam: Religion and Society in the Modern Middle East*. London: I. B. Tauris.
Ginsburg, Faye D.
1994 Embedded Aesthetics: Creating a Discursive Space for Indigenous Media. *Cultural Anthropology*. 9(3): 365–382.
2002 Screen Memories: Resignifying the Traditional in Indigenous Media. In *Media Worlds: Anthropology on New Terrain*, ed. Faye D. Ginsburg, Lila Abu-Lughod, and Brian Larkin. Pp. 39–57. Berkeley: University of California Press.
Girouard, Percy
1908 The Development of Northern Nigeria. *Journal of the Royal African Society* 7(28): 331–37.
Gitelman, Lisa, and Geoffrey B. Pingree, eds.
2003 *New Media 1740–1915*. Cambridge, Mass.: MIT Press.
Givanni, June
2001 *Symbolic Narratives/African Cinema: Audiences, Theory and the Moving Image*. London: BFI.
Gledhill, Christine
1987 *Home Is Where the Heart Is: Studies in Melodrama and the Woman's Film*. London: BFI.
Gondola, Didier
Forthcoming Tropical Cowboys: Westerns, Violence and Masculinity among the Young Bills of Kinshasa. *Afrique et Histoire*.
1996 Popular Music, Urban Society and Changing Gender Relations in Kinshasa. In *Gendered Encounters: Challenging Cultural Boundaries and Social Hierarchies in Africa*, ed. Maria Grosz-Nagate and Momori H. Kokole. Pp. 65–84. New York: Routledge.
1999 Dream and Drama: The Search for Elegance amongst Congolese Youth. *African Studies Review* 42(1): 23–48.
Graham, Stephen, and Simon Marvin
1996 *Telecommunications and the City: Electronic Spaces, Urban Places*. London: Routledge.
2001 *Splintering Urbanism: Networked Infrastructures, Technological Mobilities and the Urban Condition*. London: Routledge.
Griffiths, Alison
2001 *Wondrous Difference: Cinema, Anthropology and Turn of the Century Visual Culture*. New York: Columbia University Press.
Gumi, Sheikh Abubakar Mahmoud, with Ismaila A. Tsiga
1992 *Where I Stand*. Ibadan, Nigeria: Spectrum.
Gunning, Tom
1986 The Cinema of Attraction: Early Film, Its Spectator and the Avant Garde. *Wide Angle* 8(3–4): 63–70.

1994 An Aesthetic of Astonishment: Early Film and the (In)credulous Spectator. In *Viewing Positions: Ways of Seeing Films*, ed. Linda Williams. Pp. 114–34. New Brunswick, N.J.: Rutgers University Press.

1997 In Your Face: Physiognomy, Photography, and the Gnostic Mission of Early Film. *Modernism/Modernity* 4(1): 1–29.

2004 "Now You See It, Now You Don't": The Temporality of the Cinema of Attractions. In *The Silent Cinema Reader*, ed. Lee Grieveson and Peter Kramer. Pp. 41–50. London: Routledge.

Hannerz, Ulf

1987 The World in Creolisation. *Africa* 57: 546–59.

Hansen, Karin Tranberg

2000 *Salaula: The World of Second-Hand Clothing and Zambia*. Chicago: University of Chicago Press.

Hansen, Miriam

1991 *Babel and Beyond: Spectatorship in Silent American Films*. Cambridge, Mass.: Harvard University Press.

1995 Early Cinema, Late Cinema: Permutations of the Public Sphere. In *Viewing Positions: Ways of Seeing Film*, ed. Linda Williams. Pp. 134–52. New Brunswick, N.J.: Rutgers University Press.

1997 Introduction to *Theory of Film*, by Siegfried Kracauer. Pp. vii–xlvii. Princeton: Princeton University Press.

2000 The Mass Production of the Senses: Classical Cinema as Vernacular Modernism. In *Reinventing Film Studies*, ed. Christine Gledhill and Linda Williams. Pp. 332–350. New York: Hodder and Stoughton.

Harper, Philip

1999 *Private Affairs: Critical Ventures in the Culture of Social Relations*. New York: New York University Press.

Harvey, David

1989 *The Condition of Postmodernity: An Enquiry into the Origins of Cultural Change*. Oxford: Basil Blackwell.

2000 *Spaces of Hope*. Berkeley: University of California Press.

Haynes, Jonathan

1995 Nigerian Cinema: Structural Adjustments. *Research in African Literatures* 26(3): 97–119.

2005 Nollywood: What's in a Name? *Guardian*. 3 July. Available on-line at www.odili.net/news/source/2005/jul/3/49.html.

Haynes, Jonathan, ed.

2000 *Nigerian Video Films*. Athens: Ohio University Press.

Hecht, David, and Maliqalim Simone

1994 *Invisible Governance: The Art of African Micropolitics*. New York: Autonomedia.

Heussler, Robert

1968 *The British in Northern Nigeria*. New York: Oxford University Press.

Hibou, Béatrice

1999 The "Social Capital" of the State as an Agent of Deception. In *The Criminalization of the State in Africa*, ed. Jean-François Bayart, Stephen Ellis, and Béatrice Hibou. Pp. 69–113. Oxford: James Currey.

Himpele, Jeffrey D.

1996 Film Distribution as Media: Mapping Difference in the Bolivian Cinemascape. *Visual Anthropology Review* 12(1): 47–66.

Hirschkind, Charles

2006 *The Ethical Soundscape: Cassette Sermons and Islamic Counterpublics*. New York: Columbia University Press.

Hughes, Stephen P.

1996 The Pre-Phalke Era in South India: Reflections on the Formation of Film Audiences in Madras. *South Indian Studies* 2: 161–204.

2006 House Full: Silent Film Exhibition and Audiences in South India. *Indian Economic and Social History Review* 43(1): 31–62.

Huxley, Julian

1936 *Africa View*. London: Chatto and Windus.

Idahosa, Paul, and Robert Shenton

2005 The Turn toward the Local: Present and Past Development Policy in Africa. Online at www.valt.helsinki.fi/kmi/Tutkimus/Sal/Idahosa%20&%20Shenton.htm. 21 September.

Jaekel, Francis

1997 *The History of the Nigerian Railway*. Vol. 2, *Networks and Infrastructures*. Ibidan, Nigeria: Spectrum.

Jaikumar, Priya

2005 *Cinema at the End of Empire: A Politics of Transition in Britain and India*. Durham: Duke University Press.

Jameson, Frederic

1991 *Postmodernism, or, The Cultural Logic of Late Capitalism*. Durham: Duke University Press.

Johns, Adrian

1998 *Nature of the Book: Print and Knowledge in the Making*. Chicago: University of Chicago Press.

Joyce, Patrick

2003 *The Rule of Freedom: Liberalism and the Modern City*. London: Verso.

Kane, Ousmane

2003 *Muslim Modernity in Postcolonial Nigeria: A Study of the Society for the Removal of Innovation and Reinstatement of Tradition*. Leiden: Brill.

Kano Film Industry Operators

n.d. Islamization of the Film Industry. Memorandum Submitted to the Sharia Committee of the Kano State Government. 13 July 2000.

Kant, Immanuel

1952 *Critique of Judgment*. Trans. James Creed Meredith. Oxford: Clarendon.

1987 *Critique of Judgment*. Trans. Wener S. Pluhar. Indianapolis: Hackett Publishing.

Kaur, Raminder, and Ajay J. Sinha

2005 *Bollyworld: Popular Indian Cinema through a Transnational Lens*. New Delhi: Sage.

Keane, Webb

2001 Money Is No Object: Materiality, Desire and Modernity in an Indonesian Society. In *The Empire of Things: Regimes of Value and Material Culture*, ed. Fred Myers. Pp. 65–90. School of American Research Advanced Seminar Series. Santa Fe: SAR Press.

2005 Signs Are Not the Garb of Meaning: The Social Analysis of Material Things. In *Materiality*, ed. Daniel Miller. Pp. 183–205. Durham: Duke University Press.

Kern, Stephen

1983 *The Culture of Time and Space, 1880–1918*. Cambridge, Mass.: Harvard University Press.

Kirby, Lynne

1997 *Parallel Tracks: The Railroad and Silent Cinema*. Durham: Duke University Press.

Kirk-Greene, A. H. M.

1970 Introduction to *Political Memoranda: Revision of Instructions to Political Officers on Subjects Chiefly Political and Administrative*. Pp. v–xxi. London: Frank Cass.

1984 Canada in Africa: Sir Percy Girouard, Neglected Colonial Governor. *African Affairs* 83(33): 207–39.

Kittler, Friedrich

1994 Unconditional Surrender. In, *Materialities of Communication*. Hans Ulrich Gumbrecht and K. Ludwig Pfeiffer eds. Pp. 319–34. Stanford: Stanford University Press.

1999 *Gramophone, Film, Typewriter*. Trans. Geoffrey Winthrop-Young and Michael Wautz. Stanford, Calif.: Stanford University Press.

Koolhaas, Rem, ed.

2001 *Mutations: Harvard Project on the City*. New York: Actar.

Kracauer, Siegfried

1947 *From Caligari to Hitler: A Psychological History of the German Film*. Princeton: Princeton University Press.

1952a Appeals to the Near and Middle East: Implications of the Communications Studies along the Soviet Periphery. Report prepared for the Bureau of Applied Social Research, Columbia University, May.

1952b The Challenge of Qualitative Content Analysis. *Public Opinion Quarterly* 16(4): 631–42.

1995 *The Mass Ornament: Weimar Essays*. Trans. Thomas Y. Levin. Cambridge, Mass.: Harvard University Press.

1997 [1960] *Theory of Film: The Redemption of Physical Reality*. Introduction by Miriam Bratu Hansen. Princeton: Princeton University Press.

Kracauer, Siegfried, and Paul L. Berkman

1954 *Satellite Mentality: Political Attitudes and Propaganda Susceptibilities of Non-Communists in Hungary, Poland, and Czechoslovakia*. New York: F. A. Praeger.

Krings, Matthias

2006 Muslim Martyrs and Pagan Vampires. *Postscripts: The Journal of Sacred Texts and Contemporary Worlds* 1(2–3): 183–205.

Kuhn, Annette

1988 *Cinema, Censorship and Sexuality, 1909–1925*. London: Routledge.

Kukah, Matthew Hassan

1993 *Religion, Politics, and Power in Northern Nigeria*. Ibadan: Spectrum Books.

Ladele, Olu, V. Olufemi Adefela, and Olu Lasekan

1979 *History of the Nigerian Broadcasting Corporation*. Ibadan, Nigeria: Ibadan University Press.

Landau, Paul

1994 The Illumination of Christ in the Kalahari Desert. *Representations* 45: 26–40.

Larkin, Brian

1997 Indian Films and Nigerian Lovers: Media and the Creation of Parallel Modernities. *Africa* 67(3): 406–40.

1998–99 Introduction: Media and the Design for Modern Living. *Visual Anthropology Review* 14(2): 11–13.

2004 Bandiri Music, Globalization and Urban Experience in Nigeria. *Social Text* 81 (22.4): 91–112.

Larkin, Brian, and Birgit Meyer

2006 Pentecostalism, Islam and Culture. New Religious Movements in West Africa. In *Themes in West African History*. Emmanuel Akyeampong ed. Pp. 286–312. Oxford: James Currey.

Last, Murray

1967 *The Sokoto Caliphate*. New York: Humanities Press.

Latour, Bruno

1993 *We Have Never Been Modern*. Trans. Catherine Porter. Cambridge, Mass.: Harvard University Press.

Launay, Robert, and Benjamin F. Soares

1999 The Formation of an "Islamic Sphere" in French Colonial West Africa. *Economy and Society* 28(4): 497–519.

Lefebvre, Henri

1991 *The Production of Space*. Trans. D. N. Smith. Oxford: Blackwell.

Lerner, Daniel

1958a *The Passing of Traditional Society: Modernizing the Middle East*. New York: Free Press.

1958b Introduction. Special Issue in Attitude Research in Modernizing Areas. *Public Opinion Quarterly* 1958 22(3): 217–22.

Levin, T. Y., and Michael von der Lin

1994 Elements of a Radio Theory: Adorno and the Princeton Radio Project. *Musical Quarterly* 78(2): 316–24.

Loimeier, Roman

1997 *Islamic Reform and Political Change in Northern Nigeria*. Evanston, Ill.: Northwestern University Press.

Lombardi, Gerald S.

1999 Computer Networks, Social Networks and the Future of Brazil. PhD diss., New York University.

Lopez, Ana M.

2000 Early Cinema and Modernity in Latin America. *Cinema Journal* 40(1): 48–78.

Löwenthal, Leo

1991 As I Remember Friedel. *New German Critique* 54: 5–17.

Lugard, F. D.

1922 *The Dual Mandate in British Tropical Africa*. London: W. Blackwood and Sons.

Lyotard, Jean-François

1994 *Lessons on the Analytic of the Sublime*. Trans. Elizabeth Rottenberg. Stanford, Calif.: Stanford University Press.

MacGaffey, Janet, and Rémy Bazenguissa-Ganga

2000 *Congo-Paris: Transnational Traders of the Margins of the Law*. African Issues. Oxford: International African Institute in association with James Currey.

Maddison, John

1948 Le cinéma et l'information mentale des peuples primitives (Notes sur le travaux du Colonial Film Unit du Gouvernement Grande Britannique). *Revue internationale de filmologie* 1(3–4): 305–10.

Mahmood, Saba

2004 *Politics of Piety: The Islamic Revival and the Feminist Subject*. Princeton: Princeton University Press.

Mamdani, Mahmood

1996 *Citizen and Subject: Contemporary Africa and the Legacy of Late Colonialism*. Princeton: Princeton University Press.

Mankekar, Purnima

1999 *Screening Culture, Viewing Politics: An Ethnography of Television, Womanhood and Nation in Postcolonial India*. Durham: Duke University Press.

Manovich, Lev

2002 The Poetics of Augmented Space: Learning from Prada. Online at www.manovich.net.

Marshall-Fratani, Ruth

2001 Mediating the Global and Local in Nigerian Pentecostalism. In *Between Babel and Pentecost: Transnational Pentecostalism in Africa and Latin America,* ed. André Corten and Ruth Marshall-Fratani. Pp. 80–105. Bloomington: Indiana University Press.

Martin, Phyllis

1995 *Leisure and Society in Colonial Brazzaville.* Cambridge: Cambridge University Press.

Marx, Karl

1990 *Capital,* vol. 1. Trans. Ben Fowkes. London: Penguin.

Masquelier, Adeline

1992 Encounter with a Road Siren: Machines, Bodies, and Commodities in the Imagination of a Mawri Healer. *Visual Anthropology Review* 8(1): 56–69.

1993 Narratives of Power, Images of Wealth: The Ritual Economy of *Bori* in the Market. In *Modernity and Its Malcontents: Ritual and Power in Postcolonial Africa,* ed. Jean Comaroff and John L. Comaroff. Pp. 3–33. Chicago: University of Chicago Press.

2000 Of Headhunters and Cannibals: Migrancy, Labor, and Consumption in the Mawri Imagination. *Cultural Anthropology* 15(1): 84–126.

2002 Road Mythographies: Space, Mobility, and the Historical Imagination in Postcolonial Niger. *American Ethnologist* 29(4): 829–56.

Mattelart, Armand

1996 *The Invention of Communication.* Trans. Susan Emmanuel. Minneapolis: University of Minnesota Press.

2000 *Networking the World, 1794–2000.* Minneapolis: University of Minnesota Press.

Mbembe, Achille

2001 *On the Postcolony.* Berkeley: University of California Press.

Mbembe, Achille, and Sarah Nuttall

2004 Writing the World from an African Metropolis. *Public Culture* 16(3): 347–72.

Mbembe, Achille, and Janet Roitman

1995 Figures of the Subject in Times of Crisis. *Public Culture* 7: 323–52.

McLagan, Meg

2002 Spectacles of Difference: Cultural Activism and the Mass Mediation of Tibet. In *Media Worlds: Anthropology on New Terrain,* ed. Faye D. Ginsburg, Lila Abu-Lughod, and Brian Larkin. Pp. 39–57. Berkeley: University of California Press.

2003 Human Rights, Testimony, and Transnational Publicity. In *Scholar and Feminist Online* 2.1. Online at www.barnard.columbia.edu/sfonline/ps/mclagan.htm.

Mead, Margaret, and Rhoda Metraux, eds.

1953 *The Study of Culture at a Distance.* Chicago: University of Chicago Press.

Meyer, Birgit
2003a Visions of Blood, Sex and Money: Fantasy Spaces in Popular Ghanaian Cinema. *Visual Anthropology* 16: 15–41.
2003b Ghanaian Popular Cinema and the Magic in and of Film. In *Magic and Modernity: Interfaces of Revelation and Concealment*, ed. Birgit Meyer and Peter Pels. Pp. 200–222. Stanford, Calif.: Stanford University Press.
2004a Praise the Lord. . . . : Popular Cinema and Pentacostalite Style in Ghana's New Public Sphere. *American Ethnologist* 31(1): 92–110.
2004b Christianity in Africa: From Independent to Pentecostal-Charismatic Churches. *Annual Review of Anthropology* 33: 447–74.
2006 Impossible Representations: Pentecostalism, Vision and Video Technology in Ghana. In *Religion, Media and the Public Sphere*, ed. Birgit Meyer and Annelies Moors. Pp. 290–312. Bloomington: Indiana University Press.
Meyer, Birgit, and Peter Pels, eds.
2003 *Magic and Modernity: Interfaces of Revelation and Concealment*. Stanford, Calif.: Stanford University Press.
Miller, Daniel
1997 Why Some Things Matter. In *Material Cultures: Why Some Things Matter*, ed. Daniel Miller. Pp. 3–24. Chicago: University of Chicago Press.
Mitchell, Timothy
1991 *Colonising Egypt*. Berkeley: University of California Press.
2002 *Rule of Experts: Egypt, Techno-politics, Modernity*. Berkeley: University of California Press.
Moore, Henrietta, and Todd Sanders, eds.
2001 *Magical Interpretations, Material Realities: Modernity, Witchcraft and the Occult in Postcolonial Africa*. London: Routledge.
Moore, Rachel
2000 *Savage Theory: Cinema as Modern Magic*. Durham: Duke University Press.
Morel, E. D.
1968 *Nigeria: Its Peoples and Problems*. London: Frank Cass.
Morris, Rosalind C.
2000 *In the Place of Origins: Modernity and Its Mediums in Northern Thailand*. Durham: Duke University Press.
Morton-Williams, Peter
1954 *Cinema in Rural Nigeria: A Field Study of the Impact of Fundamental Education Films on Rural Audiences in Nigeria*. Ibadan: West African Institute of Social Research.
Mrázek, Rudolf
2002 *Engineers of Happy Land: Technology and Nationalism in a Colony*. Princeton: Princeton University Press.
Mustafa, Hudita
2002 Portraits of Modernity: Fashioning Selves in Senegalese Popular Photography. In *Images and Empires: Visuality in Colonial and Postcolonial Africa*,

ed. Paul S. Landau and Deborah D. Kaspin. Pp. 172–92. Berkeley: University of California Press.

Myers, Fred

2001 Introduction to *The Empire of Things: Regimes of Value and Material Culture*, ed. Fred Myers. Pp. 1–64. School of American Research Advanced Seminar Series. Santa Fe, N.M.: SAR Press.

2002 *Painting Culture: The Making of an Aboriginal High Art*. Durham: Duke University Press.

Nandy, Ashis

1995 *The Savage Freud and Other Essays on Possible and Retrievable Selves*. Princeton: Princeton University Press.

1998 Introduction to *The Secret Politics of Our Desires: Innocence and Culpability and Indian Popular Cinema*, ed. Ashis Nandy. Pp. 1–18. New Delhi: Zed.

Ngugi wa Thiong'o

1986 *Decolonising the Mind: The Politics of Language in African Literature*. London: Heinemann.

Nixon, Rob

1994 *Homelands, Harlem and Hollywood*. New York: Routledge.

Nye, David E.

1994 *American Technological Sublime*. Cambridge, Mass.: MIT Press.

Obiechina, Emmanuel

1971 *An African Popular Literature: A Study of Onitsha Market Pamphlets*. Cambridge: Cambridge University Press.

O'Brien, Susan

2000 Pilgrimage, Power and Identity: The Role of the *Hajj* in the Lives of Nigerian Hausa Bori Adepts. *Africa Today* 46 (3/4): 11–40.

Odunton, G. B.

1950 One Step Ahead. *Colonial Cinema* 8(2): 29–32.

Oguibe, Olu

2004 *The Culture Game*. Minneapolis: University of Minnesota Press.

Ogundele, Wole

2000 From Folk Opera to Soap Opera: Improvisations and Transformations in Yoruba Popular Theater. In *Nigerian Video Films*, ed. Jonathan Haynes. Pp. 89–130. Athens: Ohio University Press.

Okome, Onookome

2002 Writing the Anxious City. In *Under Siege: Four African Cities, Freetown, Johannesburg, Kisnshasa, Lagos*, ed. Okwui Enwezor, Carlos Basualdo, Uta Meta Bauer, Susanne Ghez, Sarat Maharaj, Mark Nash, and Octavio Zaya. Pp. 315–34. Ostfildern, Germany: Hatje Cantz.

Okome, Onookome, and Jonathan Haynes

1995 *Cinema and Social Change in West Africa*. Jos, Nigeria: Nigerian Film Corporation.

Olukoju, Ayodeji
2004 "Never Expect Power Always": Electricity Consumers' Response to Monopoly, Corruption and Inefficient Services in Nigeria. *African Affairs* 103: 51–71.
Oshin, Olasiji
1988 Colonial Railway Policy in Northern Nigeria, 1898–1914. *Odu* 35: 161–87.
Paden, Jon N.
1986 *Ahmadu Bello, Sardauna of Sokoto: Values and Leadership in Nigeria.* Zaria, Nigeria: Hudahuda.
Palmer, Sir Richmond
1934 Some Observations on Captain R. S. Rattray's Paper, "Present Tendencies of African Colonial Government." *Journal of the Royal African Society* 33(130): 37–48.
Pearson, George
1948 The Making of Films for Illiterates in Africa. In *The Film in Colonial Development: A Report of a Conference.* Pp. 22–27. London: British Film Institute.
1949 Health Education by Film. *Colonial Cinema* 7.1: 17–20.
1954 Commentary Huts *Colonial Cinema* 1954 12(2): 29–30.
Pemberton, John
Forthcoming The Ghost in the Machine. In *Photographies East: The Camera and Its Histories in East and Southeast Asia*, ed. Rosalind C. Morris. Durham: Duke University Press.
Perham, Margery
1937 *Native Administration in Nigeria.* London: Oxford University Press.
Pfaff, Françoise
2004 *Focus on African Films.* Bloomington: Indiana University Press.
Pines, Jim, and Paul Willemen, eds.
1990 *Questions of Third Cinema.* London: BFI.
Pinney, Christopher
2004 *Photos of the Gods: The Printed Image and Political Struggle in India.* Oxford: Oxford University Press.
Pittin, Renée
1979 Marriage and Alternative Strategies: Career Patterns of Hausa Women in Katsina City. PhD diss., University of London.
Powdermaker, Hortense, ed.
1953 *Mass Communications Seminar: Proceedings of an Interdisciplinary Seminar.* New York: Wenner-Gren Foundation for Anthropological Research.
Prakash, Gyan
1999 *Another Reason: Science and the Imagination of Modern India.* Princeton: Princeton University Press.
Rajadhyaksha, Ashis
1993 The Phalke Era: Conflict of Traditional Form and Modern Technology. In

Interrogating Modernity: Culture and Colonialism in India, ed. Tejaswini Niranjana, P. Sudhir, and Vivek Dhareshwar. Pp. 47–82. Delhi: Seagull.

Rajagopal, Arvind

2001 *Politics after Television: Hindu Nationalism and the Reshaping of the Public in India*. Cambridge: Cambridge University Press.

Ranger, Terence

1983 The Invention of Tradition in Colonial Africa. In *The Invention of Tradition*, ed. Eric Hobsbawm and Terence Ranger. Pp. 211–62. Cambridge: Cambridge University Press.

Ray, Gene

2004 Reading the Lisbon Earthquake: Adorno, Lyotard and the Contemporary Sublime. *Yale Journal of Criticism* 17(1): 1–18.

Rogers, Peter A.

1994 Hausa Blacksmiths and the Great Train Robbery: Iron Theft and the Moral Economy of Technological Change in Northern Nigeria, 1910–1935. In *Paths toward the Past: Essays in Honor of Jan Vansina*, ed. Robert W. Harms, Joseph C. Miller, David S. Newbury, and Michael D. Wagner. Pp. 371–91. Atlanta: African Studies Association Press.

Roitman, Janet

2005 *Fiscal Disobedience: An Anthropology of Economic Regulation in Central Africa*. Princeton: Princeton University Press.

Rostow, W. W.

1960 *The Stages of Economic Growth: A Non-Communist Manifesto*. Cambridge: Cambridge University Press.

Sassen, Saskia

1998 *Globalization and Its Discontents*. New York: New Press.

Sassen, Saskia, ed.

2002 *Global Networks, Linked Cities*. New York: Routledge.

Schivelbusch, Wolfgang

1986 *Railway Journey: The Industrialization of Time and Space in the Nineteenth Century*. Berkeley: University of California Press.

1995 *Disenchanted Night: The Industrialization of Lights in the Nineteenth Century*. Berkeley: University of California Press.

Schneider, Friedrich

2000 Dimensions of the Shadow Economy. *Independent Review* 5(1): 81–91.

Scott, David

1999 *Refashioning Futures*. Princeton: Princeton University Press.

Scott, James C.

1998 *Seeing Like a State: How Certain Schemes to Improve the Human Condition Have Failed*. New Haven, Conn.: Yale University Press.

Sellers, William

1948 Address to the British Kinematograph Society, 1947. *Colonial Cinema* 6(1): 9–11.

1953 Making Films in and for the Colonies. *Journal of the Royal Society of the Arts* 101: 829–37.

1954 Mobile Cinema Shows in Africa *Colonial Cinema* 1954 12(4): 75–81.

Shea, Philip J.

1982–85 How Indirect Was Indirect Rule? A Documentary Approach to an Administrative Problem. *Kano Studies* 2(3):154–63.

Shenton, Robert

1986 *The Development of Capitalism in Northern Nigeria*. Toronto: University of Toronto Press.

Simmel, Georg

1950 *The Sociology of Georg Simmel*. Trans. Kurt H. Wolf. Glencoe, Ill.: Free Press.

Simone, AbdouMaliq

1998 Urban Social Fields in Africa. *Social Text* 56: 71–89.

2001 On the Worlding of African Cities. *African Studies Review* 44(2): 15–41.

2004 *For the City Yet to Come: Changing African Life in Four Cities*. Durham: Duke University Press.

Singer, Ben

2001 *Melodrama and Modernity: Early Sensational Cinema and Its Contexts.* New York: Columbia University Press.

Singh, Bhrigupati

n.d. Aadamkhar Haseena and the Anthropology of the Moment. Unpublished MS.

Smith, John

1968 *Colonial Cadet in Nigeria*. Durham: Duke University Press.

Smyth, Rosaleen

1979 The Development of British Colonial Film Policy, 1927–1939, with Special Reference to East and Central Africa. *Journal of African History* 20(3): 437–50.

1983 Movies and Mandarins: The Official Film and British Colonial Africa. In *British Cinema History*, ed. James Curran and Vincent Porter. Pp. 129–43. Totowa, N.J.: Barnes and Noble.

1988 The British Colonial Film Unit and Sub-Saharan Africa, 1939–1945. *Historical Journal of Film, Radio and Television* 8(3): 285–98.

1992 The Postwar Career of the Colonial Film Unit in Africa, 1946–1955. *Historical Journal of Film, Radio and Television* 12(2): 163–77.

Spitulnik, Debra

1998–99 Mediated Modernities: Encounters with the Electronic in Zambia. *Visual Anthropology Review* 14(2): 63–84.

2002 Mobile Machines and Fluid Audiences: Rethinking Reception through Zambian Radio Culture. In *Media Worlds: Anthropology on New Terrain*, ed. Faye Ginsburg, Lila Abu-Lughod, and Brian Larkin. Pp. 227–54. Berkeley: University of California Press.

Stallybrass, Peter, and Allon White
1986 *The Poetics and Politics of Transgression*. London: Methuen.
Stoler, Ann
1992 "In Cold Blood": Hierarchies of Credibility and the Politics of Colonial Narratives. *Representations* 37: 151–89.
Sundaram, Ravi
1999 Recycling Modernity: Pirate Electronic Cultures in India. *Third Text* 47: 59–65.
Tahir, Ibrahim A.
1975 Scholars, Saints, and Capitalists in Kano, 1904–1974: The Pattern of Bourgeois Revolution in an Islamic Society. PhD diss., Cambridge University.
Taussig, Michael
1993 *Mimesis and Alterity: A Particular History of the Senses*. New York: Routledge.
Thompson, Elizabeth
2000 *Colonial Citizens: Republican Rights, Paternal Privilege, and Gender in French Syria and Lebanon*. New York: Columbia University Press.
Thwackway, Melissa
2003 *Africa Shoots Back: New Perspectives in Francophone African Film*. Oxford: James Currey.
Tibenderana, Peter K.
1988 The Irony of Indirect Rule in Sokoto Emirate, Northern Nigeria, 1903–1944. *African Studies Review* 31(1): 67–92.
Tsivian, Yuri
1994 *Early Cinema in Russia and Its Cultural Reception*. New York: Routledge.
Ubah, C. N.
1982 The Political Dilemma of Residential Segregation: The Example of Kano's Sabon Gari. *African Urban Studies* 14: 51–70.
Ukadike, Nwachukwu Frank
1994 *Black African Cinema*. Berkeley: University of California Press.
2000 Images of the "Reel" Thing: African Video-Films and the Emergence of a New Cultural Art. *Social Identities* 6(3): 243–61.
Ukah, Asonzeh F.-K.
2003 Advertising God: Nigerian Christian Video Films and the Power of Consumer Culture. *Journal of Religion in Africa* 33(2): 203–31.
Umar, Muhammad
1993 Changing Islamic Identity in Nigeria from the 1960s to the 1980s: From Sufism to Anti-Sufism. In *Muslim Identity and Social Change in Sub-Saharan Africa*, ed. Louis Brenner. Pp. 154–78. Bloomington: Indiana University Press.
2005 *Islam and Colonialism: Intellectual Responses of Muslims and Northern Nigerians to British Colonial Rule*. London: E. J. Brill.

Vasudevan, Ravi
2000 The Political Culture of Address in a "Transitional" Cinema: A Case Study of Indian Popular Cinema. In *Reinventing Film Studies*, ed. Christine Gledhill and Linda Williams. Pp. 130–64. New York: Hodder and Stoughton.
Vaughan, Megan
1991 *Curing Their Ills: Colonial Power and African Illness*. London: Polity.
Verrips, Jojada, and Birgit Meyer
2001 Kwaku's Car: The Struggles and Stories of a Ghanaian Long-Distance Taxi Driver. In *Car Cultures*, ed. Daniel Miller. Pp. 153–84. Oxford: Berg.
Virilio, Paul
1984 *War and Cinema: The Logistics of Perception*. London: Verso.
1997 *Open Sky*. London: Verso.
2000 *The Information Bomb*. London: Verso.
2003 *Unknown Quantity*. London: Thames and Hudson.
Wang, Shujen
2003 *Framing Piracy: Globalization and Films Distribution in Greater China*. Lanham, Md.: Rowman and Littlefield.
Warner, Michael
2002 *Publics and Counter-Publics*. New York: Zone.
Waterman, Christopher
1990 *Jùjú: A Social History and Ethnography of an African Popular Music*. Chicago: University of Chicago Press.
Watts, Michael
1992 The Shock of Modernity: Petroleum, Protest and Fast Capitalism in an Industrializing Society. In *Reworking Modernity: Capitalisms and Symbolic Discontent*, ed. Allan Pred and Michael Watts. Pp. 21–63 New Brunswick, N.J.: Rutgers University Press.
1996 Place, Space and Community in an African City. In *The Geography of Identity*, ed. Patricia Yeager. Pp. 59–97. Ann Arbor: University of Michigan Press.
2004 Baudelaire over Berea, Simmel over Sandton? *Public Culture* 17(1): 181–92.
Wedeen, Lisa
1999 *Ambiguities of Domination: Politics, Rhetoric and Symbols in Contemporary Syria*. Chicago: University of Chicago Press.
Wendl, Tobias
2001 Entangled Traditions: Photography and the History of Media in Southern Ghana. *Res* 39: 78–101.
Werthmann, Katja
2002 Matan Bariki, "Women of the Barracks": Muslim Hausa Women in an Urban Neighbourhood in Northern Nigeria. *Africa* 72(1): 112–30.
Westerlund, David, and Eve Rosander, eds.
1997 *African Islam and Islam in Africa: Encounters between Sufis and Islamists*. London: Hurst.

Wheatland, Thomas

2002 Isolation, Assimilation and Opposition: A Reception History of the Horkheimer Circle in the United States, 1934–1979. PhD diss., Boston College.

2005 Not-Such-Odd-Couples: Paul Lazarsfeld and the Horkheimer Circle on Morningside Heights. In *Exile, Science and* Bildung*: The Contested Legacy of German Intellectuals*, ed. David Kettler and Gerhard Lauer. Pp. 169–84. New York: Palgrave Macmillan.

White, Bob

2002 Congolese Rumba and Other Cosmopolitanisms. *Cahiers d'études africaines* 42(4): 663–86.

2004 Modernity's Trickster: "Dipping" and "Throwing" in Congolese Popular Dance Music. In *Drama and Performance in Africa*, ed. John Conteh-Morgan and Tejumola Olaniyan. Pp. 198–218. Bloomington: University of Indiana Press.

White, Luise

2000 *Speaking with Vampires: Rumor and History in Colonial Africa*. Berkeley: University of California Press.

Whitsitt, Novian

2002 Islamic-Hausa Feminism and Kano Market Literature: Qur'anic Reinterpretation in the Novels of Balaraba Yakubu. *Research in African Literatures* 33(2): 119–36.

Williams, Linda

1995 Film Bodies, Gender, Genre and Excess. In *Film Genre Reader 2*, ed. Barry Keith Grant. Pp. 140–58. Austin: University of Texas Press.

Yakubu, Mahmood

1996 *Aristocracy in Political Crisis: The End of Indirect Rule and the Emergence of Party Politics in the Emirates of Northern Nigeria*. Aldershot, U.K.: Avebury.

Zhen, Zhang

2006 *An Amorous History of the Silver Screen: Shanghai Cinema, 1896–1937*. Chicago: University of Chicago Press.

Index

Page numbers in italics indicate an illustration.

BRIAN LARKIN

is an associate professor of anthropology

at Barnard College, Columbia University.

He is a coeditor of *Media Worlds: Anthropology on New Terrain* (2002).

Library of Congress Cataloging-in-Publication Data
Larkin, Brian.
Signal and noise : media, infrastructure, and urban culture in Nigeria / Brian Larkin.
p. cm.
Includes bibliographical references and index.
ISBN-13: 978-0-8223-4090-4 (cloth : alk. paper)
ISBN-13: 978-0-8223-4108-6 (pbk. : alk. paper)
1. Mass media and technology—Nigeria—History.
2. Mass media and culture—Nigeria—History.
3. Nigeria—Civilization—20th century. I. Title.
P96.T422N65 2008
302.2309669—dc22
2007043854